"LET'S GET 'EM!"

About fifteen miles northwest of Bremen, I spotted five Focke-Wulf 190s at two o'clock, heading southwest at about fifteen thousand feet. We were above them and up-sun, so they didn't see us. "Let's get 'em!" I radioed to the flight. "Everybody take one." My plan was to make one pass and keep going because we were all getting low on fuel, especially Taylor. We didn't have enough for a prolonged dogfight.

Back up to full power, I started the dive toward the two 190s on the left. Perry went after the three on the right. My speed built up considerably as I closed on the one at the left of the formation. I started firing at about three hundred yards, closing to a hundred yards, firing all the way from dead astern and slightly above.

He never knew what hit him. . . .

AN ACE OF THE EIGHTH

An American Fighter Pilot's Air War in Europe

Norman "Bud" Fortier

PRESIDIO
PRESS

THE RANDOM HOUSE PUBLISHING GROUP • NEW YORK

A Presidio Press Book
Published by The Random House Publishing Group
Copyright © 2003 by Norman J. Fortier

Published in the United States by Presidio Press, an imprint of The Random House Publishing Group, a division of Random House, Inc., New York, and simultaneously in Canada by Random House of Canada Limited, Toronto.

Presidio Press and colophon are trademarks of Random House, Inc.

www.presidiopress.com

ISBN 0-89141-806-7

Manufactured in the United States of America

Map © Eric Hammel

First Edition: May 2003

OPM 9 8 7 6 5 4

To Jane
My loving wife and best friend

High Flight

John Gillespie Magee Jr.

Oh, I have slipped the surly bonds of earth
And danced the skies on laughter-silvered wings;
Sunward I've climbed, and joined the tumbling mirth
Of sun-split clouds—and done a hundred things
You have not dreamed of—wheeled and soared and swung
High in the sunlit silence. Hov'ring there,
I've chased the shouting wind along, and flung
My eager craft through footless halls of air.
Up, up the long, delirious burning blue
I've topped the windswept heights with easy grace
Where never lark, or even eagle flew.
And while with silent, lifting mind I've trod
The high untrespassed sanctity of space,

Put out my hand, and touched the face of God.

Contents

Acknowledgments	xi
Foreword	xiii
Map	xvii
Prologue	1
Flight Training	7
Operational Training	31
Steeple Morden	47
September 1943	55
October 1943	66
November 1943	70
December 1943	85
January 1944	96
February 1944	106
March 1944	122
April 1944	145
May 1944	159
June 1944	185
July 1944	212
Rest and Recuperation	239
October and November 1944	249
December 1944	269
January 1945	280
February 1945	299
March 1945	310
April 1945	322
May and June 1945	335
Epilogue	341
Glossary	345

Acknowledgments

"Memory isn't the first thing to go," I'm told, but it certainly doesn't improve with age—at least not in my case. I had to rely on several sources—and people—to fill in large gaps. Among the many whose help was invaluable:

Burt Sims, whose contribution to this book was written more than fifty years ago, when he wrote the diary-style *History of the 354th Fighter Squadron*. Without the squadron's history to jog my memory, I couldn't have written it with any degree of accuracy. A professional writer, Burt also gave me helpful tips when I started working on this book.

Colonel Ray Shewfelt, USAF (Ret.), flew combat missions with the 2d Scouting Force at Steeple Morden, and was assigned to the 358th Fighter Squadron for administration. Ray took on the monumental task of copying the histories of all 355th Fighter Group units from microfiche records at the USAF Historical Society at Maxwell Air Force Base, Alabama. He is the acknowledged, though unofficial, group historian. He allowed me to borrow his copy of the 354th Squadron history—more than a thousand pages—for months at a time. More importantly, Ray was an invaluable font of information about our chain of command, other Eighth Air Force units, bomber tactics, and even Luftwaffe units. He was a constant source of encouragement and support.

Bill Marshall is the son of 355th legend Bert Marshall, and the author of *Angels, Bulldogs, and Dragons*. He furnished details of Bert's career before and during World War

II, and important information about another 355th legend, Clay Kinnard. He gave me unlimited access to his large albums of photographs of 355th people, aircraft, and events.

My thanks also to my friend Gordon Smart, who helped edit my first draft. When I review that draft today, I realize what a chore that must have been.

The one indispensable person in all this was Eric Hammel, author, historian, and publisher at Pacifica Press, California. It was Eric who told me—four years ago—that I had to write a book, and he wouldn't take no for an answer. I dragged my way through the first draft. In retrospect, I wonder why he didn't return it to me with a short note: "I was wrong!"

Instead, he went through it page by page, making marginal notes as well as corrections, all the while recording a running commentary on audiotape. He was not only editing my early effort, he was also teaching me to be a better writer. This book would not have been written without his help. I shall always be grateful to him.

My sincere appreciation to all.

Foreword

"What did you do in the big war, Daddy?" My children have never asked me that question, but if they ever get curious, they can find some of the answers in this book. Time has made a few dents in my memory, so the details in my accounts may be somewhat inaccurate, but they represent the essentials as I recall them. To keep my memory on track, I have relied heavily on these sources:

Historian Roger Freeman's outstanding books on "The Mighty Eighth" are invaluable sources of detailed and accurate information about the people, aircraft, weapons, and airfields of the Eighth Air Force in England.

Bill Marshall's book *Angels, Bulldogs, and Dragons*, a diary-style account of all the missions flown by the 355th Fighter Group, with statistics, summaries, and photographs.

The History of the 354th Fighter Squadron, the "official" unit history, contains the required mission reports transmitted by the squadron intelligence section to higher headquarters, plus pilot encounter reports and a daily narrative of the day-to-day activities. Captain Burton R. Sims, who went overseas with our squadron as a combat intelligence officer and took on an added duty as the fighter group's public information officer (PIO), wrote most of it. Burt had been a sportswriter and picture editor of the *Los Angeles Examiner* at age twenty-two. When Burt was transferred to Eighth Air Force headquarters on February 1, 1945, Capt. Mike Glantz, squadron intelligence officer, took over the duties of 354th historian.

Without the narratives, the history is a dry recitation of

statistics; with them, it reads like a story. Instead of a roster of pilots, we have a cast of characters.

One bit of trivia: As a second lieutenant, I flew "tail-end Charlie" (the last plane in the group formation) on the group's first combat mission; I led the group on its last mission of the war, as a major.

The business of shooting down airplanes is, to my mind, sometimes a bit overrated. In some instances, there was no aerial combat involved. I know there were many victories gained in the course of exciting dogfights, and I had a few of those, but my guess is that for every one of them, there were at least three in which the victim was a sitting duck—unaware he was being attacked. That worked both ways. Sometimes we shot down one of them; sometimes they shot down one of us. Either way, it was a deadly game.

This is not to denigrate the exploits of those pilots who excelled at the game. We had a few of those in the 354th Fighter Squadron: Henry Brown, Ace Graham, Bert Marshall, and Clay Kinnard come easily to mind. Walter Koraleski would certainly have been in that group had he not been forced to bail out over Holland when his engine failed. They were the hunters who were usually a thousand yards ahead of the rest of us, chasing enemy aircraft. There were other leaders, not quite at that level, who knew what had to be done and how to do it. The squadron was rich in leadership talent.

Strafing was a different ball game.

In his introduction to *Angels, Bulldogs, and Dragons*, Bill Marshall makes the point that destroying enemy planes on the ground was usually accomplished at considerable risk. He refers to it as "perhaps the most dangerous fighter mission of all." Strafing heavily defended airfields in the heart of Germany exacted a much greater toll than did aerial combat. Of the twenty-one aces of the 355th Fighter Group, six were shot down by flak while strafing, not one in aerial combat. All German airfields were heavily defended, and the attacking fighters had to cross a level, wide-open expanse in a straight line to the targets, making it easier for

German gunners to track their targets. The minimum-altitude, high-speed attacks left no room for error. There was always the element of luck—or fate. In a strafing attack, you could be sure of one thing: A lot of people would be doing their best to kill you.

World War II was the pivotal, formative event of my life. Looking back, I'm amazed at how little I knew about the world around me, how naive I was about the war, its causes, and its consequences. I wasn't a gung-ho, let's-go-kill-Nazis-and-Japs type, but I was convinced that Hitler had to be stopped, and I considered it my duty to serve. In the deeper recesses of my mind, I understood that killing would be involved in the performance of that duty; and even now, the fact that I did kill people is sometimes troubling. Killing people who were intent on killing me—or my comrades— does not upset me. What *is* troubling is the fate of innocent civilians who happened to be in the way of errant bombs I dropped, or the .50-caliber bullets I sprayed around marshaling yards and other targets. War *is* hell!

Gilford, New Hampshire
February 2002

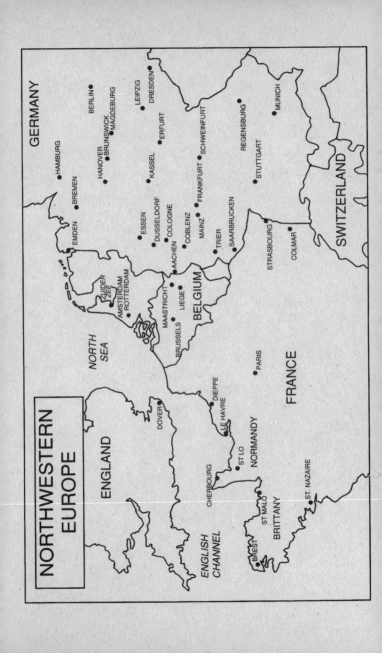

Prologue

The idea that I might someday fly an airplane never entered my mind until my second year at St. Anselm College, just outside Manchester, New Hampshire. I had never built a model airplane or even read an aviation magazine; I wasn't interested in the occasional barnstormers who came to the local airport. I had never yearned to "slip the surly bonds of earth," as Pilot Officer McGee later put it in his classic poem "High Flight." It never occurred to me.

As early as November 1938, President Roosevelt recognized the probability that the United States would sooner or later become involved in Europe's war. Perhaps disturbed by reports of German airpower, and notably by the assessment of that airpower by Charles Lindbergh, Roosevelt pushed through Congress the Civilian Pilot Training Program (CPTP) to provide a source of trained pilots for future military requirements.

The CPTP was offered to colleges and universities, with government funding, throughout the United States. St. Anselm College accepted the program—maybe it helped pay the bills in otherwise lean years—but soon ran into a problem: getting students to sign up for it.

During my freshman year, Father Houde, the college proctor (proctor defined as "a university official appointed from the academic staff to see that undergraduates observe the regulations"), tried to recruit me into the program. He was about six feet, four inches tall, with a stern demeanor and an unsmiling face. In his black garments he was an intimidating figure. I was only seventeen and the minimum entry age was eighteen, so I was able to decline with thanks, hoping he'd forget I existed.

He didn't. He collared me the following year shortly after my eighteenth birthday, and I signed up for the 1941 program but my heart wasn't in it. I just wanted Father Houde off my back.

Ground school started in mid-June 1941 at Howard Hartman's Flight School at Nashua Municipal Airport, about two miles from home. The instructor was Henry Gosselin, predictably nicknamed "Goose."

We studied air navigation, meteorology, theory of flight, aircraft engines, and civil air regulations. Just as we were beginning to wonder if we'd ever get into an airplane, ground school ended and flight training began.

There were ten of us in the class. Goose was flight instructor for half the class; George Harmon had the other half, which included me. He wasn't much older than I, in his early twenties. He and Goose had both logged about three hundred hours of flying time, but there the similarity ended. Goose was a roly-poly five-feet-five with an ever-present smile and good nature; nothing seemed to bother him. George was a slender five-feet-ten, pleasant, but more reserved and serious.

July 8—my first flight. "This is a Piper Cub J-3," George announced. "It has a Franklin engine that delivers 60 horsepower—not much, but enough to get us off the ground, we hope." He wasn't exactly boosting my confidence. He showed me what to look for in a preflight inspection, then motioned me into the backseat and showed me how to buckle and adjust the seat belt.

The engine-start procedure was simple: magneto switches on, yell "Contact," somebody spins the propeller, and the engine sputters to life. He taxied to the end of the runway. This was an orientation flight; I wasn't expected to do anything. He increased power to check the magnetos. "Just checking the mags!" he yelled. I was still a bit apprehensive—I had never been higher off the ground than in an ill-fated skiing episode. He released the brakes and pushed the throttle on full. The Cub lurched forward. I felt the tail section raise a little; we picked up speed, then lifted easily off the runway.

I cannot describe my feelings of the moment when that small Piper Cub lifted off the ground. We were no longer a part of the earth below—we were in our own detached world. I had "slipped the surly bonds of earth," and it was love at first flight. The course of my life had been changed.

I flew thirty-two of the next forty-two days, sometimes two or three times a day, and by August 22 I had logged forty hours of flight time. I was hooked on flying, and I had earned my private pilot license, certificate 98293-41.

The CPTP included a secondary program—forty hours of advanced flying training in a Waco UPF-7 at Pete Goldsmith's Flight School at Nashua Municipal Airport. I needed no urging from Father Houde.

The Waco UPF-7 was an open-cockpit biplane that looked like a holdover from World War I. It had a Continental engine that produced 220 horsepower, cruised at 105 miles per hour, and had a maximum level-flight speed of 125 miles per hour. My instructor was Al Hirsch, a ham-fisted pilot from nearby Pelham, the town of my birth. He was just under six feet tall, heavyset, with a round, jovial face under a fast-receding hairline. About forty, he looked and spoke like an old New England farmer, but he knew how to fly that UPF-7, and he knew how to teach flying.

Al sat in the front cockpit. He shouted at me through the gosport, a simple rubber tube about half an inch in diameter that ran between the cockpits. At his end was a cone, similar to the relief tube cones in later fighter planes. In the rear cockpit, the tube divided into two branches, one for each earflap of my cloth helmet. It was a one-way communication system: He yelled into the cone and I tried to figure out what he was saying. When I knew what he said, I nodded my head; he could see me in his rearview mirror. He called it his profanity strainer, but the strainer worked only when I was doing things right. When I really screwed up, he stuck the cone into the slipstream to wake me up.

Al is high on my list of unforgettable people, and the UPF-7 is high on my list of favorite airplanes. Unlike the Piper Cub, it was rugged enough to withstand the aerobatics that were part of the flight training program. It was great for loops, slow rolls, snap rolls, Immelmans, lazy eights, Cuban eights, hammerhead stalls, and even an "outside spin," which, once experienced, I was never tempted to try again. The course started on October 19, when much of New Hampshire was at peak foliage, turning the landscape below us into an artist's easel of red, gold, brown, and green mingled with the deep blue of the lakes. It was the first time I'd seen it from the air—right side up and upside down.

As autumn phased into winter, the panorama changed to a dreary dull brown, and then a brilliant white with the first snowfall. We bundled up in bulky fleece-lined leather pants and jackets, put on fleece-lined helmets, and enjoyed every minute of it, no matter which way was up.

It was warm for December, in the sixty-degree range. The dinner table had been cleared (dinner was always at noon, supper in the evening), and everyone had settled down to the usual Sunday routine. Dad was reading the Sunday paper; Mom was knitting or sewing. The radio was on, but no one was paying much attention to it. I was getting ready to go to Freddie Doucet's house to listen to records and talk about any number of things. Freddie had been my best friend since high school days; we shared a passion for music. By then I played a little bit of guitar, saxophone, and clarinet—all by ear and none of them well. Freddie didn't play a musical instrument, but he had a large collection of 78-rpm records that we loved to listen to.

"We interrupt this program to bring you this special bulletin. The Japanese have bombed Pearl Harbor! We repeat: The Japanese have bombed Pearl Harbor, our naval base in Hawaii. We'll provide details as they become available."

Our first reaction was disbelief. Was this another *War of*

the Worlds scare like the one that Orson Welles had produced a few years back, or was it real? As more details became available, it was apparent that this was no hoax—we were in a war.

Later that afternoon, Freddie and I talked about how the war would affect our future. It never occurred to us that the United States might lose the war. Most people had no idea of the serious losses our navy had suffered at Pearl Harbor. "How long do you think it'll take for us to beat 'em?" asked Freddie. Then, answering his own question, "It shouldn't take us more than a year."

Three years later, Freddie was killed in the snows of the Battle of the Bulge.

Now that we were at war, the flight training took on a new meaning. It was still fun, but Al and I were aware that flying was a wartime skill.

The training schedule included two cross-country flights in Pete Goldsmith's pride and joy, his Stinson 105. Al went with me on the first one and checked me out on the Stinson's controls, gauges, and instruments. Each cross-country flight consisted of three legs, with landings at different airports at the end of each leg. I had to do all the flight planning, get flight clearance, and do all radio calls on each leg. This was a side-by-side enclosed cockpit, so Al didn't have to yell at me to give me instructions. It was a comfortable, enjoyable day.

The second cross-country was solo. The weather was generally fair all around the cross-country route: Nashua to Concord to Fitchburg, Massachusetts, and back to Nashua. Total flight time was three hours. The flight was uneventful until I approached Nashua Municipal Airport. The wind had become strong and gusty, and was a direct crosswind for a landing on the runway. I was in radio contact with Pete and Al, in the control tower. They told me to land into the wind, at a right angle to the runway, and to be aware of the very gusty conditions.

This meant landing across the shortest part of the airfield, over the chain-link boundary fence and directly toward the main hangar. Al told me later that Pete was really worried that I would smash up his pride and joy, and he kept reassuring Pete that I could handle it with no problem. He probably had his fingers crossed.

Unaware that this was a big problem, I landed the plane with little difficulty. Goldsmith was so relieved, he almost hugged me when I got out. Al just stood there with a huge grin on his face.

My final test flight of the secondary CPTP was on December 31, 1941. Three weeks later, I left St. Anselm College and enlisted as a flying cadet in the Army Air Corps.

Flight Training

On January 21, 1942, I raised my right hand at the army recruiting center in Manchester, New Hampshire, and was inducted into the U.S. Army Air Corps as a flying cadet. I didn't look closely at the "Agreement to Serve" I signed. I agreed to serve for "the duration of the war plus six months," but I also agreed that I would not marry while still a cadet. According to my pre-induction physical, I was 5 feet, 7 inches tall and weighed 135 pounds.

The finality of what I had done was beginning to sink in. I was alone, and for the first time in my life, cut off from the security of home and family—and I was scared.

Within two hours, I was on my way to Maxwell Field in Montgomery, Alabama, along with Clarence (Bo) Beauregard from Marlborough, New Hampshire; Maurice (Moe) Cashman from Franklin, New Hampshire; Jim Owens from Haverhill, Massachusetts; and Henry J. (Hank) Pascho from Somerville, Massachusetts. At twenty-six, Bo was the oldest of the group; at nineteen, I was the youngest.

We didn't get to know each other until after we changed trains in Washington, D.C., and found ourselves in adjoining berths on the Seaboard Atlantic Railroad headed south. We had two small compartments, each with pull-down bunks and enough room to sit around and socialize before bedtime.

We were playing cards early that evening in one of the compartments when someone suggested that we might be able to get a bottle of whiskey from the porter. "I'll see what I can do at the next station," he promised. After the next stop, we had a rather expensive bottle of rotgut whiskey and a bottle of ginger ale to help chase it down.

I was out of my element. I was not a drinker. I hadn't had anything stronger than a glass of wine in my life. But I was now in the army. And army people drank liquor. So I had a few whiskeys and ginger ale, and soon the small compartment became a more pleasant place. I was no longer with strangers, no longer scared; I was among friends!

We played poker, for small stakes because none of us had much money, but we were in the army now, and our perception was that army people drank whiskey and played poker. I did not win any money that night, but I did learn three valuable lessons: Never drink whiskey when you play poker, never play poker with people who really know how to play the game, and there's no such thing as "a friendly little game of poker."

About noon on January 23, the porter came through the cars announcing that we were approaching Montgomery, Alabama. We gathered our luggage and stood by the exit as the train lurched to a stop. As we stepped down, a tall, rugged-looking sergeant directed us to a waiting army bus. We were surprised that about thirty other cadets were on the same train. With more than thirty cadets and their luggage, the bus to Maxwell Field was full.

We didn't quite get to Maxwell Field. The bus stopped in front of an old, shabby-looking two-story building. "This is where you get off," said the sergeant. "Welcome to the Old Mill."

The Old Mill was an old textile mill, condemned as unsafe and closed—until the crunch of hundreds of cadets exceeded the capacity of Maxwell Field to absorb them. This was a "temporary" facility: two floors with roughly fifty cadets on each floor, in two-tiered bunks. We were issued sheets and blankets, and a bunk number: A was bottom bunk, B was top. Bo and I shared the same bunk number; he chose top.

In the next few days, we were subjected to a number of indignities: extra-short haircuts; clothing that didn't fit and had to be reissued; immunization shots to prevent smallpox, tetanus, typhoid, and yellow fever; and the ever-present drill sergeants who marched us to and from the mess hall at Maxwell Field three times a day. "Why can't you civilians understand what a column is? Don't you know how to stay in ranks? Do you *really* expect to be cadets?"

We learned. In a few weeks, we could march to and from the mess hall at Maxwell Field, about a quarter of a mile away, in some semblance of order but never to the satisfaction of the drill sergeant. We sent our civilian clothes back home: "You won't be needing those for a while," the sergeant told us.

Then came the lectures: military customs and laws, navigation, meteorology, aircraft recognition, and the like. What I remember most was the physical fitness routine. Every day, we had calisthenics: hop-straddle exercises and push-ups and all kinds of traditional drills designed to drain energy from young studs to make them more amenable to discipline. The ultimate routine was what we called the Burma Road, a tortuous two-mile run through the woods and swamps surrounding Maxwell Field, led by a physical fitness nut who set the pace while another brought up the rear to discourage stragglers. There were streams to jump over and hills to climb, but the worst part was the stretch along the edge of the golf course where we could see women playing golf in the distance. They looked young and attractive from our vantage point, but it may have been a blessing that we never saw them up close. We could dream.

At the end of the third week, we were given "open post" (permission to leave the base) while at the Old Mill. We went into town and I drank two "Zombies," strong rum drinks popular at the time. I have no recollection of getting back to the Old Mill that night; Bo guided me to my bunk. I do recall that the old building rocked and swayed and even did a few aerobatic routines that buildings are not designed to do, and I was sicker than I had ever been before. The next morning's calisthenics were brutal.

In late February we were assigned to Craig Field in

Selma, Alabama. Finally, we thought, we were being assigned to primary flying school. We were wrong. At Craig Field, we were, as we called it, in "cold storage" until openings for primary flight training became available. There was no Old Mill at Craig Field. We were in cadet barracks, four to a room with adjoining bathroom facilities shared with the four cadets next door.

The routine was the same: Morse code, aircraft recognition, calisthenics, close-order drill, obstacle course, the "Burma Road" torture trail, and all the classroom lectures we had almost memorized by then.

On our second weekend, we were given open post and ordered to return by midnight. Bo and I found a small dingy bar in Selma. He ordered a rye and ginger. Still a neophyte at the drinking game, I ordered the same. I was three months shy of my twentieth birthday, but that didn't bother the bartender. I suppose he figured that anyone in uniform was old enough to drink. We had a few more. Bo had to help me home again.

The weeks dragged by. Craig Field was an advanced flying school, so we saw AT-6 advanced trainers taking off and landing, but we never got near the flight line. It was a frustrating and monotonous time.

We were in Class 42-K, scheduled to graduate in December 1942. When May rolled around, we figured that Class 42-K would be leaving for primary flight school soon. We were right. There was a problem, however. There were too many cadets in cold storage and not enough slots in primary flying schools. So half of the cadet corps went on to primary flight schools in the Southeast Training Command; the rest—including me—were reassigned to class 43-A and given a thirty-day furlough, whether we wanted one or not.

So four months after becoming a "flying" cadet, I was back home, without once having left the ground, except in the hop-straddle exercises of daily calisthenics. It was nice being home, of course, and I was treated like a hero even though I had done nothing approaching heroic.

The thirty days passed at a snail's pace, and finally I headed back to Maxwell Field for assignment to my first flying school.

Primary

Special Order 48 read, "The following named aviation cadets are transferred to AAFTD Embry-Riddle Company, Dorr Field, Arcadia, Florida," followed by the names of 240 cadets. We left Montgomery via troop train on July 5 and arrived at Arcadia at 10:00 A.M. the next day. This was not an express train. We were tired and hot by the time we were loaded onto the army trucks for the trip to Dorr Field, about five miles east of Arcadia. This was cattle country; there was not a hill to be seen on any horizon.

Though technically an Army Air Forces Training Detachment, Dorr Field was an Embry-Riddle civilian flight school supervised by the Army Air Forces. All the flight instructors were civilians, but USAAF lieutenants were stationed there for the express purpose of weeding out the unfit. We called them the washboard; they gave the flight checks at the end of each training phase. If you had trouble on your first flight check, you were given one more, by a different lieutenant. If he didn't like the way you flew either, you washed out. Most of the cadets who washed out were reassigned to navigator or bombardier training.

Cadet quarters were in rectangles, four quarters to a side. Each quarter had eight cadets, four in each room connected by one bathroom to the next room. There were thirty-two cadets on each side of the rectangle.

As usual, quarters were assigned alphabetically, so I was in a room with Bob Damico, Vic DeSoto, and Carmen Felice. Carmen was one of those people who look like they need a shave one hour after they've shaved. He was also one of those cadets who seemed to be marching out of step even when they weren't. For some reason, when his feet were in step, his head wasn't, so his head was always bobbing up when the rest of the heads were bobbing down. "Keep in step, Felice!" the drill instructors yelled.

"Yes, sir!" he would respond, though he was convinced that he *was* in step.

Vic DeSoto was from Tarrytown, New York, and his accent sounded typical Brooklyn to the rest of us. He was short, probably close to the lower limit for acceptance in the Cadet Corps, and stocky. He was a worrier. He didn't have much confidence that he could get past primary flight school. He was well liked, and when his own worst scenario came true and he washed out, we were all sorry to see him leave.

Bob Damico was the quintessential character. Always good-natured and upbeat, he was the constant provider of funny stories, pranks, and good cheer. It didn't take long for his reputation to reach the upperclassmen, and he soon became one of their favorite targets.

Hazing of incoming cadets by upperclassmen was a tradition in the prewar flying cadet program. It consisted entirely of drill-instructor-style, in-your-face shouted commands and comments designed to humiliate and demean the lowly incoming cadets. Physical abuse was never permitted—upperclassmen were even required to ask permission to touch another cadet—but underclassmen were expected to obey all reasonable commands of their tormentors. The favorite expression was "Hit a brace, Mister!" A brace was an exaggerated position of attention. The victim was then subjected to verbal abuse and commands such as "Suck that gut in, Mister!" and "Get those shoulders back! Keep your head up, Mister!" and "Don't look at me, Mister! Eyes straight ahead!" An underclassman had to hold that position until he appeared to be on the verge of fainting, at which time the upperclassman barked, "At ease, Mister!"

In primary flight school, hazing by upperclassmen was not officially permitted, but was not discouraged either. After the evening meal, they were allowed to roam the quarters of newly assigned cadets, making life miserable with their overbearing orders and comments. Hazing time was

limited to one hour, however, because everyone needed
time to study or just relax.

Bob Damico was a favorite target, which was not good
for the rest of us, because he always came up with a funny
remark that started us giggling, and that brought down the
feigned wrath of the upperclassmen, who also had great difficulty in trying to keep from laughing. One evening when
he heard upperclassmen coming, Bob squeezed into one of
the clothes lockers. He was in his underwear, but it was still
a tight fit. "Close the door," he told us, "and tell them I'm
not here." As expected, three upperclassmen came into the
room, looking for Damico. After putting the rest of us in a
brace, they demanded to know where he was. We maintained a stony silence.

After about five minutes of badgering, we still hadn't
given him away, but he was quite uncomfortable in the
locker and started squirming to ease the strain. They heard
him. One of them walked to the locker and yelled, "Are you
in there, Damico?"

In a high falsetto, Bob replied, "Ain't nobody in here but
us clothes."

That broke us all up, even the upperclassmen, who
quickly recovered their composure and laced into us with
renewed vigor. It was mid-July and hot. They left him in
that locker for about ten more minutes. When he finally was
released, he could hardly stand at attention, much less in a
brace. The upperclassmen roasted him a bit, then departed.
After all, they enjoyed him too much to make him really
angry.

The hazing rankled, especially in view of the fact that the
upperclassmen were only about one month ahead of us in
the training schedule. Some of them were washing out of
the cadet program at the time they gave us grief. We put up
with it, believing we had no other choice. A month later,
when we were upperclassmen, a few of our classmates took
up the practice, but most of us felt it was silly and we left
the new cadets alone. Hazing was officially prohibited
shortly thereafter.

Bob and I became close friends. Felice washed out soon after DeSoto did, so Bob and I had the room to ourselves. We spent our off-post time together, but there was little to do in Arcadia on weekends.

Neither of us had any difficulty with the flying program. The primary trainer was the Stearman PT-17, exactly the same as the PT-13 except that the PT-17 had a Continental engine rather than the Lycoming engine in the PT-13. It was also nearly identical in appearance and performance to the Waco UPF-7 that I had flown during secondary CPTP back in New Hampshire. I had more than forty hours in the UPF-7, and there were no maneuvers in primary that I hadn't done before, so I had no difficulty completing the flying phase in the PT-17. The washout rate was nearly 50 percent, most of them in Phase One, during which the student was expected to solo.

The most unusual and dramatic washout occurred when a cadet, flying alone shortly after his first solo, flew his airplane directly into the roof of a barn while on final approach for landing. The barn was at least a hundred yards to the left of the glide path for landing, but he seemingly made no effort to avoid it. The airplane was severely damaged, but he escaped with only a few bumps and bruises. It was his last flight in the cadet program.

N.K. McCoy, a slender southern gentleman in his early thirties, was my instructor. Lieutenant John Folan was the check pilot who flew with us at the end of each training phase. I was nervous on the first checkride, but gradually I realized that he was not a threat to me. He was just doing his job, probably wishing he were somewhere else.

We had the usual close order drill and calisthenics routines, except that there was no "Burma Road" in Florida: no hills, no woods, and no streams to leap over. We had an obstacle course that served the same purpose. And, of course, we had ground school subjects to absorb and memorize, with periodic written exams supposedly "just as important" as the flying phase. No one believed that.

I wrote a weekly letter to my mother, but with the flying schedule, ground school, calisthenics, and close order drill, we had very little time to be homesick.

At the end of August we graduated after nine weeks and sixty hours of flying the PT-17; we were ready for the next phase of our training, Basic Flight School. Bob and I scanned the assignment orders. We were both assigned to Shaw Field in Sumter, South Carolina.

Basic

Shaw Field was strictly army—no civilian instructors. Our barracks were wooden two-story buildings overlooking the parade ground, which looked like an overgrown paved parking lot. There were two cadets to each room. My roommate was John Gregor, from McAdoo, Pennsylvania, a few miles south of Hazleton. We were different in nearly every respect. He was a bit shorter than I, but stockier and more muscular; he was neat and meticulous in everything he did, I tended to be careless; his footlocker was always just right, with everything in its place; mine was more likely to be haphazard. One might say that we had different priorities. He liked everything tidy and orderly; I liked everything a bit loose and comfortable.

On the first day of duty, I expected to go to the flight line to get acquainted with the BT-13, our basic trainer. Instead, we were given a long, narrow package wrapped in crinoline—a stiff fabric made of flax and horsehair. Inside was a Springfield rifle, coated with Cosmoline, a thick, heavy grease, presumably designed to preserve the rifle for centuries. We were told where to find gasoline and rags, and ordered to restore this rifle to its pristine condition before the next morning. "Did I get on the wrong bus?" I asked John. "I thought this was a flight school!"

Cleaning a rifle preserved in Cosmoline is a long and dirty job, but by the next morning we were all proud temporary owners of a rather heavy, and clean, Springfield rifle.

We were not expected to fire it—just keep it clean and carry it. We even learned a little of the manual of arms, which taught us how to do all kinds of things with a rifle that had absolutely nothing to do with flying airplanes but plenty to do with order and discipline.

There were the usual routines: calisthenics, close order drill, and lectures on everything from military customs and courtesy to VD—the dreaded venereal diseases the flight surgeons warned us about and showed us graphic movies of its consequences. About every two weeks, we were lined up for "short arm" inspection, when the flight surgeon passed along a line of cadets with pants and shorts down around our knees. As he passed slowly along the line each cadet was expected to "milk" his penis, which meant to squeeze it forward. A milky discharge indicated gonorrhea, which resulted in immediate expulsion from the cadet corps and several monstrous shots of penicillin.

The obstacle courses and Burma Roads looked just like the ones we had at Maxwell and Craig, and the physical fitness zealots who herded us around them resembled those we had come to know.

There was one big difference. At Dorr Field, we were expected to keep our quarters neat and orderly, and were regularly inspected to ensure that they were. Discrepancies were dealt with on the spot. Shaw Field had a demerit system. Each cadet was designated CQ (charge of quarters) for one week; then his roommate took over CQ duties the following week. The CQ was responsible for the cleanliness and general condition of the room. Each discrepancy was one demerit charged to the CQ of the week. A cadet accumulating more than a specified number of demerits had to walk "tours" around the parade ground on Saturday afternoon, shouldering a rifle, one hour for each demerit over the allowable limit, with a ten-minute rest between tours.

Each Saturday morning, a lieutenant wearing white gloves and a fixed scowl, accompanied by a sergeant taking notes, came through the cadet quarters and inspected each room. He checked beds, footlockers, and desks, then ran a finger or two along each shelf, ridge, cabinet, window ledge, and any other location likely to accumulate dust. If anything was out of place, or if his glove became the least bit dusty, it meant at least one demerit for the room CQ, no matter where the dust came from.

When John was CQ, our room passed inspection with few if any demerits, so we were both allowed open post that weekend. When I was CQ, the lieutenant always found dust on his white glove, and I spent many of those Saturday afternoons walking tours on the parade ground while John went to town by himself. I sometimes suspected that the lieutenant, when he came to our room on those Saturdays when I was CQ, muttered to the sergeant, "Give me the dusty gloves."

Powered by a Pratt & Whitney R-985 engine generating 450 horsepower, the Vultee BT-13 "Valiant" (we called it the Vultee Vibrator) was heavier, faster, and more complex than the PT-17. It was an all-metal, low-wing monoplane with a greenhouse cockpit enclosure and a sliding canopy for each pilot. It had a two-position variable-pitch propeller, a fixed landing gear, landing flaps, and a two-way radio that had to be hand-cranked to the desired frequency. The radio was on tower frequency for nearly all of our flights, but it also had a function switch for the intercom between the front seat and backseat.

Five cadets were assigned to each instructor, most of whom were recently graduated second lieutenants and unhappy with their lot in life. My instructor was Lieutenant Gulley, about five feet, ten inches tall, slender, and obviously displeased with his assignment. He probably saw himself trapped in Training Command while the war was going on without him. About halfway through basic, he was transferred, and I imagine he was much happier. Royal Air Force Pilot Officer Benham replaced him. Benham was a recent graduate of the Army Air Forces flight training program, and was assigned to instructor duty as part of an agreement between the United States and Great Britain whereby some of the graduating RAF officers stayed behind as instructors for about six months.

Soft-spoken and invariably polite and sensitive, Benham, five feet, four inches tall, was not the typical hard-nosed instructor. He was an excellent pilot and teacher. He not only told us what he expected, he also showed us what he meant. He never raised his voice nor criticized a cadet in the presence of others. He was a gentleman, and he expected his students to be gentlemen.

The seventy-hour flight program was a transition from the fundamentals of flying learned in Primary to the more demanding requirements of military flying. It was also the point at which a career decision was made about a cadet's future assignment—whether he would go to single-engine or twin-engine advanced flying school, thence to fighters or bombers.

We reviewed the basic maneuvers learned in Primary, then went on to formation flying, instrument flying, night flying, and point-to-point cross-country flying—all while getting used to a heavier, more powerful, and faster airplane.

Flying close to another airplane made me a little nervous at first, but soon it became second nature. I tucked my wing just inside Benham's wing and was quite comfortable as long as he was flying straight and level. Then he made level turns, then climbing turns, then diving turns until I was comfortable with those. One memorable afternoon, I was tucked in tight on his right wing as he dove to pick up speed and pulled up into a loop. When we bottomed out of the loop, I had learned that in a tight formation, the only thing that mattered was maintaining position relative to the lead aircraft, no matter what the lead aircraft did. Later, while climbing through solid overcasts in England, I used that lesson well.

Instrument flying was another matter. We didn't have the sophisticated instrumentation available in later aircraft. We had two basic instruments: the turn-and-bank indicator (needle and ball) and the airspeed indicator. Here's how they worked.

If the needle was centered, the aircraft was not turning. If it was off to the right, the aircraft was turning right; off to the left, the aircraft was turning left. Rudder pedals were used to stop the turning action. If the ball was centered, the wings were level. If it was off to the right, the right wing was lower; off to the left, the left wing was lower. The control column—the stick—was moved laterally to keep the ball centered. The airspeed indicator told us if we were accelerating or decelerating. If airspeed was increasing, the aircraft was diving; if decreasing, the aircraft was climbing. Forward or backward movement of the stick stabilized the speed. The sequence was drilled into our heads: Center the needle—center the ball—adjust the airspeed.

We were taught to rely primarily on those two instruments. "Needle, ball, and airspeed!" was shouted into our earphones enough times that it became an automatic response.

There was a good reason for this. Other instruments used for flying through clouds and fog, the artificial horizon and gyrocompass, were based on the gyroscopic principles of rigidity in space and precession. Once the limits imposed by the principle of rigidity in space were exceeded, as in aerobatics or unusual flight conditions, these instruments precessed, or "tumbled," and became totally unreliable. The needle, ball, and airspeed instruments were not gyroscope-based and therefore never tumbled. There were other instruments in the cockpit of the BT-13—altimeter, rate-of-climb indicator, artificial horizon, and engine instruments—but the "needle, ball, and airspeed" were smack in the middle of the instrument panel.

We learned instrument flying two ways: in the Link Trainer and in the air. Link Trainers were primitive flight simulators used to teach proper procedures of instrument flight, including the use of radio ranges. The trainer was a boxlike affair with stubby wings and tail to give it a superficial resemblance to an airplane. Though firmly attached to the floor, the small "airplane" duplicated the pitch and roll of actual flight but was not designed to do loops and rolls. When the pilot was seated in the cockpit, a hinged cover was lowered around his head and shoulders, shutting out everything but his cockpit instruments.

At a nearby control unit, an operator was in radio contact with the pilot. The operator simulated the actual ground-to-air transmissions and controlled the radio range signals that enabled the pilot to "fly the beam" to an airport. The pilot then flew the prescribed landing pattern to a letdown and a landing. The operator could follow the progress of the airplane by watching an electronic "bug" that left a trail of red ink on a map, recording the flight path of the trainer. After each flight, the pilot and the operator studied the red-line course to critique the mission.

It didn't feel like an airplane—though the operator could introduce rough, turbulent air, making the little box bounce up and down—but it was useful for learning the correct air-to-ground radio procedures, use of navigational aids, and basic instrument flying techniques. And it was safe! To my knowledge, no Link Trainer ever crashed and burned.

Then came night flying. "The aircraft," Pilot Officer Benham informed us, "does not know, nor does it care, if it is daylight or midnight. So it flies exactly the same way all the time." That sounded reasonable, but we weren't entirely convinced. Whether the aircraft knew or not, *we* did.

Our first night flight was really a dusk flight. We took off in the daylight just before sunset, milled around in our assigned zone until it was dark at ground level—it was still light at 5,000 feet—then entered the landing pattern and landed. Gradually we became more comfortable with night flights and began to enjoy the view of the city lights of Sumter and the scattered lights of small villages and farmhouses.

We were ready for our next challenge, night cross-country flights that involved planning every little detail—weather, headings, distances, ground speed, estimated times to checkpoints, and all required radio calls. Benham flew the first one with us; on the second, we were on our own.

We spent the whole afternoon running among the flight planning room, the weather station, and the map room. None of us wanted to be "the dumb-ass cadet who gets lost" and has to land somewhere else.

Somehow we all made it.

Ground school was the usual fare: meteorology; navigation; radio procedures; theory of flight; infantry drill (with rifles); aircraft engine systems; and, of course, twenty hours of Morse code. The only part of the Morse code I ever used after my cadet days was dit-dah for A and dah-dit for N when flying radio navigation beams. I could have learned that in ten minutes or less.

At about the halfway point in our training, one of my sisters sent me a photograph of herself, taken by a professional photographer, showing her leaning on a split rail fence with the wind blowing gently in her hair. She was eighteen and quite attractive. I left the photo on my desk, where John happened to see it one day. "Wow!" he exclaimed, "Is that your girlfriend?"

"No," I said with a laugh, "just my sister."

"Wow!" he said again. "Do you think if I wrote to her, she'd write back?"

"She probably would."

John did write to her and she did reply, and that was the beginning of a lifelong relationship. They married a year after the war ended and raised a lot of lovely children and grandchildren. Just call me Cupid.

We had checked into Shaw Field on September 7, and our basic training ended the first week of November. By the sixth, the assignment orders were posted on the bulletin board. We gathered around anxiously. What would it be, bombers or fighters? Most of the cadets I knew wanted desperately to go to single-engine advanced training, as I did. John and I took a long look, then began to jump up and down with joy, shaking hands all around and grinning ear to ear. We were going to Spence Field—single-engine advanced!

Bob Damico also was going to single-engine advanced training, but not at Spence. We spent a lot of time together that last weekend. On November 9, we went our separate ways, promising to write and keep in touch. We corresponded sporadically for a short time, but our paths did not cross again until many years later.

John and I boarded the bus to Moultrie, Georgia.

Advanced

With Primary and Basic behind us, there was one last hurdle between us and those coveted silver wings: advanced flying school. The North American AT-6 was the most sophisticated airplane we had encountered so far, with a 750-horsepower engine, variable-pitch propeller, retractable landing gear, and a .30-caliber machine gun. Our training would include advanced aerobatics and formation flying, instrument flying, night navigation flights, simulated combat, and live firing at the Eglin Field ground and aerial gunnery ranges in Florida.

Ground instruction was intensified: meteorology, air navigation, aircraft recognition, Morse code, aircraft propulsion systems (hydraulic, electrical, fuel, and the like), and all the military customs and standards of behavior designed to mold us into officers and gentlemen. In our spare time we had close-order drill with rifles and strenuous physical fitness training to keep us from getting bored. I had no trouble getting to sleep at night.

There were the usual two-story barracks. Assignments to rooms and flights were alphabetical. There were four cadets to a room, sharing latrine and shower facilities with four other cadets in the adjoining room. Sometimes it got hectic. I shared a room on the second floor with Joseph Troy Folkes, William Jackson Ford, and Sammie Vincent Florance. That's right: Sammie—not Sam or Samuel—from Texas. John Gregor, my roommate in Basic, was a few doors down the hall.

Our instructor was RAF Pilot Officer Kenneth Locke, a recent graduate of the Army Air Corps flight program. He was eager to get back to the RAF in England but had one more class to instruct: ours. He was close to 6 feet tall, about 180 pounds of rugged muscle.

Locke had no trouble with Folkes, Ford, and Fortier, but Sam Florance was different. Sam was twenty-one, almost as tall as Locke, but slim and wiry at about 170 pounds. It would be fair to say that Sam and Pilot Officer Locke did not speak the same language. Sam spoke Texan; Locke spoke British. From the first day, it was clear that those two would find little common ground.

There were cultural differences besides the language barrier. Sam was raised on a farm in rural Texas, and a grin was never far from his face. Locke was from an upper-middle-class village in south-central England; he seldom smiled. He didn't smoke. Sam didn't smoke, either, but he *did* chew tobacco, a habit that Locke considered loathsome. Sam was gregarious, with that easy familiarity typical of most Texans; Locke was reserved and proper—a typical English gentleman.

Skeet shooting was designed to teach us deflection shooting—trying to hit a moving target by "leading" it, trying to visualize its trajectory and aiming ahead of it. It was our first day on the skeet range. I had never fired a 12-gauge shotgun in my life, and I was nervous. The only instruction we were given was, "Hold the butt of the shotgun tight against your shoulder" to minimize the recoil force.

The skeet range had eight stations spaced in a semicircle between a "high house" on the left and a "low house" on the right. Each station presented a different angle of deflection, hence a different challenge. The small saucer-shaped clay pigeon targets were propelled high from the left or low from the right. For the "doubles" phase, clay pigeons were projected from both houses simultaneously, and the challenge was to "kill" both birds before they flew beyond the boundary stakes.

"Pull!" I yelled. The clay pigeon shot out of the high house. I was on station 1, so it was an easy shot—straight-away, little deflection. I fired; the clay pigeon disappeared in a puff of black dust, and my shoulder felt like it had been hit by a baseball bat. I had forgotten the caveat, had held the gun loosely against my shoulder, and it had kicked me hard.

"Mark!" This time the pigeon came from the low house, heading in my direction, a more difficult shot. I missed. Sam snorted, "Ain't you Yankees ever shot a gun before?" I hadn't, but he had hunted birds since he was big enough to hold a shotgun, so he didn't miss those clay pigeons often. By the end of our training I had become reasonably proficient at killing the clay pigeons, and I knew how to hold a shotgun.

Locke was even worse at skeet shooting than his "Yankee" cadets. He was painfully aware that Sam and most of his other students were better at this than he was. He had a good day at the skeet range when he hit half the pigeons. It was his turn. "Pull!" It was that easy, straightaway shot, and Locke missed.

Sam laughed and said, "The only way you'll kill that bird is to chase it behind the low house and club it with the butt." We snickered.

Locke's face reddened. He stared at Sam for a few seconds; then, carefully laying the shotgun against the low house, he walked slowly to where Sam was standing. For a split second, I thought he was going to hit him. That same thought must have occurred to Sam; he backed off a step.

"I shall not tolerate such remarks from you!" Locke said in a low, menacing voice.

Sam had intended his remark to be funny, not insulting, so he was taken aback by Locke's reaction. Snapping to attention, he said, "I'm sorry, sir!"

Locke turned to the rest of us. "Do I make myself clear?"

We were all standing at attention. *"Yes, sir!"* we answered in unison. We were not about to do anything stupid so close to graduation.

———

"Today, we start our simulated combat training," Pilot Officer Locke said. "Here's the way it works: I take off with one of you on my right wing, and we climb to ten thousand feet. I'll then alert you by saying, 'ready . . . *now!*' At that point, we both start a sharp turn; I shall turn left, you turn right. Then you're on your own. Any questions?"

"Sir, do we have to stay in that turn?" asked Sam, who had been treating Locke with almost obsequious respect since the skeet range episode.

"You can do anything you like," replied Locke, "but the idea is to get behind the other aircraft in a shooting position and stay there. There is a gun camera in the left wing, and when you press the trigger on the stick, the camera will take pictures. Does everyone understand?" We nodded.

"Very well. Florance, you shall be first. Don't forget to turn the gun camera switch on." He smiled and added, "By the way, the guns aren't loaded."

"I won't forget, sir," replied Sam. He was grinning from ear to ear.

From Sam's description later, the "battle" went something like this: Sam started his hard right turn, then pulled up into a steep climb to a near-stall, kicked left rudder, and wound up behind Locke, who had continued his left turn. Sam was way out of shooting range, but gradually cut inside the turn, and after a few minutes of maneuvering was about two hundred yards behind Locke, taking pictures. Locke tried everything he knew to dislodge him—to no avail; Sam stuck like glue. Sam told us that he thought Locke had lost sight of him after starting his turn and by the time he figured out where Sam was, it was too late. Locke had taught us all well how to stay in a trail position during aerobatics.

Finally, Locke waggled his wings to signal Sam into close formation on his wing, and they returned to base. "Well done, Florance," he said at the debriefing after the flight, but his heart wasn't in it. He decided to skip that part of the training schedule for the rest of us. He also saw no reason to review the gun-camera film with Sam.

It occurred to me then that the RAF instructors—recent

graduates of the same training program that we were in—
did not have much more flying experience than we did.
They were about the same age as the average cadet and subject to the same human frailties. None had operational combat experience. They were "instructors" only by virtue of
the fact that they had graduated a few months ahead of us.
We still had plenty to learn, but so did they.

In early December 1942, Class 43-A was loaded onto a
troop train and transported to Eglin Field in Florida. Several
satellite bases were scattered throughout its large confines.
We were delivered to field number five, which consisted of
one thirty-five-hundred-foot runway, six or seven two-story
barracks, a mess hall, and not much else.

The AT-6 was not exactly a combat airplane. It had an
optical gunsight that projected a ring and bead onto the
windshield, and provisions for two .30-caliber machine
guns: one in the right wing, and one mounted on the fuselage just aft of the engine cowling, forward of the front
cockpit, and a little to the right of center. Only the fuselage
gun was installed. It was synchronized to fire through the
propeller and had a capacity of two hundred rounds. Only
once during our stay at field number five did a cadet manage
to put a hole through a propeller blade.

Ground targets were large white square panels with the
standard bull's-eye painted on them. There were about ten
targets in a line, each with a large number painted on top.
Each pilot had a specific target number assigned. This
seemed a fair system for scoring, but there was the in-
evitable claim of the low-scoring pilot that he had fired at
the wrong target, adding to the score of the pilot on his right
or left.

Locke's students did quite well in that phase. He led a
few gunnery flights, but we weren't informed of his scores.

The aerial gunnery phase was much more complicated.
We had hours of lectures and instructions on the art of deflection shooting, and warnings about breaking away from

the firing pass before shooting down the tow plane. We did all our aerial gunnery over the Gulf of Mexico. The tow plane pulled a canvas target—ten feet by forty feet—in a specified pattern: about twenty miles east to west, then it turned to a reciprocal course of the same distance.

Since we usually flew in flights of four; the ammunition from each plane was marked with a different-colored paint to distinguish each pilot's score. If I had red-painted ammo, my target hits had red fringes. At the end of the gunnery mission the tow plane dropped the target near the runway and we all rushed over to count holes.

Gunnery instructors lectured us on the mathematics of deflection shooting and led our flights on some firing runs. Pilot Officer Locke led our flight the rest of the time. He scored reasonably well, as did the rest of us—except Sam. He was by far the best marksman of our group. This may have been another source of friction between Locke and Sam, though none of it surfaced.

Christmas Day was one of those damp, raw days that are not uncommon on the Florida panhandle. There was no scheduled flying activity. Buses transported cadets to church services in the morning. By early afternoon we were all getting itchy. Then someone produced a football.

Eglin Field was a huge sprawling sandbox. There may have been grassy lawns at the main base facilities, but not where we were. It didn't matter. Soon we had two teams. Toemarks in the sand indicated where the sidelines and goal lines were, and there were very few rules. This wasn't touch or flag football; this was hard-nosed tackle football—a group of energetic, bored, restless young men blowing off steam.

Pilot Officer Locke wandered onto the scene. Sam, of course, was right in the middle of the action. Locke knew little about American football, but he had played rugby. He surveyed the scene for a few minutes and then asked if he could play. "Sure!" came the reply from several players. Locke was wearing sweatpants, a T-shirt, and sneakers. He quickly joined the team I was on, playing opposite Sam's team. I saw a broad smile on Locke's face as we resumed play.

Sam was quarterback for his team. Almost as soon as he got the ball from center, Locke smashed through the line and nailed Sam with a hard tackle. "Whew!" said Sam. "You sure hit hard!" Locke helped him up and smiled at him. On the next play, Sam handed off to another player who was trying to run around end. Sam was standing there watching when Locke hit him with another hard tackle. "Hey," yelled Sam, "I didn't have the ball!"

"Sorry," said Locke, "I guess I thought I was playing rugby." He helped Sam to his feet and smiled.

Sam had a rough afternoon. It seemed that no matter what he did, he found himself on the receiving end of a jarring block or another hard tackle by Locke. On the other hand, Pilot Officer Locke was having the most enjoyable afternoon of his brief stint as our flight instructor.

When we returned to Spence Field, I learned that I was one of the dozen or so cadets selected to fly the P-39 fighters. There were only three of them at Spence, and each flight instructor was allowed to pick one student for this extracurricular benefit. I didn't know Jim Duffy, my future wartime roommate, at the time, but he also was in that program, having been selected by his instructor.

The Bell P-39 Aeracobra was a first-line American pursuit plane when the Japanese bombed Pearl Harbor. Powered by an Allison liquid-cooled 1,200-horsepower engine, it cruised at 250 miles per hour and had a maximum speed of 375 miles per hour. Its armament included a 37mm cannon fired through the propeller hub and two .50-caliber machine guns in the nose. A unique feature of its design was the positioning of the engine behind the pilot's cockpit. This made for a sleek, streamlined silhouette, but it moved the center of gravity aft, which adversely affected its maneuverability and spin-recovery characteristics. The lack of a supercharger limited its operations above seventeen thousand feet. It was no match for the much more agile Japanese Zero, especially above fifteen thousand feet. P-39s flew mostly in strafing and ground-attack roles.

After a week of intense ground school preparation, we were ready to fly the P-39. Before each flight, the P-39 instructor gave us an instruction sheet outlining the maneuvers we were to perform or practice. The first day was just basic "getting a feel for the airplane" flying: dive and climb, steep turns, approach to a stall, and two touch-and-go landings before the final landing.

The P-39s were parked close to the takeoff end of the runway to prevent engine overheating during prolonged ground operation. I sat in the cockpit for about fifteen minutes before engine start, memorizing the position of the throttle, prop control, mixture control, gear handle, flaps, trim tabs, radio channels, and all the instruments on the front panel. Then, with the instructor kneeling on the wing at the open door of the cockpit, I started the engine and called the tower for takeoff directions. The instructor patted me on the head, closed the cockpit door, and slid off the back of the wing. I was on my way.

Taxiing was a breeze, because the tricycle landing gear allowed good visibility ahead and to the sides; no big nose blocked out the taxi strip ahead. The tower cleared me into position, then announced, "Cleared for takeoff."

I took a deep breath to calm myself down a little, then gently pushed the throttle to the full open position and released the brakes. I felt the surge of power as the airplane swiftly gathered speed, pushing me back in the seat. Just before liftoff speed, I pulled the nosewheel up a little and the P-39 seemed to leap off the ground. I pulled the gear handle up and set the throttle and prop control to the climb settings. Clean, streamlined, and responsive, the P-39 headed skyward.

At ten thousand feet I leveled off and had that heady feeling of speed and power as the streamlined fighter accelerated quickly and smoothly. I had never reached ten thousand feet in such a short time, and I felt an elation that is hard to describe. This airplane required the pilot to think ahead because it was *moving!* I felt so good that I had to do a couple of rolls, in spite of the fact that the aerobatics phase of the training was scheduled to come later.

The wide landing gear and clear forward vision made landing the P-39 easy. When I taxied to the parking spot, my instructor was waiting. I must have had a silly grin all over my face because he said, "I see you've had a good time."

I was ecstatic. I knew I had made the right move when I set my sights on flying fighters. I could hardly wait for the next flight.

Our graduation from advanced flight school was approaching, and we flew the P-39 only four times. Each flight had a different agenda—certain aerobatic exercises, stalls and spins, maximum performance exercises, and even a short cross-country flight. All too soon, the P-39 orientation ended.

Graduation day was January 14, 1943. My mother took a long train trip from New Hampshire to attend the graduation, and she proudly pinned the gold bars and silver wings on my brand-new uniform.

Operational Training

A few days after graduation, the assignment orders were posted on the bulletin board of our barracks. I was assigned to the 355th Fighter Group in Orlando, Florida. A few lines above my name was James E. Duffy, also assigned to the 355th. A lieutenant standing next to me was muttering, "355th Fighter Group in—"

"Are you Duffy?" I asked.

"Yeah." He looked at the list again. "Are you Fortier?" I acknowledged that I was.

"Looks like we're going to the same outfit," said Jim.

We shook hands, talked about our new assignment, and agreed to leave by bus the following day.

Next morning we met at the Greyhound bus terminal. "What did you say your name was?" asked Jim. Great friendships have modest beginnings.

It occurred to us that we could spend some time at Miami Beach if we could get a few days' delay before reporting for duty. Just before boarding the bus, we sent a telegram to the 355th Fighter Group, requesting a ten-day delay en route and asking for a reply via the Western Union office at the Greyhound bus terminal in Jacksonville.

There was no reply in Jacksonville, so we took the next bus to Orlando. By the time we got there, we had learned a lot about each other. We had become friends.

We took a cab to Orlando Air Base. The guard at the gate directed us to the 355th headquarters building. As we approached the flight line, we saw a row of twin-engine aircraft, all painted a dull black. Jim pointed. "What in hell are those?"

"Those," our knowledgeable cabdriver said, "are night fighters." I looked at Jim and saw the same disappointment that I felt. Suddenly our assignment to a fighter group didn't look so promising. The cab stopped just past the row of black-painted fighters. "Here you are, gentlemen," announced the driver. "Three five-five headquarters."

Carrying all our worldly possessions in our B-4 bags, we reported to the group adjutant, Maj. Glynn Williams. "What the hell are you guys doing here?" he asked. "I sent you the approval for that ten-day delay."

"In that case," I said, "we'll be on our way."

"No, you won't," said the adjutant. "Now that you're here, you stay." We knew better than to argue with a major.

We spent the next few days "clearing in" with the pay section, the medics, the chaplain's office, and all the other places that needed to know all about us. Base supply issued us our very own parachutes, complete with carrying bag. "I hope they don't expect me to pack my own chute," muttered Jim.

Then back to Major Williams. "You're assigned to the 354th Fighter Squadron," he told us. "It's temporarily at Zephyrhills, about fifty miles west of here."

"Are those night fighters there, too?" I asked.

"Oh, hell, no!" He laughed. "That's another outfit." We breathed a sigh of relief.

"Zephyrhills," said the sergeant driving the jeep next morning, "has fourteen churches, one drugstore, and a shuffleboard court. Orlando it ain't." His appraisal was quite accurate.

Zephyrhills Army Air Base consisted of about twenty tarpaper shacks, some dirt roads, and one runway newly hacked out of the swampy woods. The 354th Fighter Squadron consisted of about fifteen enlisted men and 2d Lt. James P. Murphy, the squadron armament officer. He was acting squadron commander, but his days of glory were short-lived. Duff and I were the first pilots to report to the squadron. Two other pilots on the same assignment order—

2d Lt. Roland Vincent and 2d Lt. Charles Sweat, both also graduates of Spence Field—signed in later that afternoon. The next day, January 25, two more pilots, Emil Perry and James Austin, both second lieutenants, reported for duty.

A few days later, a cadre of officers and enlisted men from the 50th Fighter Group came in to take over the key command and administrative positions. Within a few weeks the squadron had been pretty well filled in with pilots and maintenance people, and about a dozen P-40 fighters had been flown in. The 354th now had five first lieutenants: Joe Williams assumed command of the squadron, Henry Kucheman became operations officer, Ralph Berg and Walter J. Koraleski were designated flight leaders. Bob Woody had transferred from the infantry as a first lieutenant and had just graduated from Spence Field in Class 43-A, so his flight experience was the same as ours. Two second lieutenants also came from the 50th: Les Minchew and Albert Starr.

Duff and I were assigned to A Flight, along with Bob Woody and Emil Perry. Our flight leader was Koraleski, who had about seventy-five hours in the P-40. We soon learned that Korky was an outstanding pilot and leader.

After two weeks of intensive instruction on the P-40's systems—electrical, hydraulic, fuel, oil, coolant, and so forth—and memorizing emergency procedures for worst-case scenarios and how to survive in the swamps of Florida, we were ready to fly the beast. My first flight in the P-40 is still etched in my memory.

Challenge no. 1 was keeping the thing on the runway during the takeoff roll. I couldn't see over that huge nose in front of the cockpit, and I was standing on the right rudder to keep the engine torque from pulling me off the left side of the runway into a swamp.

As the tail lifted, I could see over the nose, and that helped. When the airspeed increased, the P-40 came alive and lifted into its own element. It began to act like an airplane.

Challenge no. 2 was getting the landing gear up. It was no simple matter, like just pulling the gear handle up. I did that, but the gear stayed down. Then I remembered that the hydraulic system had to be actuated before the gear could come up. There was a little ring on the end of a wire attached to the stick. First you had to find the little ring without letting the airplane get away from you, and then you hooked your little finger in the ring and pulled. This opened the valve that allowed hydraulic fluid to get to the gear— and presto! The gear came up. The engineer who devised this system obviously never flew the P-40.

By the time I got the gear up, the engine throttled back, and the propeller pitch adjusted, I was over Big Cypress Swamp, climbing through five thousand feet. I saw the Gulf of Mexico ahead and Tampa to my left, and it occurred to me that I'd better not let the airfield out of my sight. I was not familiar with this part of the world.

I turned back and located the field. The rest of this orientation flight was flown in a wide circle of the base, trying to memorize checkpoints to keep from getting lost in case I was ever talked into flying a P-40 again. I did a few rolls and lazy eights. Finally, I thought, I'm getting used to the feel of this airplane. At about fifteen thousand feet I started a shallow dive to build up airspeed for a loop. I needed ever-increasing pressure on the left rudder to keep the nose pointed straight ahead; as I pulled the nose up, I had to apply more and more right rudder as power increased and airspeed decreased. On the back side of the loop, just the opposite—less power, more speed, and more left rudder were needed. I felt I was learning a foot-stomping dance step.

My first landing was uneventful, unless you consider a jarring, bouncing, jackrabbit landing eventful. I was just glad to get back on terra firma.

At Spence Field, Jim and I had been among the dozen or so cadets chosen to fly the P-39 at the end of our regular training. It was a sweet-flying airplane, except for its unfortunate tendency to "flatten out" in a spin, often with fatal results. After the P-39, the P-40 felt like a Mack truck. It required a heavy hand on the stick, and we always seemed to be standing on one rudder or the other to counter the engine torque. I flew it only about five times. To put it mildly,

I didn't like it, and I hoped we would not have to go into combat with it.

Second Lieutenant Myron (Mike) Glantz, a lawyer, reported to the 355th early in December 1942. He was assigned to the 354th early in February as intelligence officer. Dr. Reed Fontenot, from the Cajun country of Louisiana, joined us from Orlando on February 13, just in time to hop onto a convoy of trucks en route to . . . Orlando. We now had legal and medical expertise. Two days later, the entire group began its move via troop train to Philadelphia, with stops along the way at Richmond and Norfolk, Virginia.

At Norfolk two more pilots—2d Lt. William (Bill) Boulet and 2d Lt. Lawrence (Pop) Allard—joined us, as did 2d Lt. Burt Sims, combat intelligence officer. The 354th Fighter Squadron was gradually approaching full strength.

On March 4 we were aroused at 2:00 A.M. We were moving out. "Why in hell can't we move in the daytime?" Duff groused. We left Langley at 4:30 A.M. by troop train, and arrived at Philadelphia at ten-twenty that night. By the time we got to the airport and to our assigned billets, dawn was breaking. We slept most of that day. We got our first look at the flight line and our operations buildings on March 6. There were no P-40s in sight. Brand-new Republic P-47 Thunderbolts, the newest and most advanced fighters in the Army Air Forces, were waiting for us.

The "Jug," as it became known, because of the shape of its fuselage, was a big, heavy airplane. It was more than 14 feet high, 36 feet long, and had a wingspan of nearly 41 feet. Fully loaded, it weighed more than 6 tons. Its eighteen-cylinder R-2800 radial engine produced 2,300 horsepower, later increased to 2,430 with water injection, and it had a top speed of 433 miles per hour in level flight. Designed as a high-altitude fighter, with a turbosupercharger for efficient engine performance above 20,000 feet, it later earned a reputation as an excellent low-level fighter-bomber because of its ability to absorb a lot of damage and keep flying.

As Duff and I stood outside our operations building,

staring at those huge airplanes and wondering if we could ever learn to fly them, one of them landed and taxied to the parking area in front of us. When the engine shut down, we watched open-mouthed as the canopy slid open and a slender young woman, about five feet, four inches tall, climbed out of the cockpit, slid down the wing, and jumped to the ground. We learned later that she was a WASP—Women's Air Force Service Pilot—and that she needed block extensions on the rudder pedals to control the aircraft. Jim shrugged. "I guess if she can fly them, so can we."

We had to learn all about the P-47's systems—engine, electrical, hydraulic, fuel, oil, brakes, flight controls and flaps, instruments, heating/ventilation, and so on—before we flew it. That was a full week of ground-school classes, complete with written exams for each phase.

My first flight in the P-47 was on March 8, 1943. It was a C model with the "greenhouse"-style canopy; later models came with a streamlined bubble canopy. The size of the airplane with that big, powerful radial engine was quite intimidating, but I kept reminding myself of that little lady ferry pilot. Taxiing required constant "essing" because of the huge nose up front. At the end of the runway, as I checked the magnetos, I had the feeling that the airplane was in a hurry to get into its own element. The tower cleared me into takeoff position. I checked all the instruments and the trim-tab settings. "Cleared for takeoff."

I eased the throttle to about half power, released the brakes, and advanced the throttle all the way forward. The Thunderbolt accelerated smoothly, pushing me back in the seat, and I was on my way. The tail came up, and the airplane lifted easily off the runway.

The Jug was easy and a pleasure to fly. The engine-torque effect was similar to that of the P-40, but the wide landing gear made it easier to control on takeoff and landing. In spite of its size, it was much lighter on the controls than the P-40; it didn't *feel* like a big airplane. After a few flights, I forgot how big it was.

Second Lieutenants Bob Kurtz and Chuck Lenfest, recent graduates of West Point and Cadet Class 43-A, joined us in Philadelphia on April 12. I watched from a second-floor window of the operations building as they walked to the orderly room to sign in. Kurtz marched ramrod-stiff, as if on parade. Lenfest ambled along about half a step behind, looking more like a midwestern farmer behind a plow than a West Point graduate.

Richard Brown, Arvid (Swede) Benson, Harold Culp, Alfred Del Negro, Byron (Sammy) Houston, Lee Mendenhall, Thomas (Jeeter) Neal, Brady Williamson, F. W. Moeller, and Kenny Williams, all second lieutenants, joined us that same day. Our family was expanding.

Philadelphia Municipal Airport was our base for operational training prior to going overseas. We suspected we would be going to Europe—we didn't know for sure—but we were quite sure that we'd soon be headed for combat.

Ground school subjects included meteorology, air navigation, radio procedures, aircraft recognition, escape and evasion techniques, and the T. O. "dash one"—the technical order that detailed all the P-47's engine and aircraft systems and emergency procedures. In groups of four, pilots were sent to Bolling Field in Washington, D.C., for altitude chamber training, where we learned firsthand about the effects of high altitude on bodily functions and the warning symptoms of anoxia. We learned later in combat situations that anoxia could be—and often was—a killer.

Flight training focused on formation flying, combat tactics, navigation, and gunnery. The aerial gunnery range, off the coast of New Jersey, was under the control of the naval air station at Cape May, temporary home of a squadron of F6F Hellcats fighters. We were allotted blocks of time each day for our gunnery flights. An Army air base in Millville, New Jersey, provided a ground gunnery range, with blocks of time reserved for the Navy fighters. We were constantly encouraged to make simulated attacks on military aircraft we saw in the course of our daily training flights, and the Hellcats provided plenty of eager playmates for our mock dogfights. The Thunderbolts and Hellcats were fairly evenly matched in performance, so our encounters were quite exciting.

One squadron at a time, we moved to the Army base at Millville for concentrated gunnery training. Millville was a sleepy little town just outside of Vineland, which had several nightspots that were happy to provide entertainment for energetic fighter pilots. Many an early-morning gunnery mission was flown with an aching head.

In the course of our "friendly" encounters with our Navy counterparts, one of our flights decided to show off their Thunderbolts, up close, to the Navy folks at Cape May Naval Air Station. The thorough buzz job disturbed the admiral in charge, and he sent a formal complaint through channels to our group commander, Col. William (Wild Bill) Cummings, who replied, as expected, with an apology. A week later, a flight of four P-47s flew over the naval air station at a thousand feet, slowed down to less than two hundred miles per hour. As they approached the flight line and administration buildings, the pilots slid their canopies open and threw out dozens of pink powder puffs.

The next day, eight F6Fs put on an impressive demonstration of low-level flight at Philadelphia Municipal Airport as four others worked over the base at Millville.

The commanders at all levels then called a truce.

On April 5, Duff and I were flying a training mission in the local flying area, practicing aerobatics and formation flying, and alternating the lead and wing positions. About an hour into the flight we spotted a C-47 transport plane about two thousand feet below us, heading south. I was leading. It was a military airplane with an olive drab U.S. Army paint job, so we considered it fair game and made two simulated "shooting" passes at it, breaking off at a reasonable distance. The C-47 pilot wasn't even aware of our presence.

Then I decided to put on a little show for that poor transport pilot destined to drive that truck around for the duration. I dove in behind him and well to his right, and at three hundred miles per hour overtook him quickly, and did a barrel roll to the left after I shot by and was well ahead of him. Duff had the good sense not to follow. That, I thought, will impress the truck driver. It did. I soon found out just how much.

When we returned to base and taxied to our parking area, there was a reception committee waiting for us. The deputy group commander, the group operations officer, and our squadron commander were there, along with a few officers I didn't recognize. I wondered what the fuss was all about, but one thing was clear: They were not happy. No one was smiling. As soon as I hit the ground, they started making comments that reflected adversely on my IQ. I finally got a word in to ask what it was all about.

That transport airplane just happened to contain Mr. Henry L. Stimson, secretary of war. He had apparently *not* been favorably impressed by my exhibition of flying prowess. He was, according to my reception committee, quite angry. Proclaiming my innocence was not an option, since large numbers were painted in yellow on both sides of my airplane. Had this been a run-of-the-mill Army C-47, I doubt the pilot would have reported the incident, but this was a C-41, a C-47 converted for VIP use. Because it contained the secretary of war, a whole bunch of people soon got into the act.

The chief of air staff in Washington demanded an investigation by the air inspector, Maj. Gen. Follet Bradley. He in turn demanded an investigation by the I Fighter Command at Mitchel Field, New York. Brigadier General Barcus, commander of the I Fighter Command, sent a colonel to Philadelphia to conduct the investigation. The colonel's first order of business was to find out who did it.

Only two airplanes with yellow identification numbers were flying in the area at the time. The other one was nowhere near Philadelphia, so it didn't take a Sherlock Holmes to figure out who did it. Besides, I never denied it.

Nevertheless, the colonel called fourteen "witnesses," only two of whom had witnessed the incident: James Duffy and Norman Fortier. I don't recall if the colonel was a pilot, but if so, he was not a fighter pilot. He asked four witnesses, including me, if they had ever performed a slow roll *to the right*. Considering that I had actually performed a barrel roll to the left, I didn't understand the relevance of the question. He also did not seem to understand the difference between a slow roll and a barrel roll. I guess he just wanted to show his boss how thorough he was.

I thought they were going to court-martial me, and I doubted that I'd have a jury of my peers—fighter pilots. My only defense, and it was flimsy at best, was that the C-47 *was* a military airplane, and we had been urged to simulate attacks against military targets. "A barrel roll is *not* a simulated attack!" I was told emphatically. Only the group air executive officer, Lt. Col. Thomas "Speed" Hubbard, came to my defense by pointing out that we *had been urged* to be aggressive. He was ignored. For the first time in my short military career, I was dejected and frightened. I had visions of going back to New Hampshire in disgrace—drummed out of the service because of a stupid stunt.

The decision finally came down from Washington: no court-martial. Maybe they needed combat pilots, or maybe they figured I'd get killed off in combat anyway, so why bother?

Under the provisions of the 104th Article of War, General Barcus fined me seventy-five dollars and reprimanded me for performing a "slow roll in close proximity" to the C-41. My pending promotion was deferred for at least three months. I received another letter of reprimand, from Henry L. Stimson. It included several unflattering references to me, all synonyms for idiot. He also implied that I might as well get used to being a second lieutenant, because I might still be one when the war ended. Duff looked at it and said, "I'll bet Stimson didn't even see your little show. He was probably taking a nap in the back of the airplane."

The reprimands made their way up and down the chain of command through a series of RBIs. This was the Army's way of ensuring that you got the message. "You will *r*eply

*b*y *i*ndorsement hereon, acknowledging receipt . . . etc."
After sixteen indorsements (that's the way they spelled it)
involving five levels of command, the fifty-seven-page report—classified CONFIDENTIAL—wound up in my personnel file on July 8, more than two months after the
incident.

Early in 1943, the mood of the American people was one
of apprehension. The West Coast appeared vulnerable to attack by the formidable Japanese navy, and German submarines were believed capable of attacking cities on the
East Coast. All the large cities on the eastern seaboard had
some form of modified blackout—more like a brownout—
to minimize the risk of attack.

The 354th took turns with the other two squadrons to
keep four P-47s on alert at all times after normal duty hours.
We were neither equipped nor trained to find and destroy
submarines in the dark sea, nor to locate and shoot down
German bombers in the unlikely event they made their way
to our continent at night, but someone at higher headquarters
had decided to have an alert force, so we found ourselves on
alert every other week or so. We spent the night at the alert
facility—a room with four cots, a table, four chairs, and a
telephone that was our link with "headquarters" (wherever
that was). Our crew chiefs were in an adjoining hut.

Duff and I were on alert one night with Emil Perry and
the flight leader, Ralph Berg. Heavy rain was doing a drum-
roll on the roof of the alert shack, and the wind was rattling the windows. Duff and I were engrossed in our usual
chess match. Perry was reading. Ralph was trying to get to
sleep.

The phone rang. We looked at each other in disbelief.
We had all been on alert before, but the phone *never* rang.
Ralph shook the cobwebs away and picked up the receiver.

"Alert flight, Captain Berg." He listened intently. "You
want us to *what?*" We strained our ears and watched his
face turn red. "What are the colors of the day?" he asked.
That apparently drew a blank, because he said, "You know!

What are the color codes of the day? How are we going to identify the thing?"

Another blank. Ralph's short fuse blew. "Listen to me," he yelled, "we're not going up through all this shit and not know if we're supposed to shoot it down or not. Give me the code of the day!" Five seconds went by.

He hung up the receiver. "They said forget it."

He went back to his cot, muttering about stupid idiots, Perry picked up his book, and Duff said, "Check!"

An inbound airliner had neglected to identify itself, and the people at headquarters decided to send us up to investigate. What they didn't know was that their alert force had little experience flying at night and none at all flying in a flight of four, through clouds, at night. We were hardly an all-weather alert force. Had we been ordered to take off that night, I might not be writing this.

As far as I know, the alert phone never rang again while we were in Philadelphia, though we kept four aircraft and pilots on alert until we left for Camp Kilmer.

On June 2, 1st Lt. Curtis Johnston joined us, the last pilot assigned to our squadron prior to our departure for England.

On June 11, the 354th Fighter Squadron suffered its first casualty. Second Lieutenant F. W. Moeller was flying Bob Kurtz's wing in a four-ship formation led by 1st Lt. Les Minchew. The flight penetrated a stratus cloud layer at about two thousand feet and began a slow right turn. At this point Moeller's plane broke off from the formation, dove straight into the ground, and exploded on contact. It was our first weather-related loss, but it would not be our last.

By the middle of June it became obvious that the time for departure to a combat zone was near. We were not told our destination, but most of us had already figured out that we were headed for Europe, though the powers-that-be tried in various ways to keep us in doubt. Our aircraft recognition sessions included Japanese Zeros and Bettys as well as Me-109s and FW-190s; our immunization shots included those for yellow fever and malaria.

On June 15, we were told that we'd better be ready to leave early the next morning if we didn't want to be left behind. It was breakfast at 5:00 A.M., and into the trucks to the railroad station. Loaded down with all our earthly possessions and only half awake, we boarded the train, which finally got under way at 9:00 A.M. "Why in hell do they get us up at four-thirty in the morning to get on a train that doesn't leave until nine o'clock?" asked Duff.

"They want to make sure you don't miss the war!" replied Brady.

"Fat chance!" said Duff.

We arrived at Camp Kilmer, New Jersey, at 11:05 A.M. on June 16. I can't remember being in a more disorganized military installation. We were really just waiting for sea transport, but so were thousands of other guys—infantry, artillery, air corps—and no one seemed to know what was going on. We were issued mosquito netting and given another malaria shot; we attended lectures on surviving in a dinghy and keeping the sharks away. We were even given heavy impregnated clothing and gas masks in case we were exposed to chemical warfare. We stayed at Camp Kilmer for two weeks, and all we did that whole time was eat, sleep, and mill around.

"Did you hear the latest rumor?" asked Perry.

"Yeah," said Korky. "We're going by train to San Francisco, and shipping out to Australia."

"The one I heard," said Perry, "is that we're leaving here tonight."

It was June 30, and we were more than ready to leave the place. Later that day we were informed that we would leave right after evening chow. We jam-packed our B-4 bags and duffel bags, but most of us "forgot" to pack our gas masks, mosquito netting, and impregnated clothing. Others "accidentally" dropped them on the way to the waiting trucks. Fortunately, our parachutes had been returned to the supply people at Philadelphia.

"Where to?" I asked the driver of our truck.

He shrugged. "I don't know," he replied. "I just follow

the truck ahead of me." When we finally got rolling, it was only about an hour's drive. We tumbled out of the truck and found that we were at the ferry pier in Hoboken, New Jersey.

"My Gawd," said the usually taciturn Perry, staring at the ferryboats, "are we going to England on one of those?"

By the time we were ferried across the Hudson River to the piers on the Manhattan side, it was after midnight. That's when we got our first look at the *Queen Elizabeth*.

The Queen

She was massive. She dwarfed the dock buildings and the other ships nearby. The *Queen Elizabeth* was the largest ocean liner ever built to that time. A steady stream of uniforms inched up several gangplanks. An MP directed us to one of them.

At 1:00 A.M., 37 officers and 252 enlisted men of the 354th Fighter Squadron followed the group ahead, lemming-like, up the gangplank and into the bowels of the ship. We stopped by an official-looking Navy type labeled Purser, who checked us off in his book; then another Navy type labeled Billeting handed each of us a little ticket telling us where to sleep and when to eat—two meals a day, breakfast at 7:30 A.M., dinner at 5:30 P.M.

Duff and I found our way to C Deck and located our assigned billet. We were in what would have been a small stateroom in happier times. Six three-tiered bunks left little room to store our baggage. There were no portholes—we were amidships—and only one bathroom.

"Welcome to the luxury liner *Queen Elizabeth*!" said Brady Williamson. "Looks like we'll be sharing this linen closet for a few days." Eighteen of our officers were in this stateroom and eighteen more in the stateroom next door.

We put our bags in a corner of the room and went up to the main deck to watch the seemingly endless procession of uniforms moving slowly into the ship. It was only after we walked all around the deck the next morning that we realized what a giant this *Queen* was—nearly 1,000 feet long and 120 feet wide.

She was built to accommodate three thousand passengers in luxury, but on this trip she would carry two fighter groups and an entire infantry division—close to sixteen thousand men—but *not* in luxury. The increase was made possible by what was called a standee bunk, a tree of metal tubes supporting up to six canvas cots or stretchers to accommodate six sleeping soldiers. They were lightweight and strong. What was once the observation lounge was a maze of five-tiered bunks, and the boarded-over swimming pool was a forest of frames. Three GIs took turns sleeping, each for eight hours over a twenty-four-hour period.

"Boy," said Duff, "this is a juicy target for German U-boats!" We were not told that though she carried well over sixteen thousand men, including crew, she had lifeboat space and life jackets for only six thousand.

We slipped out of New York harbor at 6:00 A.M. It was July 2, a beautiful day. Officially, we didn't know where we were going, but by then we had all figured out that our destination was England. The decks were crowded as we passed the Statue of Liberty, many of us wondering if we'd ever see her again.

The *Queen Elizabeth* cruised at better than thirty knots, too fast to be part of a convoy and too fast to be caught by a single submarine. She depended on speed and an unpredictable zigzag course to evade the German U-boats—it *is* a big ocean. There were several 40mm antiaircraft gun positions on the upper deck, but we derived little comfort from them when we thought of torpedoes.

The weather was great for an ocean crossing, with warm, sunlit days and bright, moonlit nights, and also ideal for German submarine hunter-killer packs. Many of the troops spent the nights on the open decks. Not only was it cooler than belowdecks, but also I suspect they wanted to be near the lifeboats. The sea was quite calm, and there was very little pitch and roll. Except for the ever-present danger of being blown out of the water, it was almost monotonous.

Early on July 6, word spread quickly throughout the ship: land! We were in sight of land! For the first time since leaving New York Harbor, the threat of German submarines was lifted. RAF antisubmarine patrols were above us all day, a flock of eagles protecting a pregnant hen.

The *Queen* dropped anchor at Greenock, Scotland, in the Firth of Clyde at nine o'clock that evening. The 355th was scheduled to debark at seven the next morning. We were advised to wear our steel helmets during the debarkation. I asked one of the crewmen if that was because of possible enemy activity. "No, sir," he replied, "it's the seagulls."

We were loaded aboard the Royal Navy tender *King George V* for the short trip to the dock at Greenock. They packed so many of us on that small vessel I didn't think we'd make it to the dock. The seagulls were indeed out in force. The steel helmets protected our heads, but most of us wore messy badges of passage on our uniforms when we reached the dock.

We were herded to the nearby train station, and with the usual confusion that attends such affairs, everyone was finally aboard by 11:00 A.M. A few toots of the whistle and we were on our way.

It was a long train ride. We stopped about midafternoon for chow, which consisted of cans of C rations heated in buckets of boiling water. The train stopped at a few stations in the middle of the night, and some nice ladies gave us hot tea and tiny parsley sandwiches. At 3:00 A.M. we arrived at Royston, about five miles from the airfield. By the time we were all loaded on 2½-ton trucks and transported to the base, it was about 5:30 A.M. The mess halls were open for us, and we all had a hearty SOS breakfast. SOS ("shit on a shingle") was the GI term for what looked like creamed chipped beef on toast, except that it was hamburger, not chipped beef. That morning, it tasted great.

Steeple Morden

Station F122, as the airfield at Steeple Morden was designated by the USAAF, was a farm until World War II broke out. In 1942 it was a training base for RAF bomber crews checking out in Blenheim and Wellington bombers. Early in 1943, rumors began to circulate that it would soon be home to an American flying unit. Confirmation of the rumors came in late June, when an advance party arrived from the United States to prepare for the arrival of the 355th Fighter Group in July.

The airfield was about a mile east of the village of Steeple Morden. It was closer to Litlington, the town directly abutting the base on the east. The 354th A Flight dispersal area was almost inside the village of Litlington. The main runway, 04-22, was 4,760 feet long. With prevailing winds, we usually took off on runway 22, heading 220 degrees. The no. 2 runway, 16-34, was 3,320 feet long. The third runway, 10-28, was 3,100 feet long. We occasionally used the shorter runways during periods of high winds before we began carrying external fuel tanks; then they were too short for fully loaded Thunderbolts and Mustangs.

The 354th officers were billeted in what had been known as WAAF Site 1 when the base was a Royal Air Force station. It was nearly a mile from the officers' mess and from the flight line. Pilots were quartered in two oversized Nissen huts, each containing fourteen beds, one stove, and little else. Sandwiched between the Nissen huts was a smaller rectangular ablutions hut. It featured ten showerheads along one wall—no stalls—and washbasins with mirrors beside the doors on each end. Opposite the showers were latrine stalls. These consisted of a large drain in the middle of the stall with two platforms in the shape of large feet, one on each side of the drain. You stood, or squatted, on these platforms, facing the showers, and went about your business. On the back wall was the water tank and pull chain to flush everything down the drain. "Primitive" is too kind a description for such an arrangement. Those poor WAAFs! Even in the middle of July, it was a dank and dreary building. I fervently hoped that the Big Wheels would find more suitable accommodations for us soon.

Because we were so far from the flight line and officers' mess, we were each issued a bicycle. This typical Army Band-Aid solution to a problem had unintended consequences. Late one afternoon, five pilots from the 357th Squadron set out to visit the nearby town of Royston on their bikes. Traffic on the country road was very light, so they decided to cycle in a vee formation right in the middle of the narrow road. It was great fun until an army truck came around a bend in the road, heading their way. The vee formation broke up, with bicycles and riders bailing out into roadside ditches. One pilot suffered a broken arm and others had cuts and bruises. There were more cuts-and-bruises incidents when pilots rode their bikes back to the WAAF site after imbibing a few too many at the officers' club.

The officers' mess was of typical Nissen hut construction, with two large sections joined in the shape of an off-center letter T. Coming through the main entrance, the mess hall was straight ahead, the bar off to the right, and a games room—snooker, darts, Ping-Pong, and cards—to the left. The entryway had a storage area for hats, coats, boots, umbrellas, and the like.

The club bar was quite primitive at first, but it gradually took shape as a circular carousel-style bar was built, and tables and comfortable chairs sprouted along the edges. English beer and Scotch whiskey were in plentiful supply; American bourbon or Canadian blended whiskies appeared only when someone returning from R&R in the States brought in a few bottles, and they didn't last long.

The mess hall consisted of two long rows of tables, each seating ten people, with a cafeteria-style counter on the right side. It was a typical army mess hall.

Our "ready room" on the flight line was a patchwork blend of a rectangular cement-block building and a Nissen hut. To the left was a solid building housing the squadron commander's small office, and the combined operations and intelligence sections. Daily flight schedules and mission information were posted on a large bulletin board outside this section. On the right was the pilots' lounge, a Nissen hut containing a Ping-Pong table, record player, dartboard, two cots, and assorted furniture used by pilots between missions. A later addition provided space for parachutes, Mae West life jackets, G suits, helmets, and other personal effects.

Eventually a snack bar was installed in the area between the intelligence section and the pilots' lounge, and this evolved into an excellent breakfast facility, because our enterprising noncoms traded cigarettes and candy with local farmers for fresh eggs—no more powdered eggs with the Spam.

The entryway was between these two sections. Above the entrance was a sign designed by Burt Sims. It featured the squadron insignia—a large bulldog in front of the Statue of Liberty. Beneath the insignia was "GREMLIN VILLA," and below that was "Be It Ever So Humble . . ." It was Burt's attempt to provide a home away from home.

P-47Bs were flown in daily until we reached our full complement of sixty aircraft. As more planes became available from ever-increasing production in the United States, our full complement was increased to seventy-five. Each squadron had its distinctive designator painted forward of the national star insignia. The 354th squadron designator was WR, the 357th OS, and the 358th YF. Individual designators were single letters aft of the star.

My P-47 was designated WR-N, as was my P-51 later. Most of the pilots gave names to their airplanes. Some were names of sweethearts or wives back home; others, like Henry Brown's *Hun Hunter from Texas*, were more like job descriptions. Duff's plane was *Dragon Wagon;* Korky's was *Miss Thunder*, a fine example of Cpl. Arthur DeCosta's outstanding nose-art paintings. DeCosta worked in the NCO mess hall, "stirring gravy in a huge tub with a broken canoe paddle," as he put it years later. Though most of the airplanes were named, I never heard a pilot refer to his airplane by name. For instance, Duff never said, "Old *Dragon Wagon* was really purring today," or anything of the sort.

I decided to keep my nose clean—unnamed. I explained it this way to Duff: "If the Krauts see a fancy painting on a P-47's nose, they figure that the pilot must be a big wheel, so they go after him. But a guy with no artwork on the nose must be just a peon—not worth shooting at."

Each squadron was assigned a radio call sign. The 354th was Haywood, the 357th was Blowball, and the 358th was Trooptrain. In a combat formation, each flight had a designated color code: The lead flight was red, the next flight was yellow, the next flight was blue, and the fourth flight was green. If a fifth flight was needed, as in a maximum effort mission, it was designated white. The group leader was Sunshade no matter which squadron he led.

The squadron's operational organization followed a similar pattern. Each pilot had an individual call sign for use on test hops, orientation, or other solo flights. Our organization in early September 1943 is shown—with call signs—in the following table:

Squadron Commander—Haywood 10
Operations Officer—Haywood 11

A Flight		B Flight		C Flight		D Flight	
Koraleski	H-20	Starr	H-30	Johnston	H-40	Vincent	H-50
Woody	H-21	Allard	H-31	Sweat	H-41	Lenfest	H-51
Perry	H-22	Kurtz	H-32	Minchew	H-42	Neal	H-52
Duffy	H-23	Austin	H-33	Del Negro	H-43	Mendenhall	H-53
Boulet	H-24	Benson	H-34	Williamson	H-44	Williams	H-54
Culp	H-25	Houston	H-35	R. Brown	H-45	Bauman	H-55
Fortier	H-26	Murdoch	H-36	H. Brown	H-46	Morris	H-56
				De Siena	H-47	Wright	H-57

My first crew chief at Steeple Morden was Sergeant MacArthur, but he was transferred to C Flight before our first combat mission. Herbert L. McKibbin was the crew chief on P-47 WR-N, and Lt. Harold Culp and I were the first two pilots assigned to fly it. After Culp was shot down, I was the primary pilot assigned to WR-N, and McKibbin was my crew chief until the end of the war.

Mac was at least fifteen years older than I, and looked old enough to be my father. He was from North Carolina and spoke with that slow and easy drawl typical of the area. He was known as a man who "could hold his liquor"— which meant that he was a fairly heavy drinker—and his face was a road map of where life had led him. He was a sergeant when I first met him. For the rest of the war, he fluctuated between sergeant and staff sergeant, depending on how much trouble he had gotten into at any given time.

Mac had a reputation for being very knowledgeable about the P-47 and later the P-51, but sometimes I wondered how much of that reputation really belonged to his young assistant, Cpl. (later Sgt.) Richard Dawe from Maine. "Dickie," as Mac called him, was a typical Maine man, quiet and reserved. Mac could ramble all around the answer to a question, but Dawe usually answered with a simple "yup" or "nope." He was the perfect balance for McKibbin's sense of comedy. Cpl. (later Sgt.) Henry Lowry, from Bedford, Virginia, was the armorer on WR-N. Like Dawe, he was a quiet man. He spent most of his spare time listening to fine music and reading.

McKibbin often appeared for work in the morning unkempt, unshaven, and red-eyed from his previous night's partying. Dawe and Lowry were always neat and cleareyed. They stayed away from the NCO club; it was Mac's second home. Somehow they worked well together to keep the aircraft in top shape for the combat missions.

Mac was a free spirit—translation: a character. Shortly after we arrived at Steeple, he and a few of his buddies boarded a train to London to celebrate his promotion to staff sergeant. English trains were compartmentalized, with each little compartment seating about eight people. He and his friends took up all the space in one compartment. A cord ran above the windows along the length of each compartment, through the whole train. Beneath the wire cord was the message PULL CORD FOR EMERGENCY STOP ONLY, and beneath, in smaller letters, "Penalty for improper use: £5." Mac and his friends had been sipping a little Scotch and were discussing whether pulling the cord would actually stop the train. Mac took up a collection totaling five pounds and pulled the cord.

The train hissed and shuddered to a stop, and the conductor ran through the compartment corridor, shouting, "What's the emergency? Who pulled the cord?"

When he got to Mac's compartment, Mac said, "I pulled the cord. There's no emergency. Here's your five pounds."

He soon found out that it was not quite that simple. The English police met the train at the next stop and took him to the station. They called the base, and Mac was soon on his way back to Steeple in a Military Police jeep.

The next day, he was a sergeant again. He had been a staff sergeant for nearly forty-eight hours.

In spite of his shortcomings, Mac was a hard worker, as were all the crew chiefs and assistants in our squadron. They and their counterparts in armament and communications worked long hours every day to make sure the fighters were in top mechanical condition for combat. They were the backbone of the outfit.

From mid-July to the first part of September we were immersed in all kinds of training and getting acquainted—from the air and on the ground—with the English countryside that would be our home. There were aircraft recognition sessions so we wouldn't shoot down our compatriots or our British allies; escape-and-evasion (E&E) lectures told us how to evade capture if we were shot down, or how to escape from POW camps if captured; and, of course, there were the VD lectures.

In the air and on the ground, Korky worked hard getting A Flight ready for combat. We spent hours in discussions of tactics, formations, performance of the Me-109s and

FW-190s, and many hours in simulated dogfights in the skies above Steeple Morden.

Our basic flight formation was known as the "finger" formation—if you hold out your right hand, palm down with fingers close together, the tips of your fingers indicate the position of each aircraft in the flight, as shown in this sketch:

1

2   **3**

4

Number 1 is the flight leader, 2 is his wingman; 3 is the element leader, and 4 is his wingman. In the lead flight, 1 was red leader, 2 was red two, 3 was red three, and 4 was red four. In a combat situation, the flight was spread out, looking like the back of your hand with the fingertips spread apart. The role of the wingmen—numbers 2 and 4—was defensive; 2 covered the rear of the second element, and 4 covered the rear of the lead element. The flight leader and his element leader were the hunters.

A squadron formation usually consisted of four flights: Yellow Flight was behind and slightly below Red Flight; in the second section, Green Flight was behind and slightly below Blue Flight, as shown below.

```
        T                            T
T               T          T                 T
    Red Flight      T          Blue Flight        T

        T                            T
T               T          T                 T
    Yellow Flight   T          Green Flight       T
```

We practiced the basic formation for hours, from section level to whole-group formations.

As we did in operational training, we engaged any and all aircraft passing through our flying area in mock dogfights. We soon learned that the Jug was no match for RAF

Spitfires in maneuverability. The Spitfire was much lighter and smaller than the Jug; it was designed to intercept and shoot down German bombers, and it excelled in that role. On the other hand, Spits had a much shorter range and seldom ventured above twenty-five thousand feet. "They're great at what they were designed to do, but they can't go very far from their own backyard" is the way Korky put it.

By the end of August, we were getting antsy.

September 1943

When September came we were ready for the Luftwaffe, or so we thought. The VIII Fighter Command thought so, too, but the bosses didn't want us to jump in over our heads right from the start. They scheduled us for "fighter sweeps," which were designed to ease us into the unfriendly skies over Europe and to show us what flak looked like.

September 9, 1943. Our group was now on operational status. Briefing was scheduled for 5:30 A.M., the mess hall opened at four-thirty, and takeoff was set for seven forty-six. "If this is just a fighter sweep," said Duff, rubbing the sleep out of his eyes, "why can't they have it in the afternoon?"

"It's because those guys in Fighter Command are up all night planning these things, and this is their bedtime," I explained.

Like most of our buildings, group headquarters looked like a huge oil drum that had been split down the middle and laid on a cement slab. The end pieces were flat, but the arch was corrugated for structural strength. The briefing room took up most of the available space on the east end; the west end housed the group headquarters offices. A large illuminated map covered the semicircular end wall of the briefing room. England was squeezed into the upper left side of the map, part of Denmark and the Baltic Sea were at the top of the ceiling arch, and Russia sprawled on the far right. Except for Switzerland, the rest of the map showed countries under German control. A stage in front of the map enabled the briefing officer to reach all those places with a long pointer. Backless wooden benches filled the room, and a few chairs on either side of the stage were reserved for the briefing officers.

The briefing room was already half full when Duff and I arrived, ten minutes early. Colonel Cummings stood in the back of the room, calm and silent. The group flight surgeon, Maj. Herschel Burns, had grounded him a few days earlier because of a painful ear infection. The tension and sense of excitement in the room were almost palpable. Five minutes later, all available seats were taken, and a number of spectators lined the back wall. Duff looked around and said, "Half these guys aren't even on the mission!"

"They're just curious," I said. I looked at the map. Heavy black twine traced a route from our base in England to Dunkerque, France, then southwest to St.-Omer, back to the coast near Calais, and back to base. A chart on the left side of the stage listed the timing information—start engines, takeoff, set course, landfall, rendezvous, break escort, and so on. "That sure as hell doesn't look like a fighter sweep to me!" I said. Duff just grunted; he was busy writing numbers on the palm of his hand.

Major Daniel Lewis, the group intelligence officer, was helping the weather officer set up his charts to the left of the stage. The intelligence officer usually began the briefings, but this was not a usual briefing.

At exactly five-thirty, all the lights in the briefing room went out except for the floodlights illuminating the map and the stage. Major Phillip Tukey, an experienced combat pilot on loan from the 56th Fighter Group to lead our first few missions, was onstage. "Well, we're in the big league. Right from the start!" he said with a smile. "This is not a fighter sweep. We'll be escorting B-17s into France!" I thought maybe I was expected to applaud, but no one else did, so I sat on my hands. "I expect you've already figured that out."

He signaled to Danny Lewis, who took center stage to tell us about the target, where we could expect flak, and locations of airfields likely to harbor the Luftwaffe. He briefly reviewed escape-and-evasion techniques before turning the briefing over to the weather officer.

Foggy Schmucker—all weather officers were nicknamed either Foggy or Stormy—tried to be optimistic. "Once you get off the ground, the weather will be great," he said, "but ground fog might close in by takeoff time." He motioned for the lights to be turned off; then the bright light of the slide projector cut through the darkness and cigarette smoke. It showed a cross section of the weather we could expect throughout the mission.

The lights came back on, and the communications officer reviewed the radio-channel assignments. Then Major Tukey went over each squadron's assignment, and gave us a little pep talk about staying in formation, radio silence, and tactics if attacked. "Any questions?" Silence. "Time hack!"

The communications officer gave the time hack: "It will be 0556 in twenty seconds . . . ten seconds . . . five, four, three, two, one, hack!"

We poured out of the briefing room—and our hearts sank. A wispy fog was beginning to swirl in slowly from the east. Our ready room was full of speculations. Maybe the fog will lift enough for takeoff. Maybe the mission will be delayed. Maybe the bombers haven't taken off yet. On and on. Then it was time to go.

Duff and I piled into the CO's command car with Korky, Curt Johnston, Al Starr, and Burt Sims, who just wanted to share the excitement. It was slow going through the thickening fog, but it wasn't a long ride. Before we had gone a hundred feet, we heard someone bellow, "Go back to the ready room. Takeoff is canceled!" The visibility had dropped to less than half a mile.

I had mixed feelings. I was eager to get going—this, after all, was what all that training was about—but I didn't relish the idea of taking off on my first combat mission with less than half a mile of visibility. The morning passed with the usual grousing and groaning, along with the familiar Ping-Pong games and hangar flying. After lunch, the sky brightened a bit and hopes were rekindled that we might get off the ground after all.

"Briefing at 1630!" came the voice from the Tannoy

speaker. The ready room erupted in cheers, but in the back of my mind I was thinking that if we took off late, we'd be landing after dark—not a comforting thought, since the runway lighting system at Steeple was primitive at best.

The scenario had been changed. Instead of escorting the bombers to St.-Omer, France, we would be sweeping the area ahead of their withdrawal route to keep German fighters away. The mission in other respects was essentially as briefed earlier.

A 25-knot wind was now blowing from the west, so at 6:06 P.M. we took off on runway 28, which was only 3,100 feet long. This was no problem for takeoff, but not the best choice for a night landing, when we'd be approaching directly over the A Flight dispersal area to a short runway with minimal lighting. The already active butterflies in my stomach doubled their tempo.

Major Tukey led the group with our squadron, which consisted of three flights. The deputy group commander, Lt. Col. "Speed" Hubbard, flew Tukey's wing. Korky led Blue Flight with Duff on his wing; Perry and I were his second element. I was "tail-end Charlie" of our squadron.

It took three orbits over the field to assemble the group, then Major Tukey headed southeast as the sun dipped closer to the horizon behind us. Shortly after setting course, Tukey had to drop out because his radio failed and his "prop control went haywire." Hubbard took over the lead and Pop Allard, one of the spares, filled in the no. 2 slot. Our formation was picture perfect as we approached the North Sea. As we passed through twenty thousand feet, the voice of the mission controller cut through our complacency. "Hello, Sunshade. This is Jackknife. Return to base and pancake." A barely audible obscenity broke the ensuing silence as we turned back into the setting sun.

We landed just as dusk became night. My butterflies subsided.

So we were operational, but we had yet to fly a mission. The next day was one of those typical English days: low clouds, drizzling rain, and lousy visibility.

Tom Lea of *Life* magazine, the artist whose paintings *Life and Death of the USS* Hornet and *North Atlantic Patrol* drew international acclaim, visited our station. He was on a tour of all USAAF combat units, collecting sketches that he intended to transfer to canvas on his return to the States. He spent the next three days with us, sketching people, buildings, airplanes, and everything else that caught his interest. He was quiet, unobtrusive, friendly, and interested in everyone and everything.

When he saw the artwork that Corporal DeCosta had painted on the nose of many P-47s, he had a long chat with Colonel Cummings. "This is an artist!" he told him. "You could make better use of him than what he's doing now. He should have his own studio." Colonel Cummings agreed. He not only gave Art DeCosta his own studio, he also promoted him to sergeant. His studio was a small Nissen hut, with this sign above the entrance:

DeCosta's Art Studio
By the Grace of God and Colonel Cummings

DeCosta set to work creating beautiful murals on the curved walls of the mess hall. His theme was the *Rubáiyát of Omar Khayyám,* and he illustrated it with creative imagination and voluptuous beauties. Our mess hall soon gained a reputation that brought in many visiting pilots from bases throughout East Anglia. It was no longer a typical Army mess hall.

The weather next day was more of the same; the standdown continued. We spent most of our time looking over Tom Lea's shoulder as he sketched Korky, who tried to look bored but succeeded in looking embarrassed.

Three B-26 medium bombers provided a bit of excitement when they landed at Steeple Morden late in the afternoon because the weather was even worse at their home base. It was a short runway for the bombers, and two of them blew tires trying to avoid going off the end. Chaplain Zeigler was on hand to give each crew member a T.S. Ticket, with one punched hole. Whenever anyone in the

Eighth Air Force complained of having a tough time—in the line of duty or with a personal problem—he was told to "go tell the chaplain and get a T.S. Ticket." The T.S. stood for Tough Shit, and the chaplain, after listening to his problem, handed him a T.S. Ticket. If he already had one, he punched a hole in it. Chaplain Zeigler always carried a supply of tickets and a hole puncher. He called them Tough Situation tickets.

September 11, 12, and 13 were monotonous extensions of the dismal English weather—overcast, rain, drizzle, fog. Six pilots reported for duty from a replacement depot: Ray Morris, James Donovan, Ray Murdoch, and Al Desieno—all second lieutenants—and Flight Officer Gil Wright and Flight Officer Henry Brown.

"Replacement pilots?" said Jeeter. "You guys are a little early, aren't you? We haven't been to war yet!"

We sprawled around Gremlin Villa, writing letters, playing Ping-Pong, reading, and becoming convinced that the weather gods were on the side of the Luftwaffe. We were kept busy with aircraft recognition films, E&E lectures, and censoring mail.

Officers were exempt from having their outgoing mail censored, but the enlisted men's mail had to be screened to delete all references that might give the Germans valuable information. Originally the nonflying officers were given this chore, but soon it was evident that even if that was their sole function, they couldn't possibly handle that volume of mail. So the pilots were recruited—after all, they spent most of their time hanging around the ready room, waiting for somebody to tell them to go to war.

We hated the job; we didn't like the idea of intruding in the lives of these men, and we considered it unnecessary. Axis Sally, a German version of Tokyo Rose, had welcomed the 355th Fighter Group to Steeple Morden the evening after we arrived and had informed us that the Luftwaffe was looking forward to shooting down our new P-47s. It seemed to us that the Germans already knew all they needed to know about us. She even mentioned some of our names. We groused, but we all took turns with the scissors or razor blades.

On September 14 the weather cleared and we saw the sun for the first time in a week. At 10:20 A.M. the Tannoy blared, "All pilots to the briefing room immediately!" For some reason known only to higher headquarters, this was a hurry-up mission scheduled for an eleven-o'clock take-off. The hasty briefing left only fifteen minutes until takeoff time. The mission was a fighter sweep: Rendezvous with the 4th Fighter Group at eleven-thirty over Bradwell Bay; cross the enemy coast north of Dunkerque, France; turn left after a short penetration; and cross out of enemy territory at Oostende, Belgium. Weather would be no factor.

I had instructed Sergeant McKibbin to have my parachute in the cockpit at takeoff time. When I reached the airplane, there was no chute! Master Sergeant Buck Wrightam, the line chief, happened to be riding by in his jeep. Mac flagged him down and explained the situation. Wrightam screeched off in the direction of Gremlin Villa and returned in a few minutes with my chute. I made it, with not much to spare. At Gremlin Villa, Burt was yelling, "Who in hell forgot his chute?" The image I had projected with the Stimson affair in Philadelphia was getting a bit more tarnished.

Major Tukey led the group with the 357th Squadron this time, and the 354th was in the middle. I was flying Woody's wing in Korky's Blue Flight, with Duff in the no. 2 slot. Our takeoff was uneventful, but Capt. Walter Kossack, leading the 358th right behind us, struck a tree just after becoming airborne. His left wing and horizontal stabilizer clipped about ten feet from the top of the tree. The P-47 flipped dangerously low, but Kossack was able to right it, and he belly-landed in a field just southeast of Litlington. Except for a bruised forehead, he was uninjured.

The mission that we had anticipated for so long turned out

to be a bore. The Luftwaffe totally ignored us; the Germans didn't even bother to show us what flak looked like. We could as easily have flown this one over Philadelphia.

The group launched a second mission later that afternoon. Pilots who had missed the morning flight flew this one. As they approached the enemy coast, they met a wall of towering cumulus clouds and had to return to base without crossing into enemy territory, for which they received no mission credit. We were beginning to realize that one of our most formidable adversaries in this war would be the weather.

On September 16 I was promoted to first lieutenant along with Brady Williamson and Sammy Houston. Jim Duffy's name was not on the list, which was disappointing to both of us, but not surprising. We recalled an incident that had occurred about ten days earlier.

We were returning from an evening at the officers' club. I was feeling no pain, but Duff had absorbed a snootful and had become quite talkative, an Irish trait that I had become accustomed to. Unfortunately, as we approached our quarters, we encountered the squadron commander and operations officer in a seemingly serious conversation. Duff decided that this was the time for him to deliver his critique of the manner in which the commander was doing his job.

It quickly became obvious to me that Duff was about to shove his foot deep inside his mouth, so I yanked him by the arm and said, "Come on, Duff! Let's get to bed." But he persisted. He started to lay it on the CO thick and heavy, so again I tried to pull him physically away. He would not be put off.

"Let him talk, Bud," the commander said. "Let him get it off his chest." I replied that he was just getting himself in trouble. The commander assured me, "Don't worry. Tomorrow morning, this will all be forgotten. Let him get it off his chest. It won't be held against him."

I stood there helplessly as Duff got it all off his chest—in spades. When I told him about it next morning, he said, "Me and my big mouth!" Ten days later, the promotion list came out and Jim's name wasn't on it.

Clouds, rain, fog, and minimum visibility kept us grounded until September 22, when we flew two fighter sweeps that introduced us to heavy flak but no enemy fighters.

Next day I was awakened at 3:30 A.M., but not for a mission. Wing headquarters wanted six P-47s to orbit over the English Channel to protect any air/sea rescue operations that might be required. Stud Starr, Bob Kurtz, Jim Austin, Emil Perry, Bill Boulet, and I had been selected for the task. We took off sleepily at six thirty-five, landed at Thorny Island RAF station to refuel, then went on to our patrol. We milled around over the Channel until after one-thirty, then back to base by two o'clock. We had seen nothing but clouds and water and an occasional boat way below us. This did not count as a mission—just a waste of time and fuel—but it probably made some colonel at wing headquarters feel good.

While we were boring holes in the sky over the Channel, the group flew a fighter sweep, which turned out to be just as monotonous as our task, except that they did get to see a little flak, and it did count as a mission.

Most of our pilots were sent to the Goxhill RAF aerial gunnery range to sharpen shooting skills. I wasn't selected to go, and neither was Duff. Either the brass didn't think we needed it, or they thought we were beyond redemption. On September 25, 2d Lt. James Donovan was killed en route to Goxhill when his flight encountered bad weather and he spun out of a low overcast and crashed. He had been assigned to our squadron only a few days earlier, so we did not get to know him well. He was our first weather casualty in England.

On September 24 and 25, the 354th Fighter Squadron was ordered to stand down while its Thunderbolts were fitted with shackles to hold seventy-five-gallon belly tanks. This additional fuel would enable our Jugs to take the bombers deeper into enemy territory, but it wasn't enough to take them all the way to Berlin.

On September 26, equipped with seventy-five-gallon belly tanks, we flew our first escort mission. "It'll be a little slower on takeoff," said Korky, "but once we get airborne, you won't know you have it. Switch to the external tank on climbout."

"Do we jettison the tank when it's empty?" asked Woody.

"Hell, no!" replied Korky. "Those things are expensive. We jettison only if attacked."

I was beginning to understand the importance of the extra fuel. That fuel tank was buying time—time we needed to stay with the bombers longer, and time to fight off Luftwaffe attacks and still get home. But on deeper penetrations, even the extra seventy-five gallons wouldn't be enough to stay with the bombers all the way to the target. Bomber crews said sarcastically that when the P-47s left, the Me-109s and the FW-190s took up the escort duty. The B-17s bristled with .50-caliber machine guns, but the German fighters took a heavy toll—while suffering heavy losses.

The Eighth Air Force was determined to prove that daylight pinpoint bombing could be accomplished without sustaining prohibitive losses. Fighter escort was an increasingly important factor in this equation.

We took off at 4:38 P.M. I was in my accustomed no. 4 slot on Woody's wing in Korky's flight. We picked up the bombers deeper in enemy territory and stayed with them for nearly twenty minutes, until the 4th Fighter Group relieved us. We saw plenty of flak but no Luftwaffe, and we were back on the ground by 6:30 P.M.—with belly tanks. Korky was right: I forgot the tank was there.

The next day, we flew a sweep, clearing the way ahead of the bomber stream, for more than two hours. This time I was on Perry's wing, still no. 4. There was little flak and no Luftwaffe reaction.

Late in September we were issued RAF leather helmets, much superior to the USAAF cloth or leather helmets, and RAF combat boots. The latter were a combination boot and shoe. The top part of the boot was fleece-lined leather reaching just below the knee. The bottom was a low-cut black shoe, sturdy but drab and nondescript. If we had to bail out, we could rip off the top leather section, and the remaining shoe looked like the typical footwear of ordinary workers in occupied countries. Anyone trying to avoid capture by posing as a French laborer, for instance, would not attract attention because of his shoes.

By the end of September we had listened to fifteen briefings and flown only eight missions. "We're going to get briefing fatigue long before we get battle fatigue," said Chuck Lenfest.

We had been exposed to flak, but none of it was close or threatening. "Flak isn't close," according to bomber crews, "unless you can hear it and feel it." We had seen not one German fighter. We had heard about the Abbeville Boys, supposedly Göring's select fighter group, flying yellow-nosed FW-190s. The rumor mill had it that a Luftwaffe pilot had to have at least five aerial victories to become a member of this elite group, but this turned out to be just propaganda.

Axis Sally said that we would soon encounter these pilots, and they would teach us a bitter lesson about combat flying. "Bring them on!" said Duff, but I'm not sure he was serious.

October 1943

October was no improvement; it opened with a heavy fog that lasted all day. October 2 dawned bright and sunny, so we were up for an early briefing. We were to fly to Shipdham—about sixty miles northeast of Steeple—to refuel, then off again to escort B-17s headed for Emden, a German seaport believed to be harboring U-boats. Colonel Cummings led the group with our squadron. I was no. 4 in Korky's flight again.

Blue Flight was delayed about ten minutes when Korky's brakes failed as he began taxiing to the runway. He shut down the engine immediately but was unable to stop or steer the heavy airplane as it headed directly toward a P-47 being worked on by two mechanics on a workstand. Korky waved his arms and yelled at them to get out of the way. When they saw what was happening, they jumped off the workstand and dove under the airplane, rolling away from the oncoming Thunderbolt. Neither was seriously hurt—just a few cuts and bruises.

Immediately, a procession of fire trucks, ambulances, staff cars, jeeps, and even bicycles streamed from the tower area—and turned into the wrong dispersal area! When they finally found the accident, Korky had already changed airplanes, and Blue Flight was taxiing to the runway. The procession filed slowly back toward the control tower. We caught up with the group a few minutes before landing at Shipdham.

"I hope the wheels have this all figured out," I said to Korky as we watched the refueling operation. "I would think that landing here and topping off the tanks, then taking off and having to form up again wouldn't add much to our range."

"Probably just enough to let us stay with the bombers an extra fifty miles," he said, "and that's pretty important to those guys," he replied. "Just remember that old saying 'The only time you have too much gas is when your plane's on fire.' "

Except for moderate flak near the target, the mission was a boring milk run. We had good weather all the way, but the Luftwaffe did not react.

The 355th Fighter Group got its first victory two days later while escorting B-17s headed for Frankfurt. The extra fuel in the belly tanks gave the group enough range to escort the bombers two hundred miles from the Belgian coast to Eupen, twenty miles beyond Liège. I was a spare for this one, but my services were not needed, so I was sent back when the group made landfall at Blankenberge; no mission credit.

This time the Luftwaffe did react. As the group completed its 180-degree turn to head home—the 56th Fighter Group had just taken over escort duty—about twenty Me-109s and FW-190s jumped the 358th Squadron from above, pressed their attack on the bombers, then headed for the deck. Captain Carl Ekstrom fired at an Me-109 as it streaked by and managed to get a few hits. To his surprise, the 109's canopy flew off and the pilot bailed out.

"Pure luck!" said Ekstrom later at debriefing. "That guy was at least a thousand yards away!"

First Lieutenant Ralph Dean of the 358th wasn't so lucky. A Focke-Wulf 190 nailed him hard, leaving him slightly wounded, with his airplane full of holes and the left gear hanging down. The Jug was still flying, and he barely made it back to England. He couldn't get the right gear down, and the left one wouldn't go up. In his attempt to crash-land at a small airfield at Monkton, he suffered severe head injuries and died in a Canterbury hospital later that night.

Bob Kurtz and Pop Allard were bounced by two Me-109s and performed a few aerobatics with them, but the 109s split-essed for the deck before any scoring was done. On his way home, Bob was surprised when he noticed a bullet hole in his right wing. "I wasn't scared until I saw that hole!" he said at debriefing. "I kept staring at it all the way back." After he landed, a group of mechanics gathered around to admire it and stick their fingers in it. All too soon, battle damage would become a routine sight for them and would lose its novelty.

Rain and fog kept us grounded for the next three days. October 8 brought another escort mission with a refueling stop at Hardwick, and another long milk run. We saw plenty of flak but no Luftwaffe. Flak always added excitement to an otherwise boring milk run. Even at the high altitudes we were flying, flak was often uncomfortably close. My blood pressure and adrenaline levels rose as we took radical evasive action to get away from it. The bombers had no choice. They had to plow straight ahead, right through it, and it took its toll.

Colonel Cummings, not one to give long speeches, reminded us of our function in no uncertain terms later in the month at one of our briefings. "General Kepner telephoned me a while ago," he said, "to emphasize this close support of the bombers. Stick with them all the way. If we're jumped, and it's possible to turn into the attack, give them a squirt to drive them off, and get back to the bombers. We may lose some fighters, and we may not all come home heroes, but we've got a job to do. Let's do it!" Frustrating or not, we had clear instructions about what our role was in the Eighth Air Force at that time.

On October 14 the bombers went to Schweinfurt, Germany, a hotbed of enemy fighter activity. Unfortunately, heavy fog kept most of the VIII Fighter Command on the ground, and the bombers caught hell. Sixty bombers failed to return, and many more were badly damaged. It was their worst day so far.

On October 18, the 358th lost another pilot over France on an otherwise uneventful sweep. First Lieutenant Eugene Maben dropped out of formation over Cambrai and was last seen in a spinning dive at about ten thousand feet. There was neither flak nor Luftwaffe activity in the area. Anoxia was thought to be the most probable cause—a loose-fitting oxygen mask, a disconnected oxygen hose, or a malfunctioning regulator.

On October 20 we were assigned to escort B-17s to Düren, about twenty miles southwest of Cologne. Captain Kucheman led the 354th with our flight. I was no. 4 on Woody's wing. As we approached the rendezvous point, we saw about twenty-five Me-109s swarming around the bombers. With throttles jammed to the firewall, we sped toward them, but as soon as they saw us, they dove for the deck. The P-47 could dive faster than any German fighter, and it crossed my mind that we could have caught them, but we stayed with the bombers. I saw two B-17s going down in flames—four chutes blossomed from one of them, none from the other. It hit me hard then that if we had arrived a few minutes earlier, we might have saved two bombers and sixteen lives. And if we had chased the 109s, we might have exacted a price for those losses. The policymakers would have argued that if we had pursued the Me-109s, another group of German fighters might have attacked the unprotected bomber force. Wars shouldn't be fought with ifs.

October ended as it began: foggy, drizzly, wet, and muddy. The group flew only seven missions, three of which were hampered and complicated by weather. The 355th had flown only fifteen missions since becoming operational. The 358th Squadron had shot down two Me-109s but had lost two of its pilots—Ralph Dean and Eugene Maben. All in all, it was not an auspicious beginning.

November 1943

Burt Sims's squadron history narrative for November 1 starts out: "Watery mud lies two to three inches deep on all the roads, the squadron area and the site in which the officers are quartered are quagmires and still the rain comes down and the clouds droop low."

That morning, the 354th Squadron pilots were transported by truck to the 65th Fighter Wing headquarters at Saffron Walden for dinghy drill. Duff was not much of a swimmer—"I *know* I'll drown!"—and he developed an instant head cold with sore throat and sniffles. When he reported to the base hospital, Doc Fontenot took one look at him and promptly ordered him to bed in the sick ward. By the time we returned from dinghy drill, Duff had made a miraculous recovery and was ready to leave the hospital, but Doc Fontenot kept him there "for observation" until after lunch the next day. His rapid recuperation was attributed to the hospital bill of fare.

It was a half-hour ride to Saffron Walden. As befitted a higher headquarters, there was a large indoor swimming pool on the premises. We were led into the dressing room, where we were issued a flight suit—it didn't matter if the size was wrong, this was just for the drill—then out to the chilly pool area.

A major wearing a warm jacket explained the procedure: "The dinghy drill consists of jumping from this ten-foot platform into the deep part of the pool, wearing the flight suit, Mae West, and a parachute harness [no chute] with dinghy attached. Once in the water, you are to shed the harness, inflate the Mae West, deploy and inflate the dinghy, climb into it, then paddle to the shallow end of the pool." I think he had memorized this routine. "Any questions?"

"Yes, sir," said Jeeter. "What if I drown?"

The major smiled. He had fielded this question before. "If you drown," he replied, "you don't have to paddle to the other end of the pool."

To give the event a competitive dimension, each pilot was timed from splashdown to arrival in the dinghy at the far side. I don't remember what the prize was—probably twenty free laps in the pool.

Though the pool was indoors, it was not heated, so there were whoops and hollers each time someone entered the water. For those of us awaiting our turn, shivering in flight suits, that was not comforting. It soon became apparent that this was not a fun event.

Finally it was my turn. The water seemed a lot farther down than only ten feet, but I jumped—or was pushed—off the platform. Like those who had gone before, I whooped as I hit the cold water and went under. I came up spluttering, then wiggled and squirmed out of the harness and inflated the Mae West.

It took a while to get the dinghy out of its pack and inflate it while I tried to keep from freezing to death. Then came the hard part (not that the preceding maneuvers had been easy)—getting into the dinghy, which was wet, slippery, and cold. The inflated Mae West compounded the problem. After what seemed like a couple of hours, I finally flopped into the dinghy. It had about six inches of cold water in it, but I was intent on getting it to the other end of the pool, not bailing it out. I didn't even stop to find out if there were paddles on the thing. I just used my hands to paddle, slowly and erratically to the far side, and exited the pool as quickly as I could. That water was cold! Not as cold as the North Sea, maybe, but cold enough to turn our faces a light shade of blue. Someone pointed me in the direction of the warm dressing room, where I shed the sopping flight suit, toweled dry, and got dressed.

It was an exhausting but instructive exercise. The conversation in the ride back to Steeple was heavily sprinkled with comments like "That was a helluva lot tougher than I expected!" and "I damn near drowned in that bleeping pool!"

I visited Jim at the base hospital that afternoon. He was not happy. In a twelve-bed ward with two patients who were really sick, he had been diagnosed with "a minor attack of tonsillitis" and was required to stay in bed and take some awful-tasting concoction every two hours. "Doc Fontenot is doing this to me on purpose," he complained. "He thinks I should have gone with you guys!" When I described the dinghy drill and the fun time we had, he said with a moan, "I would have drowned! I *know* I would have drowned!"

November weather continued the pattern of the previous two months: fog, low clouds, rain, and drizzle. We flew only ten missions in November, but they were beginning to get more exciting.

The first one, on November 3, was a bombing attack on the German naval base at Wilhelmshaven. We took off from Steeple at about 8:00 A.M., landed at Bungay—about ninety miles northeast on the coast—to refuel, left Bungay just before noon, picked up the bombers over the North Sea just before landfall, and escorted them to the initial point.

From the IP to bombs away, the bombers had to maintain a straight, steady course through a heavy barrage of accurate flak. I thanked my lucky stars that I was flying fighters; we were able to stay wide of most of it as we turned for home. The 78th Fighter Group picked up the B-17s as they came off the bomb run and escorted them back. The Luftwaffe didn't show, and the bombers inflicted heavy damage on the large naval installation, the home port of many U-boats.

On November 5 a total of 240 B-17s—four sections of sixty—bombed Gelsenkirchen, right in the center of the German industrial heartland in the Ruhr Valley. Bomber crews had already dubbed this area Flak Alley, and with good reason. With heavy irony, fighter pilots called it

Happy Valley. The heavy concentration of 88mm antiair-craft guns formed a thick black wall of exploding shells that the bombers had to fly through to the target.

This was our first mission using the new 108-gallon belly tanks. The 354th flew high cover at 27,000 feet on the right side of our formation; Korky led the squadron, and I flew the Red-4 slot. Shortly after landfall, 1st Lt. Larry Sluga, leading the 358th Blue Flight on the low side, spotted a single Me-210 sneaking up on the tail end of the bomber task force and shot it out of the sky.

We saw an immense black cloud of flak about twenty miles ahead as we approached the rendezvous point with our assigned task force. The bombers were emerging from this barrage as we swung around in a wide right turn to take up our escort positions. The Luftwaffe stayed out of Flak Alley because flak did not distinguish friend from foe. They waited for the bombers to clear Flak Alley before pressing their attacks.

"Haywood Green Leader from Green-4. Bogey at three o'clock low!" Curt Johnston, leading Green Flight, peeled off and closed rapidly on the FW-190. The German pilot saw him coming and broke away, passing right in front of Brady Williamson, who was flying Johnny's wing. Brady let fly with a quick burst but didn't see any strikes. The 190 was now directly in front of and slightly above Charley Sweat, who was leading the second element.

Charley closed in from behind and below, and started shooting. He saw strikes on the underside of the 190 as he pressed the attack. Just as he thought he might overrun him—which would have put him in the German's gunsight—the 190 flipped over and spun toward the ground, trailing smoke and debris. The 354th Squadron's first victory!

Meanwhile, Vincent and Pete Bauman swooped down on a pair of Me-109s and wound up in a tight Lufbery with them. They managed to put a few holes in one of the 109s before the Germans decided to go home and split-essed for the deck. Jeeter Neal and his wingman chased three 109s in a vee formation, and they, too, headed homeward.

The radio crackled with excited voices. I spotted two 109s closing fast from our right rear, headed for the bombers. Forgetting radio protocol, I jammed the mike button on the throttle and yelled, "Korky! Two 109s, four o'clock high!" He racked into a tight turn toward them, but as soon as they saw us, they split-essed for the deck, bypassing the bombers. We didn't give chase.

Bill Boulet was monitoring C channel, the fighter-bomber communications channel. Suddenly he heard someone bellowing, so he answered, "Are you in trouble?"

"Hell, no!" came the reply. "You guys sure look good up there!"

With the extra fuel in the larger belly tanks, we were able to stay with the bombers until they were halfway across the North Sea on their way home. Colonel Cummings, who was leading the group, was happy. We were doing our job.

On November 6 we finally moved from the WAAF site mud hole to an area near the officers' club. We were now much closer to the flight line and within easy walking distance to the club. The Big Wheels took away our bicycles and gave them to the mechanics, who didn't have the ready access to vehicular transportation that we did. The bicycles became a familiar evening sight outside the pubs in Litlington and Steeple Morden.

"Bud, you're OD tomorrow," Chuck Lenfest told me at the mess hall that night. He wore an armband with the letters "OD" in white on a black background, and had a .45 pistol strapped to his waist. Then I remembered. Posted on the bulletin board last month was the "Officer of the Day Duty Schedule," listing all the squadron officers and their duty days. My name appeared for November 7, more than a month away, so I promptly forgot all about it.

"What does an officer of the day do?" I asked Chuck.

"You wear that armband and the gun, and hang around the base for twenty-four hours doing nothing," Brady said from across the table. He had been OD the day before. "The best part is—you have your own jeep for a day."

"That's about it," said Chuck with a grin. "You report to the orderly room at 1100 and you let them know where you are all the time. You're the officer of the day until the next day at 1100. Buster will tell you all about it."

"But I'm on the mission schedule tomorrow!"

"Not anymore. Kucheman took you off this afternoon."

At 11:00 A.M. on November 7, I reported to the orderly room. Captain Ulmer "Buster" Francis, squadron adjutant, was in charge of squadron administration—the paper mill—and all activities that did not pertain to airplanes. Stocky and gruff, he looked and acted like a man in charge. He explained my duties as officer of the day and handed me the gun and armband. "Let the CQ know where you are at all times. If you have any problems, you're in charge. Don't call me!" The CQ—charge of quarters—was an NCO who manned the orderly room during off-duty hours. All NCOs except section chiefs were on the CQ duty roster. He answered the phone and notified the OD of any situation requiring immediate attention. The OD either took care of the problem, or made the decision that the CO should be involved.

I had only one call from the CQ—at 11:20 P.M. "There's a fight going on at the enlisted men's quarters!"

"Notify the MPs," I said. Then I drove leisurely to the enlisted men's quarters where, as I had hoped, the MPs already had the situation well in hand.

November 7 was not a good day for the 355th. It was an escort mission to Düren. Rendezvous was in the southeastern corner of Belgium. The group stayed with the bombers for thirty-five minutes—a long stretch at that stage—and there were more than a few radio calls complaining about dwindling fuel supplies when the group finally headed home. Then came our first encounter with the phenomenon later identified as a jet stream—a ninety-knot wind blowing from the northwest above twenty thousand feet.

The strong wind dramatically reduced ground speed and pushed the group south of the intended course. A layer of low clouds, with only occasional breaks, made navigation difficult for the fighters. Lady Luck smiled on the 354th—all our pilots made it back home after refueling at bases on the English coast. Korky led A Flight into Manston RAF station, on the northeastern coast of England. All their fuel gauges were hugging the empty pegs. They refueled the internal tanks and made it home.

The other squadrons weren't so lucky.

Captain Norm Olson of the 357th spotted a lone Me-210 twin-engine fighter soon after he left the bombers and dove after it. His flight followed him down through a layer of clouds. He closed on the 210, firing all the way. Both engines burst into flames, and two crewmen bailed out. When Olson started to climb back up through the overcast, he saw only his wingman. First Lieutenant Edwin Carlson and 1st Lt. James Westphall, the second element of his flight, were seen to enter the cloudbank behind Olson's element in the dive, but were not seen afterward, which led to speculation that they had collided during the dive. They did not return to base.

Captain Kossack, 358th operations officer, crash-landed in Holland after running out of fuel. First Lieutenant Bill Roach of the same squadron was blown far south of his intended course. As his fuel supply reached the critical stage, he let down through a cloud layer, hoping to see the coast of England. In the poor visibility, he mistook the Cherbourg Peninsula for the English coastline and landed at what he thought was an RAF base. He was welcomed with open arms by the German tenants.

Flight Officer Chester Watson of the 358th, on his second combat mission, ran out of fuel and bailed out six miles off the coast of France. He was never seen again.

First Lieutenant Jack Woertz of the 358th ran out of fuel and crash-landed on a road just beyond a beach in southwestern England. Lieutenant Chet Butcher had to land at an RAF base with a very short runway. He tore through a fence and damaged the airplane, but he was unhurt.

Kossack, Roach, and Westphall became POWs. Carlson

and Watson were listed as killed in action. The 355th destroyed one plane, and lost six aircraft and five pilots—not a sustainable ratio.

The only bright spot in the day came in this teletype from Maj. Gen. William Kepner, commander of VIII Fighter Command: "No bombers were lost on today's mission, every Fortress and Marauder employed having returned safely to base. The splendid escort afforded by our pilots contributed greatly to the success of the mission. Heartiest congratulations on another job well done. Kepner."

The next morning, when the scheduled mission was scrubbed halfway through our briefing, Colonel Cummings gave us a little lecture: "When you're on the way home and running low on gas, don't start bleating about it on the radio. Just say you're returning to base. If the Germans had been smart, they would have sent up some fighters to intercept us on the way out—you know they monitor all our radio chatter—and a lot of others might not have made it back."

Luftwaffe strategy was to attack unprotected boxes of bombers and to avoid tangling with escorting fighters. After all, the fighters weren't dropping bombs on vital military targets; the bombers were the villains.

On November 11, while escorting B-17s, we spotted four Me-109s heading for a B-17 that had lost an engine and was straggling behind the main formation. Korky peeled off and we headed for the crippled bomber. The 109s saw us coming and headed for the deck. The bomber had turned around and headed for home, so Korky checked with the group leader and got permission to escort him back. We got him over the North Sea and close to the English coast before we had to break escort because of limited fuel. The crippled B-17 got home. The mission was otherwise uneventful.

November 12 was the 355th Fighter Group's first birthday, and there was no scheduled mission. The first order of the day was to conclude the Turkey Day skeet-shooting competition. The pilots had already conducted shooting contests to determine which five pilots would represent each squadron. Our team, consisting of Kucheman, Koraleski, Woody, Benson, and Neal, won easily; and Neal took top honors with the best individual score. The prize: Our officers and enlisted men would dine together in the Red Cross Aero Club on Thanksgiving Day, and pilots from the other two squadrons would be the waiters and provide KP services.

On November 13 we provided withdrawal support for B-17s on their way home from Bremen. We staged out of Bungay to extend our range with full 108-gallon belly tanks, and picked up our bombers—three boxes of sixty each—at Cloppenburg, about twenty-five miles southwest of Bremen. Speed Hubbard led the group with our squadron; Korky led his second element, and I flew Red-4 on his wing. Shortly after our rendezvous with the bombers, Jeeter called Vinnie, who was leading Yellow Flight behind us: "Yellow Leader from Yellow Three. Two bogeys coming in at five o'clock high!" I had my head on a swivel, but I couldn't see them. Vinnie turned his flight into them, and the fight was on. The 109s lost. Vinnie and Jeeter each nailed one, then scrambled back to the squadron formation.

From there it was a milk run until we got to Holland, where heavy flak blossomed all around. We were close enough to the bombers to be included in the welcoming barrage. It was the heaviest flak I'd encountered—close enough to hear and feel. We were turning and climbing, scrambling to get away from it, when Hubbard caught a couple of bursts in the engine section. His plane was vibrating severely, but the engine kept running, so he throttled back a bit and headed west. Just as we emerged from the flak zone, Maj. Bill Chick, his wingman, yelled, "Speed! Break left! Quick!" as two 109s bore down on them from behind. Hubbard wheeled into a sharp left turn, and his engine broke loose from its mounts. The 109s split-essed for the deck.

Korky racked into a steep turn and went after them full

bore. I scrambled after him. They had a big head start, and by the time we reached ten thousand feet, I could see them way ahead of us, on the deck, speeding south. If we ever *did* catch them, we'd be deep in Germany and low on gas. I could see Korky shaking his head as he pulled up, and we headed back to the group formation.

In the meantime, Speed's airplane—minus its engine—was performing violent aerobatics, and he had a lot of trouble getting out. He was quite low before he finally managed to clear the airplane and pull the ripcord. His chute was seen to open. Dutch underground people spirited him away before the Germans got to the scene. He was back in England six months later.

Norm Olson of the 357th took his flight down on three Me-109s trying to get to the bombers from below. Two of them broke for the deck, but the third was too slow. Norm opened a withering fire and kept shooting until the 109 struck the ground and exploded.

At about the same time, the 358th Squadron, flying top cover, was jumped by two Me-109s from above. Major Ray Myers called the break, but the Germans managed to shoot down his no. 4 man before streaking for the deck.

"All hell was breaking loose all around us," Korky lamented to Sims at debriefing, "and we were in the wrong place the whole damn time!"

So the score was three for us and two for them, but the loss of Speed Hubbard made us feel that we had the short end of the stick.

Two days later, the 357th lost two more pilots, 1st Lt. Don McNally and 1st Lt. Larry McGraw, as they flew a weather reconnaissance mission. The only radio transmission heard was that they were descending through a layer of clouds to check conditions below. McGraw's body washed ashore near Calais, France, a week later. McNally was never found. There was no enemy activity reported, and the Germans did not claim any P-47s shot down in that area, so their loss was chalked up to the weather.

Thanksgiving Day was bitterly cold and windy, and low-flying clouds obscured the sun intermittently. There was no mission scheduled. At 10:30 A.M. the three squadrons lined up in what passed for a military formation for the presentation of medals. Duff was scheduled to receive an Air Medal, but he preferred to sleep late, so he missed all the fun. I wasn't scheduled for a medal, so I decided that Jim had the right idea and elected to stay in a warm bed rather than stand in a cold, blustery wind.

At noon, the squadron assembled at the Red Cross Aero Club to reap the reward earned earlier in the month by our skeet-shooting team. The other two squadrons honored their part of the bargain—and then some. The walls of the large main room were decorated with cutouts of Pilgrims, pumpkins, colorful leaves, and even an Indian or two. From Burt's narrative: "The blackout curtains had been drawn, and white linens and silver gleamed in the light from numerous candles. Every man received half a ration of turkey and half a ration of pork, with cranberry sauce, mashed potatoes, lima beans—and ice cream and cake for dessert." A sumptuous meal in a lavish setting. The other squadrons provided waiter service and performed KP duties, and all in good humor.

Individual members of our winning skeet-shooting team were presented with trophies; there were speeches, a resounding round of applause for the KPs, and we sang a few songs, then wandered back to our quarters for a nap. "If this is war," said Jeeter, "who needs peace?"

It was only a day off from the war. The next morning, November 26, we were roused from our beds at five forty-five. Breakfast was at six and briefing at six forty-five.

Colonel Cummings led the group, staging out of Bungay again to extend our range. Takeoff was slated for 8:20 A.M. When dawn finally broke, we saw white frost and ice on the airplanes and runways.

The mechanics attached hoses from jeep and truck exhausts to blow hot air over the wings to get rid of the ice, but the runway and taxiways were too slick to permit take-off on schedule. At eight-thirty we were told that another briefing would be held in thirty minutes.

We gathered again at nine and sat on our butts on those uncomfortable benches for an hour while intelligence people hauled blackboards in and out with ever-changing targets and times. Finally Burt took the stage and announced that a mission to Africa was being planned and he was giving us the background information and what we could expect. We sat there in pretended absorption, listening as he continued: "Now, the love life of a camel is not what everyone thinks. . . ." Now he really had our attention.

"For oft on his trips through the desert, he stops to make love to the Sphinx . . .

"Now, the Sphinx's posterior annex lies deep in the sands of the Nile . . .

"Which accounts for the hump on the camel . . .

"And the Sphinx's inscrutable smile."

That did it! Others took the stage to tell ribald jokes and limericks; a quartet sang off-color parodies; and Burt, Starr, and Woody staged a simulated wrestling match that accidentally knocked over a couple of benches and dumped their occupants on the floor. Then somebody yelled "TEN HUT!" and everybody stood at attention as Colonel Cummings entered the room.

"What in hell's going on here?" he said sharply, but a little smile that he was trying hard to hide belied his anger. The room settled down, and the briefing began in earnest.

We were doing a repeat of the November 13 mission, staging out of Bungay to escort bombers on their way home from Bremen. We had swapped missions with another group, which would now be escorting the bombers on their way in.

We took off from Bungay at eleven-twenty and picked up our assigned bombers at Papenburg at twelve-thirty. As we settled into position above the bombers at thirty thousand feet, two P-47s from another group swept through our formation at right angles. One of them clipped a few inches off the top of Starr's vertical stabilizer, eliciting a few choice epithets from Stud. Their markings identified them as belonging to the 356th Fighter Group. Later that day, Colonel Cummings sent a sharp reminder to the 356th commander that we were not the enemy.

Well below us, we could see a number of dogfights involving P-47s from the veteran 56th Fighter Group and a bunch of 109s and 190s. Korky called the group leader: "Sunshade, this is Haywood Blue Leader. Okay if I take my flight down to help out?"

"Blue Leader, this is Sunshade. Negative! Our job is to protect these bombers." Then a few seconds later, "Besides, they don't seem to need our help." Korky didn't reply, but I could see him squirming.

We learned later that the 56th had racked up a record twenty-two destroyed, two probables, and six damaged, for the loss of one pilot, who bailed out over Amsterdam. I guess they *didn't* need our help.

"Yeah, it's true," said Major Kucheman. There had been rumors in recent weeks that our squadron commander was being transferred. On November 27 it became official. It was a trade: He would be taking over a squadron in another group, and one of their squadron commanders would be taking over the 354th. Some greeted the news with dismay, others with indifference. Duff and I were not unhappy to see him leave. Much of the time since we arrived in England, the CO had been plagued by ear infections, colds, and the like that had kept him grounded, or restricted to altitudes far below those required for escort duty. As a result, he had not played the leadership role in our combat missions that he might have preferred to play.

Major Claiborne H. Kinnard Jr. would be our new commander. Rumors circulated that he was "kind of an oddball," but most of us decided to wait and see. Ironically, he arrived with flight restrictions similar to those of his predecessor: Ear and respiratory infections would keep him grounded for nearly a month after he joined us. We were not told the reason or reasons for the command change. For the first few weeks of his new assignment, Kinnard stayed in the background, scrutinizing each mission minutely, asking questions, and observing.

The 354th suffered its first combat loss on November 29. It was another escort mission for bombers attacking Bremen. The 358th lost two more pilots—Charles Hecht and Richard Peery, both first lieutenants. They crash-landed in Holland after running out of gas. The 354th lost 1st Lt. Alfred Del Negro.

Colonel Cummings led the squadron. On climb-out, his no. 4 man, 1st Lt. Curt Johnston, became ill and returned to base. Lieutenant Rich Brown, one of the two spares, filled in. Then Korky's engine started cutting out, so he left, escorted by Major Kucheman, who was flying his wing. That left Bob Woody and Emil Perry in Yellow Flight. The remaining spare, Del Negro, joined Yellow Flight on Bob's right wing. As the squadron reached the bomber stream, Woody looked back and saw Perry and Del Negro in position. He followed the group leader in a steep right turn above the bombers to get in escort position. When he completed the turn and looked behind him for Perry and Del, they weren't there.

Others in the squadron heard Perry call Woody to tell him that he was heading home, but Bob didn't hear him. Nothing was heard from Del. He simply disappeared. There was no flak, and there were no German fighters anywhere near. The wreckage of his plane was never found, and to this day no one knows what happened to him. The most plausible explanation is that he had some kind of oxygen trouble—a loose connection or some other problem with his oxygen supply—and he must have passed out and crashed. The fact that wreckage of his plane was never found raises the possibility that he may have crashed into a sizable body of water. The squadron was at thirty thousand feet at the time of Del's disappearance. Anoxia comes quickly at that altitude.

Del was our first combat-mission casualty, though not actually combat-related. He was a stocky, good-natured guy with a great sense of humor—well liked by everyone in the squadron. The other two squadrons had taken quite a few losses; we had been lucky. With Del's loss came the realization that the 354th also would be paying the price.

On November 30, our engineering section began to install water-injection systems to boost the R-2800 engines to 2,300 horsepower for heavy-load takeoffs and war-emergency power.

Vincent's D Flight flew off on detached service to the RAF Interception Training School at Colerne in south-central England. There was a lot of banter about the suitability of the heavy Thunderbolt in an interceptor role, but the D Flight pilots insisted it would be a valuable and educational ten days.

The group flew only ten missions in November. Bad weather forced the cancellation of nearly as many.

December 1943

December 1 featured broken clouds with about three miles of visibility. Briefing was at a reasonable hour for a change—8:00 A.M. The target was Solingen, about twenty miles south of Essen in the heart of Happy Valley.

Vinnie's flight was still at the RAF Interception Training School at Colerne, so the 354th provided only three flights for the mission; the other squadrons had four. Colonel Cummings led the group with our squadron again, but Major Kinnard was still grounded with the ear infection. Korky led Blue Flight, with Duff on his wing; I was surprised and pleased to see my name in the no. 3 slot, with Hal Culp on my wing. Maybe the tarnish in my reputation was fading, and I was moving up in the hierarchy.

We made landfall at Blankenberge, Belgium, where we were greeted by intense and accurate flak, which necessitated radical turning and climbing to get away from it. There was more of the same as we passed Antwerp. Again, I was made aware that flak was not something that only bombers had to contend with; it didn't differentiate between fighters and bombers.

We made rendezvous with our two boxes—120 B-17s—at Julich, about thirty-five miles southwest of Solingen, at thirty thousand feet. Cummings positioned us above and slightly ahead of the lead bombers. The Luftwaffe often attacked the bomber stream in a head-on "roller coaster" pattern, starting with a shallow dive, then a climbing firing pass to rake the underbellies of the bombers, then a split-S to the deck. This technique minimized the effectiveness of the B-17's top turret, waist, and tail gunners. Cummings had put us in position to break up such attacks before they reached the bombers. It meant diving and firing at the attackers head-on to break up their formations. Closing speeds in such attacks often exceeded seven hundred miles per hour, so they were exciting, to say the least.

The 358th was a thousand feet above us and between the bombers and the sun on the right side. The 357th was down-sun, below and slightly behind the second box, to intercept attacks from the rear. Because of the difference in cruising speeds, the fighters had to weave in an S pattern along the bomber route. The flights within each squadron flew a trail, follow-the-leader pattern that kept the bombers in view and closed off potential avenues of attack.

We were just settling down in our routine when fifteen to twenty Me-109s bounced the two squadrons behind us, and tried to get through to the bombers. At the same time, a flight of four P-38s bounced *us,* apparently thinking we were Me-109s. We turned into them, and they veered off. Cummings started to turn back to join the fracas behind us.

"Sunshade from Blue Two. Bogeys at four o'clock high!" Two flights of P-47s were diving at us in a very aggressive maneuver, so once again we had to turn into them before they identified us and turned away. Cummings, usually unflappable, yelled, "What the hell's going on here?" but the aggressive P-47s were on a different radio channel. Again, he turned back to the other squadrons, but by that time the action was over. The 357th and 358th had each nailed two of the 109s as they dove away. None got through to the bombers.

"Damn!" sputtered Korky at the debriefing. "We have a knack of being in the wrong place all the time!"

"We were sure as hell in the wrong place when they threw all that flak at us on the way in!" I said.

"The other two squadrons each lost a guy to flak today," said Burt. "One guy bailed out; they don't know about the other one."

———

Rain, fog, and low clouds kept us on the ground the next two days. On December 4 the weather over the Continent was the villain, but late that afternoon we flew to Thorny Island RAF station on the southern coast of England, from which we were to take off the following morning with a full fuel load to escort bombers to targets near Bordeaux.

Just before taking off for Thorny Island, we received word that 1st Lt. Roland Vincent had been killed in an aircraft accident at Colerne. The scant information available indicated that he had entered a steep dive at about thirty thousand feet and recovered at about fifteen thousand feet. He zoomed back up and then split-essed for the deck again. He stayed in that dive for an unusually long time, according to one witness, probably fighting the effects of compressibility. He finally started to recover at about seven thousand feet, but the tail section broke off. He dove straight into the ground at more than six hundred miles per hour. He was our squadron's third loss, our second non-combat-related casualty. Burt's entry in the squadron history reflects our feelings: "The news came as a distinct shock. . . . Vinnie was, above all things, a top-notch pilot. He was held in great esteem by all who knew him, and he was one of our sturdiest leaders. His loss will be keenly felt."

It was a somber, muted flight to Thorny Island.

The mission on December 5 was uneventful—the usual flak, but no fighters—and we headed home. Long before we reached England, we were informed that a heavy fog had closed down Steeple Morden and most of the air bases in East Anglia. The group's P-47s were scattered that evening over nine different airfields, most of them RAF bases near the coast.

I was in the lead flight with Major Dix, Korky, and Captain Rosenblatt. We managed to find Thorny Island again and landed, followed by Yellow Flight—Kucheman, Minchew, and Boulet—and two flights from another group. The weather closed down Steeple and many other bases in East Anglia until December 10.

———

We were not prepared for an extended stay at Thorny Island. None of us had toilet articles or a change of clothing. There were shower facilities and we were able to find soap, but our only clothes were what we wore under our flight suits.

Thorny Island was a small RAF station—basing just one squadron of Spitfires. At first the RAF officers were friendly and helpful, but as the days wore on they found the Yanks were always first for afternoon tea, first in the bar, first in the dining hall, always occupying the most comfortable chairs in the lounge, and monopolizing the dart games and snooker tables. Their attitude turned a bit cooler, then became downright unfriendly. They were as grouchy as we were at being grounded, but they had been invaded, and they resented the invaders. There were occasional exchanges of unpleasantries but no serious altercations.

When it became obvious—by the second day—that we might be stranded at Thorny Island for a while, Major Dix got the 354th contingent together right after the RAF afternoon tea had been taken over by the Americans. "Remember that we're guests here," he told us, "and I expect all of you to mind your manners! I don't want to see any of you repeating that performance at tea this afternoon. This is *their* base. I hope we can get out of here tomorrow, but as long as we're here, the least we can do is be polite." He looked around. "Another thing. Stop by the NAAFI store and pick up some toilet articles. I don't want you looking like bums." NAAFI was the British equivalent of our PX.

Unfortunately, Dix had no control over the eight pilots from the other group, though he tried. A major was the ranking officer in that group also, and he didn't appreciate Dix suggesting what he should do. They continued their boorish behavior, and the RAF resentment of them extended to us as well.

Finally, on December 10, the weather cleared enough to allow us to return to Steeple. The RAF officers had put up with us for six nights and five days and were undoubtedly delighted to see us leave. Back at Steeple, many hilarious tales were told about the various bases the pilots had "occupied." Some of the tales were true. The more fortunate pilots had landed at bases near sizable communities with a semblance of nightlife. Thorny Island was in the middle of nowhere. The D Flight contingent, though shocked by Vinnie's death, had managed to have a great time at Colerne. "WAAFs and everything . . ." We were told in great detail about the "everything."

Weather played havoc with the mission on December 11. There was snow and ice on the runways and aircraft, forcing a delay in the takeoff. Then heavy cloud cover curtailed the escort mission, sending everyone scurrying home early. The weather at Steeple was marginal, with about a five-hundred-foot ceiling and two miles visibility, so several pilots elected to land somewhere else. A strong wind blew from the southeast, so the Jugs used Runway 16. Duff and I weren't on the mission, but we were standing next to the control tower to watch the Jugs coming in for a landing. We watched the 354th land without incident, and were about to turn back to Gremlin Villa when a 358th Squadron P-47 popped out of the overcast and tried to line up with the runway. He was too low and too slow; the airplane stalled, crashed, and exploded just a few hundred feet away from the watching pilots and mechanics. The pilot, 1st Lt. Jack Woertz, was killed instantly.

Later that afternoon came this brassy Tannoy announcement: *Attention all personnel! Attention all personnel! Effective immediately, all personnel will carry gas masks with them at all times, even off base. We repeat . . .*

"What the hell's going on?" I asked Burt. Most of the pilots were at Gremlin Villa, censoring mail or just lounging around.

"Damned if I know!"

"You're the intelligence officer! You're supposed to know!" yelled Jeeter. "Are we being attacked?"

"I don't know any more than you do," said Burt, "but

I'm going to find out!" He headed for the phone. After a few moments of conversation, he turned to the rest of us: "Nobody in Group knows anything about it, either. It's an order that came down from Wing. That's all they know."

"I left my gas mask at Camp Kilmer," said Brady.

"Better hurry back there and get it," said Duff. "You're not borrowing mine!"

The 354th orderly room was in a small building at the entrance to our quarters area. Captain Buster Francis, the squadron adjutant, handled all the squadron administrative functions with a staff of about five enlisted men. "Check the bulletin board!" he yelled as we approached. The bulletin board told us where ammunition would be available for the Thompson submachine guns, carbines, and pistols.

"One might think," said Charley Sweat, "that there's a war going on around here."

At the bar that evening, rumors were bouncing off the walls: The Germans had a new bomb capable of releasing poison gas. The Germans had perfected a rocket with a poison-gas warhead. German paratroopers, equipped with gas canisters, had been dropped in the vicinity of American air bases. And so the rumors flew. No one was armed, but everyone was carrying a gas mask—except Brady.

Early next morning, the gas mask order was rescinded— with never a word of explanation.

December continued cold and raw. Jim and I shared a small room that more closely resembled a cell. There was a small potbellied stove and a small supply of coke, a form of coal that was difficult to ignite. We started with plenty of paper and whatever small pieces of wood we could find. Once we got that going, we threw the coke on top. The paper and wood burned fine, but the coke did not, unless the bed of coals was red-hot underneath.

Later that winter, when the armament people were mixing up some napalm to heat things up for the Germans, Duff had a bright idea. "Why not get a little napalm from those guys. I'll bet that will light the damned coke." He talked Pat

Murphy into letting him have a jerry can about half full of napalm.

We filled the stove half full of coke, then poured about a cupful of napalm (Murphy had warned Duff not to use much) over it, and lighted it. In no time at all, the napalm was burning fiercely in the stove. Then, to our consternation, we saw little streams of flaming napalm leaking out around the bottom draft of the stove onto the cement floor, where they spread rapidly. Jim tried stomping them out and nearly set his shoes on fire. We finally rushed outside and dug up some dirt to cover the fiery streams and stop their progress toward the wall. The napalm streams slowly ebbed and went out. The coke was burning nicely.

On December 16 we headed again for oft-pounded Bremen, and again the weather muddled the mission. The base of the overcast at takeoff time was fifteen hundred feet, with the tops at about four thousand. Climbing through thick overcasts in a four-ship flight was becoming routine, though it was never easy, and we were getting plenty of practice in getting the group together on top. The cloud cover extended over our entire route, hampering our navigational efforts. There were high broken clouds at twenty-four thousand feet, but we managed to find our bombers at Oldenburg. We escorted them to the target, where they bombed through the clouds. An unidentified voice came through the radio: "I wonder what those bombs are actually hitting."

There was plenty of flak, but no Luftwaffe. Once again, the fuel supply became a problem for many. The 358th's Lt. Harold Macurdy made a dead-stick crash landing at Rock Heath after running out of fuel. The P-47 was completely wrecked, but Macurdy walked away without a scratch.

After we left Steeple that morning, a heavy ground fog had settled in, closing the base down to all air traffic. The group's airplanes were again scattered all along the English coast.

Perry's turbo failed on climb-out, so he returned to base

with Bill Boulet escorting him, leaving Yellow Flight as a twosome—Bob Woody and me. We followed Red Flight (Kucheman, Wright, Lenfest, and Mendenhall) into Manston, a large RAF base close to the North Sea. It had an extra-long runway and was used extensively for emergency landings.

The weather didn't allow our return to base until December 19, so once again we were guests of the RAF, this time for three nights. Manston was a busy place, and the RAF people there were used to accommodating strangers overnight or longer. It was nevertheless a long two days for us, and required another trip to the NAAFI store for toilet articles.

"Where are we going this time?" I asked Mike when he woke me up on the December 20 for the 8:30 A.M. briefing. Duff was in the base hospital, nursing a nasty cold.

"Bremen again."

"What's in Bremen that we hit it so hard and so often?"

"I guess Target Intelligence knows something we don't."

"Either that or the bombers keep missing the target."

The mission was routine—the usual flak, but no Luftwaffe—and all airplanes landed at Steeple. Here's a short excerpt from Burt's narrative history:

> Before takeoff, Bud Fortier and Charley Lenfest were seen with large Pilot's Navigation kits under their arms, and much comment was tossed at them regarding their ability to navigate—particularly when en route to quarters after a few hours in the officers' mess.
>
> Bud and Charley disclosed, with very self-satisfied smiles, that the kits now contained shaving equipment, towel, cap and other necessary accoutrements for remaining the "well-groomed man" in the event they landed at advance dromes and were unable to get home because of bad weather. If this sort of thing keeps up it's quite possible that someone may attach a footlocker to the underside of his plane instead of a bellytank.

We were back by 1:30 P.M. Shortly after that, we were told there would be another briefing at 4:30 P.M.

This was a short one. We flew to the advance base at Hardwick on the coast to be ready to fly a mission early next morning. Korky took over the squadron when Kucheman had to return with engine trouble. I was in the no. 4 slot, on Perry's wing.

It surprised no one when the mission was scrubbed the next day because of weather, and we had to wait until noon for the weather to improve just enough to let us land at Steeple. We took out some of our frustration by working the field over just below treetop level prior to landing. Some headquarters people on the ground gave Korky hell for buzzing the field before landing, but he told them the visibility was so bad, he had to make sure we were at the right place.

That night we had a brilliant display of antiaircraft fire from nearby batteries as Luftwaffe bombers passed our way. We never found out the target.

The rest of the month was more of the same. A mission scheduled for December 23 was scrubbed due to weather.

On December 24 there was a massive attack on rocket sites in the Calais area. The bombers flew between twelve thousand feet and eighteen thousand feet, and hundreds of fighters formed a protective barrier all around them. There was surprisingly little flak and no Luftwaffe reaction. I drew a pass on this one.

It was a routine mission for everyone except Curt Johnston. He saw a smoking B-24 about five thousand feet below him with two fighters closing in on it. He took his flight down, squeezed off a good burst at the lead aircraft, and saw strikes on both wings before the aircraft rolled over and split-essed for the deck. It was then that Curt realized he had fired on a P-51. From dead astern, he had been unable to identify it. There had been no mention at the morning briefing of P-51s being in the area.

When Curt walked into the ready room, he was obviously shaken. "I just shot down a P-51," he told Mike and

Burt. He handed the film magazine from his gun camera to
Burt. A few hours later, it was learned that the P-51, though
badly damaged, had managed to crash-land at an RAF base
near Dover. Curt was greatly relieved, but the Mustang pilot was "really pissed off" and offered to meet "that idiot
P-47 jockey" at twenty thousand feet and have it out with
him. Johnston apologized profusely and politely declined
the offer.

Christmas Eve festivities went on late into the evening,
and became even rowdier when it was announced around
midnight that we had been released until dawn of December
26. The weather extended our "vacation" three more days.

Just before the briefing on December 30, a fully loaded
B-17 from nearby Bassingbourne struck a tree right after
takeoff and crash-landed on the western end of our field after
barely missing the large maintenance hangar. The pilot managed to put it down between our two active runways, leaving
them clear for our mission, though I suspect that was not on
his mind at the time. The load of bombs did not explode and
no one was hurt, but the front end of the B-17 looked like an
accordion. Lady Luck smiled on the crew that day.

At the briefing, as might be expected, Major Dix point-
edly reminded everyone that Mustangs would be present in
increasing numbers from now on, and they did not appreciate being used for target practice. I wasn't scheduled on this
mission, which targeted Ludwigshaven.

It was a rough day for the 355th. As we ended our escort
stint and headed home, a gaggle of 109s was seen heading
for the bombers we had just left. The 358th tried to head
them off, but the 109s barreled right by them, and shot
down Flight Officer Charles Wambier as they sped through.

The rest of the group gave chase, but the 109s headed for
the deck. The 354th's Lt. Ray Murdoch was last seen chasing several 109s—alone. He shot down one of them before
being shot down. He spent the rest of the war in a POW
camp.

Captain Carl Ekstrom of the 358th was last seen strafing

a flak tower. He and Wambier were later reported killed in action. Cully had been the first of our group to score. He was an excellent pilot, but flak didn't take that into account.

December ended with many briefings and only ten missions. Since being placed on operational status, the 355th had destroyed thirteen aircraft and lost six pilots in air combat. Seventeen pilots had been lost to flak and weather-related accidents. Thirty-five missions had been flown. I flew fourteen of them.

January 1944

The New Year's Eve party went on well into the wee hours after Fighter Command released us from combat until January 2. We slept till noon on New Year's Day, but there were still a few throbbing heads at lunchtime.

We were at the mess hall early that evening in anticipation of the New Year's Day turkey dinner we had been led to expect. The turkey dinner looked more like GI C rations, and the moans and groans of disappointment were steadily increasing in volume. The Special Services officer, 1st Lt. Phil Haimovit, tried to explain. "We didn't get enough turkeys for everybody," he shouted above the groans, "so we decided to serve them to the enlisted men now, and have a turkey dinner for the officers as soon as the rest of our allotment arrives." He looked around the hall and added, "I'm sure you all agree that our hardworking enlisted men deserve it." That made the decision—but not the C rations—a bit more palatable.

The next day, Sunday, was a beautiful, sunny day, but we were on stand-down status to give the armament people a chance to practice loading and unloading 500-pound bombs on the P-47 fuselage shackles—a harbinger of missions to come. Korky had A Flight watch this practice session. "You might learn something useful" was his only comment.

Next morning we were summoned to the group briefing room, where 1st Lt. Pat Murphy, now the group armament officer, showed us what a 500-pound bomb looked like and explained exactly how it worked. He also gave us detailed instructions on various methods of releasing the bomb. Someone asked, "What do you do if the bomb doesn't release?"

"You get out and kick the goddamn thing off!" yelled Jeeter.

Pat Murphy offered a few other alternatives. Then Major Dix gave us a few pointers on dive bombing, but few pilots expressed enthusiasm at that prospect.

Flight Officer Clarence Barger joined our squadron on January 3, raising our pilot strength to twenty-seven. The organizational chart (pilots) showed one major (Kinnard), four captains, twenty first lieutenants, and two flight officers.

The rest of January was a continuation of December—lousy weather, over either England or the Continent, or both. The mission on January 4 featured 840 bombers pounding Kiel, plus another 140 B-17s attacking Münster. "Hitler must be getting a little nervous," said Duff as we looked at the briefing map. "Every day, we put more and more airplanes in his sky."

"And every day, we get more and more airplanes from the States," I said. "He has plenty of reasons to be nervous."

I wasn't scheduled for this one. Duff flew as a spare, but had to come home early when he couldn't get fuel from his belly tank. Korky chased two Me-109s away from a 356th Fighter Group·P-47, but couldn't match their tight turn as they dove for the deck, so he couldn't get a shot at them.

On January 7 I flew another of those "except for the heavy flak, the mission was uneventful" milk runs. It was the first time I saw a combat wing of B-24s in the bomber stream.

On January 11 the bombers were going to Brunswick, and we were to cover their withdrawal. In a small but significant change of tactics, the 357th Squadron was assigned to bounce any enemy aircraft in the area, but the other two squadrons were to stick close to the bombers. Foggy Schmucker told us that the base of the overcast was twenty-five hundred feet, tops at four thousand. From there on it would be clear. "But you might run into that super-strong wind again at higher altitudes—about a hundred miles per hour blowing from the northwest. If you do, just drop down a few thousand feet until your ground speed picks up again."

We started engines at 11:59 A.M. I wondered why they couldn't have made it noon—would it have made that much difference? That's the kind of thing that made us a little suspicious of the people who planned these missions. As we started engines, a light rain began to fall and visibility slipped to about a mile, but we were off on time.

The group went into the overcast in fairly good formation but soon broke up into squadrons, then flights, then elements, and even individuals. It was the worst flying weather we had encountered. We broke out of the low overcast as predicted, but not into a nice, clear blue sky. There were broken clouds in heavy layers between four thousand feet and ten thousand feet, and then a solid overcast to well over thirty thousand feet.

Our formation started out like this:

Red Flight	Yellow Flight	Blue Flight	Green Flight
Kucheman	Allard	Koraleski	Lenfest
Minchew	Kurtz	Fortier	Morris
Johnston	Austin	Perry	Neal
Williams	Benson	Culp	Mendenhall

Shortly after takeoff, 1st Lt. Larry Sluga, the 358th Squadron's operations officer, bailed out after blundering into a small thunderstorm. His instruments went wild and he couldn't tell the attitude of his ship. He hit the ground only seconds after his chute opened. His face was "sandpapered" by hailstones and his right ankle was sprained, but he was otherwise uninjured. His P-47 crashed in a nearby open field.

Les Minchew had problems at mid-Channel and returned to base. Shortly after that, Captain Kucheman turned back with the rest of his flight.

Korky kept climbing, hoping to top the overcast and find the bombers. The overcast was thick, and I was working hard at staying just inches away from Korky's wing. Vertigo set in every now and then, and I'd swear that we were flying upside down, but I shook it off and kept my eyes glued on his cockpit. The formation lessons learned in Basic flight training were paying dividends. Somewhere along the way, Perry and Culp became separated from us and returned to base. The clouds were so thick, I wasn't even aware of their departure. I didn't dare look at my altimeter, but learned later that at thirty thousand feet, Korky leveled off and flew the assigned heading for several minutes, then decided that was enough and turned for home. If we did get beyond the clouds, our chances of finding the bombers would be slim to nil.

We landed after an hour and a half of solid instrument flying; Korky flew the gauges, and I was tucked tight inside his left wing. I couldn't remember being so tired after a flight. When I shut down the engine, McKibbin jumped up on the wing. "How'd it go, Lieutenant?"

"Another milk run," I answered. This time, I thought, that expression was quite appropriate. I felt like I had spent the whole time flying inside a huge bottle of milk.

In his narrative, Burt Sims put it this way: "It was a rough trip. The strain showed on their faces when they returned to Gremlin Villa. . . ."

As I was slinging my parachute onto the rack, Korky came over to me, and in a rare display for him, patted me on the back and said, "Nice going, Bud."

I was a little flustered. "You didn't do too bad yourself," I replied.

January 14 was the second of several missions with the code name IQ. They consisted of a series of concentrated attacks on the launching sites of the V-1 missiles being developed by the Germans. A murmur stirred the briefing room when Major Dix revealed the altitudes at which we'd be flying: the 358th at fifteen thousand feet, the 357th at sixteen thousand feet, and the 354th at fourteen thousand feet. Our assignment was to provide a defensive "wall of fighters" on the German side to protect the bombers that would be bombing from ten thousand feet to twelve thousand feet.

Bob Woody led our flight, I was on his wing, and Perry and Duff were the second element.

The Luftwaffe stayed away—our fighters surrounded the bombers on three sides and overhead—but we saw several chutes floating down from bombers that had been hit by the intense antiaircraft barrage. The flak gunners launched quite a few shells in our direction but nowhere near what they threw at the bombers.

On the way home, Duff was short of fuel and landed at Fair Oak RAF Station, just outside London. When the rest of us got back to Steeple, the B-17s of the 91st Bomb Group were flying directly over our base on their final approach to Bassingbourne, just four miles to the north. Perry squeezed in between two bombers and landed at Steeple, but Woody couldn't find an opening. Our fuel supply was low, so we joined the bomber traffic pattern and landed at Bassingbourne. We were taken to Steeple by jeep, and returned the next day to fly the Jugs home. Duff flew back in after dark. "You damn fool," I greeted him when he walked into Gremlin Villa, "you were only a few miles from London, and you came back *here*!"

"I missed my roommate," was his sarcastic reply.

On January 21 the 355th, led by Colonel Cummings, was to patrol an area from Évreux, fifty-five miles west-northwest of Paris, to Abbeville, about eighty miles north of Paris. We were to "engage and pursue" any enemy fighters in the area. Our squadron brought up the rear of the group formation.

From twenty-five thousand feet, Abbeville and Évreux were just dots on the landscape below, so I suspect that Colonel Cummings was using Paris as a checkpoint to keep us close to our assigned area.

I was a spare for this mission. Spares were to fill in if anyone had to return to base; if no one aborted, the group leader usually released spares when the group made landfall at the enemy coast. No one aborted, but Cummings didn't give the usual order releasing the spares, so I decided to tag along behind the 354th.

I was flying above and behind Blue Flight, led by Koraleski. Green Flight, led by Stud Starr, was high and to our right. We patrolled the Évreux–Abbeville area for nearly two hours without encountering any sign of enemy activity. Finally, Cummings made a wide left turn at Évreux and said we were heading home. The turn put us over the outskirts of Paris.

"Heywood Green, this is Blue Leader. You've got bogeys coming in at four o'clock high!" Korky had great eyesight. I swiveled my head around and saw two specks against the dark blue sky background. The specks were rapidly getting bigger.

"Got 'em," replied Starr. "Green Flight, break right . . . NOW!"

When Green Flight turned into them, two FW-190s swept past Green Flight and headed for the deck in a diving turn to the right. Korky jammed full throttle and dove after them, with the rest of Blue Flight behind him. Green Flight joined the chase.

From my vantage point behind Blue Flight, I watched the drama unfold, but not as a disinterested spectator. I was scared to death that the 190s would spot me, all by myself, an easy target. I headed for Korky's flight at full throttle.

The P-47 could overtake any German fighter in a dive, and Korky soon got in shooting range of the second FW-190. His first burst probably did some damage, because the FW turned sharply left, still heading for cloud cover. We were not yet equipped with API (armor-piercing incendiary) ammunition, so we couldn't see where—or whether—we were hitting the target, except when flames appeared or pieces of the airplane tore off.

The 190's sharp left turn put him right in Jim Duffy's gunsight. "Get him, Duff," said Korky. Jim was already firing. Smoke poured from the 190's engine, and pieces fell off the fuselage as it entered the cloud in a steep dive, trailing smoke and debris.

Korky had pulled up, but the rest of Blue Flight had followed Duff, so I quickly filled in on Korky's wing. He spotted a lone FW-190 diving toward Paris below and tried unsuccessfully to get within firing range. The 190 took us on a wild chase, low over the streets of Paris—diving, climbing, weaving—and we were unable to get close enough for a lethal burst. I saw Korky firing every now and then, and when the FW turned in my direction, I fired a burst even though I knew I was out of range. At least I had finally fired at an enemy airplane, ineffective though it might have been. I probably broke a few windows in Paris.

There had to have been a few more FW-190s in the vicinity, because several other 354th pilots were chasing them all around Paris—without scoring.

Suddenly it was over. The 190s were gone. P-47s converged on Korky, and we headed home in a loose formation.

Air combat was often like that, I was learning. All hell breaks loose, confusion reigns as individual dogfights mushroom all around, then suddenly it's over. You're alone, or with only your wingman, wondering where everybody went.

As we were letting down over a peaceful English countryside, I was mulling over two glaring mistakes I had made on that mission:

1. I should not have stayed with the squadron beyond landfall. A simple radio transmission—"Sunshade, this is Haywood Spare, am I cleared to return to base?"— would have reminded Colonel Cummings that he had not released me.
2. Having made the first foolish mistake, I compounded it by sitting high above and behind the squadron—all alone. Korky didn't know I was there. If the 190s had spotted me before they attacked Green Flight, I would have been easy prey. Better to have latched onto Korky's flight and let him know.

I was also learning how to deal with fear, an emotion that probably would accompany me on most of my missions. Fear could serve useful purposes: It pumps up the heart rate and the flow of adrenaline, and it sharpens your focus on the situation and what has to be done. But it had to be controlled. You had to look it in the face, overcome it, and get on with the mission. Every time you did that, you got a little stronger and more confident.

I was learning. There's an old saying, "A good scare is worth more to a man than good advice." I had just had a good scare.

The mission on January 24 was uneventful as far as Luftwaffe participation was concerned, but heavy flak tore the wing off a 357th Squadron P-47, killing the pilot, and damaged several other airplanes in the group. "Flak isn't just for bombers," observed Charlie Sweat.

The next day, an Me-110 and a Ju-88 landed at Steeple Morden. They were part of the RAF "Flying Circus" designed to give us all a close-up look at the enemy aircraft. Shortly after their arrival, a single Me-109 gave an outstanding demonstration of a grass-clipping buzz job, to the cheers of the watching pilots, before landing. They were with us for five days, giving us all kinds of performance data and flight characteristics of the aircraft as well as demonstrations of German weapons and uniforms. When they left, they once again gave the base a thorough going-over at an altitude of about eighteen inches.

On January 26, Major Kinnard and Captain Glantz talked to the pilots about dive-bombing techniques and identification of significant targets on airfields such as Gilze-Rijen in Holland. That gave us a hint of things to come. "I don't like the way these lectures are going," I said to Duff. "They're not telling us all that stuff for nothing." I had reservations about dive-bombing heavily defended German airfields.

On January 28, Lt. Col. Everett Stewart joined the 355th as group executive officer. He came from the 352d Fighter Group, where he had been a squadron commander.

To no one's surprise, January ended with a dive-bombing attack on Gilze-Rijen airfield in Holland. Aircraft in the first eight-ship section, led by Lieutenant Colonel Stewart, carried a 500-pound bomb instead of a belly tank.

Blue Section, led by Korky, was assigned to escort and protect the "bombers." I was flying Blue-4, on Woody's wing.

Cumulus clouds covered much of the target area, so it
took a while to locate Gilze-Rijen. Finally, Stewart called,
"I see it! Let's go!" He split-essed from seventeen thousand
feet and dove straight down to about nine thousand feet, released his bomb, and pulled back up to about fifteen thousand feet. The rest of his section followed in a trail
formation.

It took a while for the bombs to reach the target, but
soon we saw explosions on the east–west runway, then in
the headquarters and billeting area. The second flight, led
by Captain Kucheman, hit an aircraft dispersal area and
an ammunition-and-fuel storage area, causing a tremen-
dous explosion that spewed flames, debris, and black
smoke high into the air. Only two bombs missed the airfield completely.

From our vantage point at eighteen thousand feet, we
were impressed. "There might be something to this technique after all," I thought. Surprisingly, there was little
flak.

Fifteen minutes after we left the area, the 4th Fighter
Group arrived on a similar mission. After they released their
bombs, they were bounced by about a dozen Me-109s. In
the ensuing dogfight, the 4th claimed six 109s destroyed. At
our briefing the next morning we were told that they also
claimed to have hit an ammunition-and-fuel storage area, an
announcement that was greeted with hoots of derision.

"Don't you ever wonder," I asked Duff, "why you and I
are not leading elements, or even flights by now?"

"Don't ask me! Ask Korky or Kucheman. They're the
ones who set up the schedule."

"Perry and Woody lead elements in our flight. They
don't have any more experience than we have. I led an element just once. You shot down an airplane and you haven't
led an element even once! Replacement pilots are leading
elements in the other squadrons."

"They've had more losses than we have," said Duff. "We'll get our chance."

"I hope so! I don't want to go through the whole bloody war as tail-end Charlie."

The 355th Fighter Group flew only ten missions in January. At least that many were scrubbed because of weather. I flew seven of the ten.

February 1944

Major Claiborne H. Kinnard had been our squadron commander for more than two months and had yet to fly a mission with us. An infection had taken up permanent residence in his ears and he couldn't shake it. The weather was no help. Our previous commander had the same problem and had flown very few combat missions prior to his reassignment.

VIII Fighter Command required that all squadron commanders of newly arrived fighter groups fly combat orientation flights with an experienced fighter group. Kinnard had flown several missions with the 4th Fighter Group and had been credited with one aerial victory and one enemy aircraft destroyed on the ground, so his reputation for aggressiveness was well established. His forced inactivity was more of a concern to him than to the rest of the pilots; he didn't want to be seen as a hypochondriac.

Kinnard may have been grounded, but he didn't spend much time at the base hospital. He attended every briefing, spoke to all the pilots in the squadron, and spent hours analyzing intelligence reports, taking notes on the disposition and dispersal of Luftwaffe units and antiaircraft defenses at Luftwaffe airfields. He studied weather patterns over Europe; he visited Bassingbourne to discuss bomber formations and tactics; he quizzed the engineering officer, 1st Lt. Walt Randall, and line chief MSgt. Buck Wrightam, about maintenance procedures and schedules. He subjected the armament, communications, supply, intelligence, and administrative sections to the same intense scrutiny.

"I think he's writing a book," said Perry as February rolled around, "and he hasn't got to the combat part yet."

"Well, he already knows a helluva lot more about this outfit than I do," said Duff.

"And about this war!" Korky added.

We were standing outside Gremlin Villa watching Kinnard wandering among the P-47s parked in the A Flight area, chatting with crew chiefs and assistants. With his easygoing manner and soft Tennessee drawl, he had them eating out of his hand, telling him their problems, complaints, and how they'd run the squadron if given the chance. They had his undivided attention.

He also had devoted a lot of time studying fighter tactics and organization—ours and the Luftwaffe's—and concluded that our squadron organization wasn't quite right. His Squadron Order 3 dated January 28 and effective February 1 created two subsquadrons: Squadron A and Squadron B. New assignments were as follows:

A Squadron

Captain Kucheman was squadron leader.

Stud Starr was A Flight commander and deputy squadron leader. Pop Allard was his deputy flight commander. Others in A Flight were Swede Benson and Jim Austin.

Chuck Lenfest was B Flight commander, and Jeeter Neal was his deputy. Others: Ken Williams, Silky Morris, and Gil Wright.

Bob Kurtz was C Flight commander; Lee Mendenhall was his deputy. Others: Sammy Houston and Pete Bauman.

B Squadron

Captain Koraleski was squadron leader.

Curt Johnston was A Flight commander and deputy squadron leader. Other members of A Flight were Brady Williamson, Henry Brown, and Fid Barger.

Charley Sweat was B Flight commander, and Rich Brown was his deputy. Others: Hal Culp and Bud Fortier.

Bob Woody was C Flight commander. Other members: Emil Perry, Jim Duffy, and Bill Boulet.

The new organization was the subject of heated discussions at the officers' club bar that night. "How in hell can that work?" asked Duff. "If a guy goes on a two-day pass to London, or somebody gets a cold, our flight is down to three guys!"

"I used to be in A Flight," I added, "and now I'm in B Squadron, B Flight. What does this do to our radio call signs? Sometimes I wonder what goes on in that guy's head."

"Two flights don't have a deputy flight commander," said Brady, brandishing a copy of the Squadron Order 3, "including the one I'm in. Why not? In fact, I wonder about the whole thing. We have twenty first lieutenants in this squadron, and there's not more than a fifteen-hour difference in our flying times. I wonder what he based his assignments on."

"If nothing else," said Perry, "he's caused a lot of confusion in what used to be a normal squadron . . . if there is such a thing."

"Give it a shot," said Burt. "Try it for a few missions. It might work."

The conversation went on until the bar closed. One thing was clear to me: Duff and I were still peons, no matter how the squadron was organized.

On the next mission, February 2, I found myself flying the no. 4 slot on Charley Sweat's wing in the lead flight, with Stewart leading and Major Rosenblatt on his wing. Korky led Blue Flight, with Captain Liston (on detached service from a newly assigned fighter group) on his wing, and Perry and Boulet in the second element. Henry Brown was flying his first mission as a second lieutenant—his promotion had come through on the first of February—on Curt Johnston's wing in Yellow Flight. Our mission was to provide area support of the bombers under radar control.

We milled around at twenty-seven thousand feet for

more than an hour, just boring huge holes in the sky. The Luftwaffe apparently had the day off. As we headed home, Stewart spotted several unidentified aircraft milling around a formation of B-26 medium bombers at about ten thousand feet, so he took us down in a hurry to investigate. From a distance, the smaller aircraft looked like Me-210s. We closed on them fast, and just as Stewart and Sweat were about to open fire, someone yelled, "They're Mosquitoes! Don't shoot!" We had not been briefed to expect RAF Mosquito fighters escorting B-26s in the area, and this incident came close to being a disaster.

No one was happy with the new flight setup, and by the next mission, on February 3, the flights began to look like the organization of old. Korky had Captain Liston on his wing, but his second element consisted of Duff and Hal Culp. Starr seemed to have his old B Flight buddies with him. Gradually the Kinnard plan eased back into the old familiar pattern. He didn't object. Quietly, he rescinded Squadron Order 3.

The early-morning mission on February 3 was an uneventful escort mission into central France, but late that afternoon, group headquarters asked for two pilots to fly a most unusual mission. "Two barrage balloons have broken loose from their moorings and they're raising hell by dragging the mooring cables across power lines near Colchester. Can you get two pilots to go up there and shoot them down?"

"You bet!" said Kucheman.

"Make damn sure you don't spray lead all over Colchester or any village in that area!"

Everyone in the squadron volunteered to go, but Kucheman volunteered himself and picked Jeeter Neal to go with him.

They had no trouble locating the sausage-shaped balloons, but picking the right angle from which to fire without shooting up the neighborhood called for some jockeying around. They finally got set up and started their firing runs, each picking out one balloon. Jeeter flamed his—a spectacular display—but Kuch's balloon simply expired without fireworks. Burt was waiting for them when they returned. "No, you *don't* get credit for a kill!"

Lieutenant Colonel Stewart, who arrived at Steeple Morden on January 28, took only one day to settle in before going to work. He led the group on January 30 and on the next eight missions, and quickly established himself as an effective and aggressive leader.

On February 4, Stewart led the group with our squadron. Colonel Jesse Auton, commander of the 65th Fighter Wing, flew Stewart's wing. I was in my usual no. 4 position in Korky's flight. We escorted B-17s on their way back from Frankfurt. Three FW-190s were spotted about three miles away, but they left in a hurry when we headed their way. Except for the usual flak, our wing commander had a nice, boring flight.

February 6 was our fifth mission in five days. Stewart led with our squadron but returned early when his prop control went haywire. Korky took over, the Luftwaffe stayed out of our way, and again, I flew no. 4—on Perry's wing this time. "This is getting monotonous!" I thought. Not dodging flak, which is never monotonous, but always flying somebody's wing—not getting a chance to lead. I *knew* I could fly at least as well as those who were leading elements and flights. Was I the only one who thought so?

Soon after his reorganization plan fell through, Kinnard came up with another brainstorm. We had been flying the basic "finger formation" since operational training. Kinnard thought it might be better to have each flight and section in a trail formation, as shown here:

```
        T                      T
        T                      T
        T                      T
        T                      T
```

The second section was directly behind the first. This formation, he thought, would allow all four planes in a flight to turn into an attack with all guns blazing.

To my knowledge, this formation was tried on only one mission, during which two serious flaws were revealed: It was a difficult formation to maintain in an overcast, and it was vulnerable to attacks from the six-o'clock-high position. The tactic was promptly dropped. Again, Kinnard didn't object. He was not dogmatic; he wanted his ideas tested, and if they failed, so be it.

On February 8, Kinnard strode into Gremlin Villa with a big smile spread across his face, walked directly to the mission board, and placed his name in the squadron leader slot for the day's mission. He turned to us, still with that huge grin. "That's right, folks!" he proclaimed, "I'm cleared to fly!"

We didn't know if we were supposed to cheer, but Korky said, "Welcome aboard, Major!"

The mission on February 8 was to cover the bomber withdrawal from Frankfurt. Stewart led the group with the 358th, Jonesy was next with the 357th, and the 354th took off last, with Kinnard leading. The prevailing winds at Steeple Morden were from the southwest, so most of our takeoffs were on Runway 22, but with a strong wind blowing from the northeast that morning, the group used Runway 04, right over the village of Litlington.

I wasn't on this mission; I was one of the spectators gathered at Gremlin Villa to watch the takeoffs. Lieutenant Walt Gresham was leading the 358th's Yellow Flight, and just as he neared takeoff speed, he suddenly swerved left and off the runway. He couldn't coax the plane back onto the runway, but he was finally able to get barely airborne—headed on a direct collision course for Gremlin Villa. I saw that big airplane coming right at us, and I thought I was dead. I dropped down flat on my stomach and covered my head with my arms as the P-47 roared overhead and managed to clear the roof of our ready room by no more than two feet.

We scrambled to our feet, resumed breathing, and started scraping the mud from our uniforms.

Kinnard led the squadron that day and soon demonstrated that he was no shrinking violet. When half a dozen 109s and 190s bounced the squadron and broke away when he turned into them, he chased them all the way down to a thick layer of clouds at nine thousand feet. "If that cloud layer had been two thousand feet lower," he said, "we'd-a had a couple of 'em!"

That evening, a message from Fighter Command signaled an important change in the fighter mission. In the early stages of escort, the shortage of fighters made "staying with the bombers" of paramount importance. The increasing numbers of P-47s and the introduction of the longer-range P-51s enabled VIII Fighter Command to enlarge the mission of its fighters to include hunting and pursuing enemy aircraft. The message from Fighter Command read: "If bombers are not being attacked, groups will detach one or two squadrons to range out searching for enemy aircraft. Upon withdrawal if endurance permits, groups will search for and destroy enemy aircraft in the air and on the ground." Everyone greeted the message with enthusiasm.

Kinnard flew five of the next six missions in February, and there was no doubt in anyone's mind that he was in charge. His ear infection had healed, but his hearing steadily deteriorated throughout the war. His plane's radio eventually had to be set at full volume.

Jim Duffy was lucky and unlucky. He was lucky getting out of tight situations, but unlucky getting into them. For instance, on February 11, the 355th escorted B-17s headed for Frankfurt. We were weaving over the bombers at twenty-seven thousand feet, in our spread-out combat formation. Duff was flying no. 2 slot on Korky's wing, and I was in the no. 4 slot on Woody's wing. Each element covered the rear of the other, so I was in position to see Jim's plane and any aircraft that might try to sneak up behind him.

Suddenly I noticed Duff's plane bobbing up and down and weaving in and out of the formation. "Oxygen trouble," I thought. I pressed my mike switch on the throttle knob: "Haywood Blue 2, check your oxygen. You're weaving all over the place!"

His answering "Roger" was slurred, like the speech of a drunk.

"Duff!" I shouted. "Check your oxygen!" There was no answer. His oxygen hose connection had pulled apart, but thinking that his mask was loose, he pushed the mask onto his face, took two or three deep breaths—and passed out. The plane pulled up in a lazy wingover, then plunged straight down.

The P-47's rapid acceleration in a dive was legendary. The Jug often reached speeds at which the "compressibility effect" froze the controls, making recovery chancy at best. With a sinking heart, I watched Duff disappear into a cloudbank at twenty thousand feet, still in a vertical dive. The odds were that I had lost my friend and roommate.

The rest of the mission was uneventful. I kept hoping to hear a radio call from Duff, but none came. When we landed and taxied to the A Flight dispersal area, I was elated to see his plane, WR-Y, in its usual spot. It was plenty battered and surrounded by mechanics. He gave us a complete account of his hair-raising adventures when we got back to Gremlin Villa.

When Duff came to, he was headed straight down, and his altimeter was unwinding crazily. He tried to pull the stick back, but it seemed set in concrete. He knew the plane had reached compressibility. He did the only thing he could do: He rolled in a little back trim and pushed the throttle wide open. It takes guts to jam the throttle open when you're hurtling toward the ground at more than five hundred miles per hour, but it was supposed to help bring the nose up. And he probably prayed.

At about ten thousand feet, the nose of the plane started to come up, agonizingly slowly at first as the ground rushed up. Then he was suddenly slammed down hard into his seat as the Jug came out of the dive and headed skyward. The heavy G forces pulled a black curtain over his eyes.

When his vision returned, the plane had gone past vertical; Duff was hanging by his seat belt. He rolled right-side-up, heaved a huge sigh of relief, and looked around.

He was at fifteen thousand feet and completely alone— no bombers or fighters in sight. He decided to head back to England at treetop level, where German radar couldn't detect him. He headed for the deck at a moderate angle this time.

Hedgehopping is great sport for any fighter pilot, and Jim was enjoying the fast-moving scenery. Soon he was skimming the canals of Holland, which were busy with barge traffic. Why not shoot up a couple of barges along the way? After all, those barges were certainly used by or for Germans.

He pulled up about five hundred feet to look around, and saw a row of barges moving slowly along a wide canal. Likely targets, he figured, so he flipped the gun switch on and slanted down toward them. He lined up the gunsight on the lead barge. All hell broke loose.

It was common knowledge that Germans packed some of the barges with antiaircraft guns, usually 20mm and 40mm stuff. As luck would have it, two of the barges in that row of targets were flak barges. It didn't take Jim long to figure out that he had stirred up a hornet's nest.

Duff felt the plane shudder, heard and felt the shells hitting the plane as the sky around him exploded in red, yellow, and black. Frantically, he turned away from the attack, a tactical error because they now had the whole underside of the plane as a target instead of the smaller and more intimidating head-on view of eight blazing .50-caliber machine guns. He forced the shuddering plane to treetop level and jammed the throttle to the firewall, desperately trying to get out of range of that deadly barrage.

In seconds that seemed like hours, he was in the clear. He could see quite a few holes in the wings, and the engine was running pretty rough, but it was still running. The controls seemed to be normal, so he headed across the North Sea. It was a nervous trip across that icy water.

As soon as he crossed the English coast, he called for a steer to base, where he landed as quickly, and carefully, as he could. As he taxied to the dispersal area, he saw the mechanics pointing at his airplane. By the time he had shut down the engine, a small crowd had gathered.

The damage was impressive. The landing gear fairings were buckled, some rivets had popped in the wings, and the right aileron was bent—all this from his recovery from that high-speed dive. The damage from the flak barges was even more impressive. There were more than two hundred holes, ranging in size from half an inch to about eight inches in diameter.

Closer inspection later that day revealed that an oil line had been punctured and there was only about a cupful of oil left in the tank when Duff landed. Had the flight been five minutes longer, he would not have made it back to base. That same inspection revealed a 20mm shell lodged under the pilot's seat. Why it hadn't exploded on impact, no one knew. More of Duff's Irish luck. "If it had," said Jim, "I'd be walking around today without an ass."

The airplane was beyond repair. Usable parts were salvaged; what was left was consigned to the junkyard as scrap metal.

The weather kept us grounded for more than a week following the mission on the eleventh. Second Lieutenant Robert Browning, a replacement pilot, joined our squadron on February 11 and was assigned to Korky's flight.

On February 20, more than six hundred heavy bombers opened up what was to become known as Big Week, with attacks on the German aircraft industry at Leipzig, Ascherleben, Gotha, Braunschweig, and Halberstadt. From Italy, the newly activated Fifteenth Air Force bombed Regensburg, Augsburg, and Stuttgart.

Kinnard led the squadron again, with Bob Woody on his wing; I flew no. 4, on Kucheman's wing. The ceiling was eight hundred feet, so penetration of the overcast was made by individual flights, and the group assembled above the cloud layers, at about ten thousand feet. Kucheman returned to base when his radio failed; Jim Duffy, the spare, joined us on my wing. I was, temporarily at least, an element leader.

We made rendezvous with four boxes of B-24s in a tight formation at twenty-eight thousand feet in the vicinity of Marienburg—we couldn't be sure about the location because of a solid cloud layer at about fifteen thousand feet. Another group of P-47s was already in place above the bombers and appeared unwilling to go elsewhere, so we positioned ourselves at and below bomber level. Just as we began the weaving pattern that allowed us to keep up our speed and stay with the bombers, the 357th reported about twenty-five Me-109s heading for bombers withdrawing from Braunschweig and Halberstadt. "Go get 'em," said Cummings, who was leading the group with the 358th. When the 357th gave chase, the 109s turned tail and dove away. Norm Olson caught one and blew it up for his fifth victory, thereby becoming the group's first ace. First Lieutenant Jim Dickson nailed another.

Meanwhile, in the 354th, six Me-109s tried to sneak by Chuck Lenfest's Yellow Flight to get at the bombers, but when Chuck and company turned into them, they dove away, headed for the cloudbank below.

Jeeter Neal closed to within a hundred yards of one fleeing 109, and just as he was about the squeeze the trigger, the German's propwash had Jeeter bobbing up and down and sideways, unable to get a shot off. By that time the German pilot became aware that he was close to extinction, and he led Jeeter into a dizzying display of aerobatics before finally dropping down into the clouds. "I just *knew* I had that bastard!" a frustrated Jeeter kept saying after the mission, "I *had* him!" He made no claim.

The three squadrons damaged several 109s, but only two

Me-109s were claimed destroyed. The rest of the mission was uneventful.

It was a great day for the VIII Fighter Command: sixty-one enemy fighters were destroyed, six probably destroyed, and thirty-three damaged, for a loss of four aircraft. The bomber gunners claimed an equal number destroyed, but without the benefit of gun-camera film, their claims were difficult to confirm.

On Monday, February 21, day two of Big Week, five combat wings attacked Luftwaffe airfields and installations in the Braunschweig and Diepholz areas. I was the spare for this mission, but no one aborted. This time, when we made landfall over Holland, I didn't even wait for release by the group leader—I turned back and went home. Survival rule no. 1: Don't make the same stupid mistake twice.

Our assigned boxes were ten minutes late, so the 355th Group was unable to escort them all the way to the target, but another P-47 group arrived as we left. On the way home, the 357th Squadron spotted fifteen FW-190s headed for the bomber stream and piled into them. Captain Olson was leading. The 190s tried to dive away, but Olson caught up with one of them and peppered it with lead. The 190 pilot bailed out of his smoking aircraft. It was no. 6 for Olson, but he was nearly shot down himself when he overran his next target and the hunter became the hunted. A 20mm shell exploded right behind his canopy, and machine-gun bullet holes appeared all over his airplane. He managed to get away—and so did the 190. It was a good day for the 357th—two other 357th pilots scored victories—but the other two squadrons were in the wrong piece of sky.

Six months after our group arrived in England, I got word that my brother-in-law, Maurice "Moe" Levesque, had arrived in England and was stationed near Portsmouth. He was in the 4th Armored Division of General Patton's Third Army. I wrote to Moe, and we arranged to meet in

London on February 23, at the Jules Club, where I had reserved a room. It was an old London hotel used as a leave
center for American officers. It was just off Piccadilly
Circus on Jermyn Street.

February 23 dawned cold and drizzly, and by ten o'clock
the group's scheduled mission had been scrubbed because
of nasty weather. The armed forces radio station reported
that the Luftwaffe had bombed London the night before.
Those Luftwaffe bombing raids had been less and less frequent in recent months, the reporter added. After lunch, I
got a jeep ride to Royston, caught the train to London, and
checked into the hotel.

I was sitting in the lobby at 7:00 P.M., our prearranged
meeting time and place, reading a magazine and looking
forward to seeing Moe again. Seven o'clock came and went,
but he didn't show up. I found out later that his leave had
been canceled and he was unable to make it, and also was
unable to let me know.

At about seven-thirty, the air raid siren sounded. The
Luftwaffe was making a second appearance over London in
as many days. It was my second experience with a London
air raid, and I was a bit nervous. I looked around at the others sitting in the lobby, but everyone sat calmly and seemingly unperturbed, so I decided to stay put and keep cool.
Heavy blackout curtains covered all the windows, the lights
remained on, and life went on as usual in the little hotel.

A few minutes later, we heard the heavy thumping of the
antiaircraft guns several blocks away, in Hyde Park. Again I
looked around nervously at the dozen or so other officers,
but they acted as if everything were perfectly normal. "Am I
the only one in here who's a little scared?" I wondered.

I rose from my chair to get another magazine when an
earsplitting explosion shook the hotel. Then another, almost
as loud. The lights went out. I was thrown to the other end
of the room, flat on my face. Plaster had fallen from the ceiling, leaving a choking dust. It was pitch black.

No one said anything. All I heard was the coughing of
people around me. Something was on top of my head, so I

moved it. It was somebody's foot, fortunately still attached to its owner. "Sorry," he said.

The English manager of the hotel lit a candle and asked, "Everyone all right?" A few minutes later, several candles illuminated the lobby. It was a shambles. Chairs and tables had been thrown around the room, and the floor was covered with fallen plaster and broken glass from lamps and chandeliers. Our uniforms were coated white.

Men were coming down the stairs, half dressed and in one case with shaving lather all over his face. Everybody was asking the same question: "What happened?"

Apparently no one was seriously hurt. I got up and checked myself over. Aside from the coating of white from the ceiling plaster, I was all right.

One of the janitors came running into the lobby. "The building's been hit by two bombs!" he shouted. "One of them went off, but the other one didn't!" That was his opinion, of course, but it never occurred to me at the time that he could not possibly have known this.

I decided there wasn't enough room in that hotel for an unexploded bomb and me, so I made my way to the blacked-out double doors and into the street. The roar of the antiaircraft guns was much louder there. I started toward Piccadilly Circus, where I intended to go down into the Underground station.

"Get out of the street, you bloody fool!" a voice bellowed from across the street. "There's shrapnel falling all over the bloody place!" Probably a Civil Defence warden. He was right. I could hear whistling noises and the clanking of metal hitting the street. But I wasn't about to go back into that building.

Searchlights probing for German airplanes reflected off the low overcast and faintly illuminated the streets. Keeping as close to the buildings as I could, I ran down Jermyn Street toward Piccadilly Circus. With the searchlights, the booming antiaircraft guns, and the occasional explosions nearby, I didn't notice the cold, wet drizzle, even though I had left the hotel in too much of a hurry to grab my coat and hat.

I finally reached Piccadilly Circus and ran down into the Underground station. All of London's subways were air raid shelters, and thousands of people actually *lived* there, so even though my uniform was covered with wet plaster dust, no one paid any particular attention to me.

When the all-clear sounded nearly an hour later, I made my way through the blacked-out streets back to the hotel, where some semblance of order had been restored. The power was still off, but there were plenty of candles and lamps. Two bombs, it turned out, had hit a large building behind the hotel, and had blown down part of the back wall of the hotel. Most of the rooms, including mine, had only fallen ceiling plaster and cracked walls to show for it. I was given a candle and went up to my room, shook the plaster off the bed, and went to sleep. By morning, electric power had been restored, the place was pretty well cleaned up, and life was going on as usual.

I decided to stay one more night in case Moe found a way to get there. Fortunately, the Luftwaffe had the night off. Moe did not show. I guessed that something had forced a change in his plans, and my forty-eight-hour pass was running out, so I took the train back to Royston.

That was the Luftwaffe's last manned bombing raid on London. Later, Hitler pinned his hopes on the V-1 "buzz bombs" and V-2 rocket bombs to demoralize the British people and force them to sue for peace terms. He underestimated them.

On February 26, our squadron received two brand-new P-51Bs, substantiating the rumors that had been floating around that we would soon be switching to Mustangs. Two days later, I checked out in the P-51 with a minimum of pre-flight preparation. I had flown P-39s, P-40s, and P-47s; this was just another airplane. There was the cockpit orientation hour, in which Korky showed me where all the switches and controls were, and told me what to expect on takeoffs and landings, what speeds were appropriate for various situations, and all other information that he thought I'd need to get the airplane up and down in one piece. I then took off on a thirty-minute orientation flight.

I had mixed feelings about the Mustang at that point. The cockpit was much smaller than that of the Jug—the whole airplane was much smaller—and the in-line liquid-cooled engine had a totally different sound. The roar of the P-47's 2,000-horsepower Pratt & Whitney radial engine sounded like a large, powerful luxury car; the P-51's 1,650-horsepower Rolls-Royce Merlin engine sounded more like a pack of motorcycles. It was obviously more maneuverable than the Jug—had a much better rate of climb, and a tighter turn radius—but it was also more vulnerable, with all the plumbing required for the liquid coolant. The Jug could take a terrible beating and still bring you home. Would Duff have made it home in a Mustang on February 11?

On February 28, we flew an area patrol in support of B-17s striking the Pas-de-Calais "rocket coast." I was on Perry's wing in my usual Blue 4 slot in Korky's flight. The Luftwaffe didn't challenge, but there was plenty of flak, especially in the Hesdin area, where I saw two bombers go down—one in flames and the other breaking up before it hit the ground—and only seven parachutes where I was hoping to see twenty. We escorted several straggling Fortresses—one was limping along with both port engines feathered—to about ten miles past the enemy coastline.

February 29 closed out the month with another milk run; I flew Kinnard's wing. It was noteworthy only in that the 8th Fighter Command reported only one claim: one Me-110 shot down by Maj. Gerald Johnston of the 56th Fighter Group. Burt's comment in his narrative: "The question on everyone's mind: Where is the Luftwaffe?" The question in *my* mind: When will I get to be an element leader?

March 1944

March started out with typical nasty English weather—cold with a biting wind, drizzle, and low visibility. The scheduled mission was scrubbed early. By 4:00 P.M. the sun was poking through some breaks in the overcast, and the pilots assembled in front of Group Operations for a presentation-of-awards ceremony. Colonel Jesse Auton, the 65th Fighter Wing commander, presented the Distinguished Flying Cross to thirty pilots. Captain Larry Sluga received the Order of the Purple Heart for wounds caused by enemy action when his face was pelted almost raw by hailstones after he blundered into a thunderstorm shortly after takeoff on January 11.

"Wounds caused by enemy action!" said Duff. "Isn't that a bit of a stretch?"

"Not at all!" I answered. "In England, the weather is the enemy."

The 358th had a good day on March 2 when they encountered two FW-190s near Charleroi and three Me-109s near Liège. The 190s were diving away when 1st Lt. Walt Gresham managed to hit the leader with a long-range, high-deflection shot that blew up the aircraft and killed the pilot. Lieutenant Roscoe Fussel and Lt. Larry Dudley caught up with the other 190 and took turns getting hits on it until the pilot bailed out. It was later established, with gun-camera film and the recollections of the wingman who bailed out, that the FW-190 destroyed by Gresham was piloted by the great German ace Egon Mayer, the Luftwaffe's top B-17 killer.

"I was just plain lucky," said Walt. "He was about a thousand yards away, in a turn. I put the pipper somewhere ahead of him and fired a long burst, and suddenly the 190 blew up." Good news for bomber crews.

Pilots of the 358th Squadron also shot down the three Me-109s. The other two squadrons didn't see a single enemy plane. The 358th had a great time at the club that night, making loud, derogatory comments about the eyesight of the rest of us.

The briefing room was buzzing with excitement the next morning, March 3, when pilots saw the red yarn showing the bomber route stretching more than halfway on the large map on the wall: target, Berlin. This was to be the first daylight raid on the German capital by the Eighth Air Force. I felt the sharp twinge in the pit of my stomach—I was becoming used to that feeling.

The 55th Fighter Group, flying P-38s, was slated to escort the bombers over the target. We were to escort B-17s on their withdrawal over Holland. We took off shortly after noon in bright sunshine. As we climbed out over the North Sea, we were informed that the Berlin mission had been scrubbed because of bad weather; the bombers were to strike targets of opportunity, and we were to patrol the area over northern Holland. Just as we made landfall over Holland, my engine began to run rough, and a thin spray of oil that soon covered my windshield restricted my forward vision. I told Korky what my problem was and turned back toward England. The North Sea looked even colder with a rough-running engine, so I stayed well above twenty thousand feet until I spotted land.

I didn't miss much. The group ran into towering clouds and never did find the bombers. The 55th Fighter Group didn't hear the recall message, so they were the first fighter group from the 8th Fighter Command to fly over Berlin. They probably were wondering where in hell everybody was.

Berlin was the designated target again the following day, and Col. Jesse Auton was on hand to fly the mission with us. Colonel Cummings led the group, with Auton on his wing. I drew the assignment of relay for this mission, with Lt. Robert Browning on my wing. None of the pilots liked this assignment, which consisted of orbiting over the North Sea at twenty-five thousand feet, just off the Dutch coast, and relaying messages between the strike force and Mission Control in England. It was boring, though the Luftwaffe occasionally sent a few fighters to entice us to chase them, and German flak batteries in Holland sometimes used us for target practice.

After the briefing, Maj. Danny Lewis read a directive from 8 Fighter Command advising pilots not to carry guns or even long knives on missions. This was to avoid intimidating people in the occupied countries who might otherwise approach downed airmen, and to preclude the possibility of shooting a German civilian, thereby becoming liable to civil prosecution.

Colonel Auton spoke briefly. He noted that in spite of the message from VIII Fighter Command to permit hot pursuit of enemy aircraft and even destroying them on the ground, most P-47 fighter groups seemed reluctant to fly at lower altitudes, where the 190s and 109s had a maneuvering advantage. He told of the probable formation of a volunteer low-level Thunderbolt group to explore the feasibility of strafing heavily defended enemy airfields and to develop tactics for such missions. He suggested that pilots interested in joining such a group submit their names to Wing headquarters.

Once again the weather forced the bombers to seek secondary targets. One box of bombers, with P-51 fighter escort, did make its way to the outskirts of Berlin, where it encountered heavy clouds and severe icing conditions, and was forced to turn back. Eleven escorting fighters didn't return. All were believed to be victims of the foul weather.

The 357th Fighter Squadron flew Mustangs for the first time on this mission. The 355th Group scoured the assigned area but found no bombers. There was no activity from the Luftwaffe, but the flak over the southern end of the Ruhr valley was intense and accurate. Several of our planes were damaged, none seriously. A chunk of flak tore off an exhaust stack from Norm Olson's brand-new Mustang.

"Big B again!" said Korky as we entered the briefing room on March 6. "I hope the bombers get there this time."

They did.

Major Danny Lewis, group intelligence officer, began the briefing at 10:50 A.M. "The bomber train headed for Berlin today will be almost a hundred miles long," he said. When the low whistles and exclamations subsided, he added, "but we're not expected to protect the whole train." That brought a few chuckles. "The 1st Bomb Division, with three hundred B-17s, will be at the head of the attacking force. On the way back from Berlin, the bombers will form a wide front, with all three bomb divisions flying line abreast. The B-24s of the 2d Bomb Division will be on your right as you approach this massive formation. We are to cover the rear boxes of the 1st Bomb Division, the northernmost B-17 formation." He went on to give us tail markings of our assigned bombers and rendezvous place and time. Pilots were scribbling short notations in the palm of their hands.

"We figure that the Luftwaffe has nearly six hundred single-engine fighters, about 75 percent of them Me-109Gs, that they can put up against this raid, and we believe they'll use every one they can—some more than once. You might see a few Me-110s and Me-410s out there. They'll each be carrying four big twenty-one-centimeter rockets—that's twenty-one centimeters, gentlemen, about eight inches in diameter! They'll be looking for unprotected bombers. They try to avoid tangling with the escort." Germans called the 410 *der Zerstörer* (the destroyer).

Foggy Schmucker said the weather would not be a problem unless we landed after 7:00 P.M., when fog might develop.

Lieutenant Colonel Stewart, who would be leading the

group with the 357th Fighter Squadron, spoke briefly and to the point. "I'll cover the rear boxes, 358th up front, and 354th will be high cover. I'm sure the Jerries will put up everything they have to stop this raid. They'll be using mass attacks against our strung-out escort fighters. Be ready. We should be able to bag a few today. Good luck!"

We had begun our conversion to P-51s, but earlier that day pilots from the 4th Fighter Group arrived to fly sixteen Mustangs of the 357th Squadron back to Debden to be used on the Berlin mission. The 355th launched three squadrons of sixteen P-47s each, and nine spares—every available Thunderbolt.

Korky led our squadron. We started out with sixteen P-47s and two spares, but by the time we made landfall at Ijmuiden, we were down to eleven aircraft because of mechanical or other problems. I was flying Red 4 in Korky's flight, but when Red 2 and Red 3 aborted, I filled in on Korky's wing. Fid Barger, last of the spares, filled in at the Red 3 position. Red Flight was now a threesome.

We were supposed to pick up the bombers on their withdrawal southeast of Vechta, a dot on the map between Bremen and Osnabrück. Dümmer Lake, about twenty-five miles northeast of Osnabrück, was a familiar landmark in that area. We were told that the bombers were running late, so we eased way back on the throttle and mixture control to conserve that all-important fuel. This later allowed us to stay with the bombers ten minutes longer than planned.

Finally we spotted an immense sky train plowing westward in the Dümmer Lake area. I had never seen that many bombers in the same piece of sky. We found our assigned task force and took up escort positions. Strong headwinds at higher altitudes forced the B-17s below twenty thousand feet; they were stacked from fourteen thousand to seventeen thousand feet, well below their usual cruising altitude.

About a dozen Me-109s tried to attack the rear of the task force, but the 357th Squadron drove them off, shooting down five in the process. There were no fighter attacks from the front or sides.

A group of P-47s took over our escort duties before the bombers reached Holland. Soon after leaving the bombers, Korky spotted several aircraft—way below us—circling a lone B-17 on the deck. "We're going down to have a look," he called. "Defrosters on!" At five thousand feet we could see that two P-47s were trying to keep three Me-109s from a crippled B-17.

Korky got behind one of the 109s and blasted away. I saw hits all around the canopy, and the 109 went into a cloud layer in a steep spiral dive, trailing thick black smoke.

"Two more at nine o'clock low, Red Leader," I called out. He turned and dove after them, closing to about three hundred yards before opening fire on the wingman. I saw strikes and explosions all over the 109, which pulled up in a climbing left turn, at the top of which the pilot bailed out.

The other Me-109 wasn't taking any evasive action until Korky got a few hits on it. It then became a difficult target, jinking and weaving at full throttle just a few feet above the ground. Korky was getting hits on the 109, but it just kept going. "I've only got one gun firing," he said. "Take over, Red 3." Fid Barger slid in behind the 109 and fired several long bursts, putting a few more holes in it. Then he ran out of ammunition.

My turn. The adrenaline level rose again. The 109 was just a few feet above the ground, and I wasn't much higher, so as I tried to get it in my gunsight, I had to be careful not to fly into the ground. I closed to about three hundred yards, firing whenever I could get him in my gunsight for more than a split second. I saw hits on the wings and tail section, but every time those eight .50s fired, the recoil slowed the P-47 down by twenty to forty miles per hour, allowing the 109 to stay well ahead of me. Then tracers warned me that I was running out of ammunition. By this time the 109 had led us on a long, merry chase over towns, farms, and airfields.

"I still have a few rounds in that one gun," said Korky. "I'm going to try to climb right up his ass and finish him off." Slowly we gained on it, but just as Korky was getting ready to fire, the 109 pilot chopped his throttle and crash-landed in a long meadow. Korky had to pull up sharply to avoid a collision. The 109 slid the length of the field, shedding pieces all along, and stopped at the far end. We swung back over the wrecked aircraft but couldn't see if the pilot was still in it. Our fuel was getting really low, so we didn't waste time looking for him.

The pilot of that Me-109 was Oberleutnant Gerd Schaedle, stationed at Creil, fifteen miles north of Paris. Thanks to Jeff Ethell and Alfred Price, coauthors of *Target Berlin,* we have a view from the other side. These are excerpts from Oberleutnant Schaedle's encounter report:

After taking off from Creil, the *Gruppen* assembled over Reims and climbed to 8,000 m to see whether the formation of enemy bombers was attacking a target in southern or northern Germany.

Reims was our waiting position. When it was clear that the bombers were flying east, we were ordered to move to Wiesbaden and land there and refuel.

Scrambled at 1340 and flew northward. My 109 carried three 20mm cannon. Sighted the bomber stream ahead, many small specks against the horizon. The Gruppe made a head-on attack on a *pulk* [section] of B-24s in the Rheine-Hopstein area. Then the escorts descended on us and there was a dogfight. Oberfeldwebel Morzinek and Unteroffizier Sens were flying with me. We had dropped our tanks on sighting the enemy, and were now beginning to run low on fuel so we broke off the engagement and dived away, intending to land at Rheine or Hopsten. Dived vertically to low altitude and headed for the airfields.

Then suddenly saw Thunderbolts coming after me. Flying low, with Sens as wingman. There was a long chase and Sens was shot down. He called *"Ich bin jetzt getroffen. Ich springe!"* [I've been hit. I'm bailing out!]

The chase continued, passing low over trees, meadows, and farmhouses. They fired whenever they could,

and my aircraft was taking hits. I wanted to land at
Hopsten airfield, but with the Thunderbolts coming up
close behind me it was too dangerous to slow down. So
I continued northward past it.

I kept as low as I could to make it difficult for the
enemy pilots to hit me. Jinking when attacked, but all
the time keeping very low and holding maximum
speed—hugging the ground. Aircraft hit in both wings.
It seemed as if I was doomed. If I continued on like
that, too low to bail out, sooner or later they would get
me. Then, suddenly beyond a small wood, there appeared ahead a long meadow.

As I passed over the trees I cut the throttle and
pushed the Me-109 down onto the ground. As the
fighter decelerated rapidly, the Thunderbolts screamed
past. There was a long, bumpy ride across the ground
before the aircraft came to a halt. Then I threw off the
canopy and dashed over to a small ditch where I took
cover, in case the Thunderbolts came back to strafe
me. But the Thunderbolts pulled up and circled the
crash before heading for home.

Schaedle returned to the 109, retrieved his parachute, and
walked to a nearby farmhouse. He was taken in a horse-
drawn cart to the airfield at Hopsten. He returned to his
home base at Creil by train. Both Sens and Morzinek had
survived their crashes, and they joined Schaedle on the
train. Schaedle concluded his encounter report as follows:
"When I chopped the throttle, the Thunderbolt behind me
almost collided with me. I imagine they had quite a story to
tell at the club that night, as we did."

After that lengthy full-power chase, we didn't have
enough fuel to return to Steeple Morden, so we landed at
Manston on the English coast. After refueling, we took off
for Steeple, coming in at treetop level and executing climbing rolls over the base.

My first "kill" was shared with Korky and Barger. I now
had one-third of a victory.

"You want me to paint one-third of a swastika on the airplane?" McKibbin asked me the next day.

"Hell, no," I replied. "Paint a whole one."

This was the first full-scale attack by the Eighth Air Force against the German capital. More than 750 bombers participated; 68 of them didn't make it back. A total of 82 German fighters were shot down, and others were listed as probable or damaged. VIII Fighter Command lost 11 fighters. For many Germans, the inability to protect their capital from Allied air attacks signaled the beginning of the end.

Two days later, we lost Charlie Sweat and damn near lost Fid Barger. I wasn't on that mission, but Barger's encounter report tells the story. He was flying Curt Johnston's wing, with Charley Sweat and Henry Brown in the second element. They looked over an airfield with several aircraft on it and decided to strafe it but were suddenly greeted with plenty of flak. Curt decided to fly upsun for several miles, then dive down to the deck and approach the field on the deck, and maybe surprise the flak gunners. When they doubled back, they missed the airfield, so they made a 180-degree turn and headed for it again. When they came out of the turn, their positions were switched. Charlie was in the lead, followed by Fid, then Johnston and Brown. Part of Fid's encounter report follows:

I saw a line of four Ju-88s with others strung out around the perimeter. Lt. Sweat opened fire at the first Ju-88 from 200 yards and practically zero feet altitude. I saw it burst into flames and black smoke started pouring out. I opened fire on the next Ju-88 from zero altitude and at a range of about 250 yards. I saw strikes on the ground in front of the aircraft and saw the pattern finally engulf it, hitting the entire fuselage and wings. It began to burn. I pulled up and in so doing my tail section hit the vertical stabilizer of the burning plane. I was too close to fire on the third aircraft so I held fire until I got the fourth Ju-88 in my gunsight. Still at zero altitude, I fired and saw strikes on the entire fuselage

and wings. I passed over it too quickly to see it catch
fire. On this pass over the field, the machine gun fire
was quite heavy and concentrated but all of us flew
through it OK.

Fid was wrong. They didn't all fly through it OK.
Charlie Sweat's luck had run out. After setting the Ju-88
ablaze on that first strafing run, he was seen making a sharp
left turn just fifty feet above the ground. Later eyewitness
reports confirmed that his right wing and part of his tail section had been blasted off by flak, and he crashed just off the
airdrome.

Fid found himself in the lead, and thinking that Johnston
and Brown were behind him, decided to make another pass.

I made a steep left turn and made another run. This
time I essed until I got in position to fire on the last two
E/A. I fired and saw strikes on both of them.

I whipped around to the left again and made a third
pass. I didn't even fire this time because the machine
gun fire from the ground by that time showed tracers
on all sides of me. I was the only one making this pass
and all guns seemed to be concentrated on me.

By this time Fid was alone, and his fuel was down to 105
gallons. Off in the distance, he spotted another Mustang,
which turned out to be Henry Brown's. Fid latched onto
Henry's wing and suddenly realized that Brown was intent
on attacking another airdrome:

When we dropped to about 3,000 feet I saw that he
was heading for another airdrome on which I spotted
an Me-110. Lt. Brown opened fire at the E/A and
smoke was coming out of it by the time I got within firing range. I opened fire on the same E/A at about 350
yards but I overshot the target and missed.
The machine gun fire was very heavy. We continued
on the deck for almost half a mile and then began to

climb. Flak was exploding on all sides of us and machine gun fire was still heavy. An explosive shell burst
at my tail and shook the plane terrifically. I called Lt.
Brown and asked him to throttle back as my plane was
hit. No sooner had I finished talking when the damn
stuff came tearing through the right side of my cockpit
through the rear panel. Some hit the armor plate so
close to the edge of it that it chipped off. The shrapnel
from this hit me in the back of the head, stunning me
for a few seconds.

I slumped forward in the cockpit for a few seconds
but not long enough for my airplane to get out of control. I didn't know just how badly I was hit and just
kept saying to myself, "I've had it this time!"

I called to Lt. Brown again and guess I sounded
quite excited. I said I was hit in the head and that my
ship was in a very critical condition. I looked at the gas
gauge again and saw I only had sixty gallons, noticing
at the same time that my airspeed indicator was reading zero. The glass of the suction pump gauge was broken, and half of the glass of my gunsight was shattered.

The control wires of my left aileron had been shot off
and it was flapping up and down in the wind. My wing-
flaps were also flapping—my hydraulic system had
been shot out. There was a hole about a foot in diameter
through the trailing edge of my left wing root; smoke
was coming out of it all the way back to England.

Captain Johnston heard our radio chatter, spotted us
and joined our formation. I didn't know how badly my
tail assembly had been shot up, so I asked him to fly in
close and have a look, since my plane was vibrating so
much that it almost shook my shoes off. Captain
Johnston said my tail looked OK—but after we landed
he told me he thought it would shake loose, but didn't
want to tell me because it might excite me.

Johnston and Brown kept essing around me to protect me from any enemy aircraft from sneaking up on
my tail. I crossed out of the enemy coast at 7,000 feet

with 1,500 RPM and thirty inches. My fuel warning
light came on while I was still over the Channel. I
weighed the two possibilities: bail out as soon as we hit
England or try to crash-land. There was a layer of
clouds 2,000 feet thick with a base at 1,000 feet.
Captain Johnston wanted me to fly through on his
wing, but I didn't want to try it as I feared that the
wires of my right aileron would give way, flicking my
airplane into his.

Coming out of the clouds I saw a large airdrome on
my right. I made one complete right hand circuit (right
hand because of the dead aileron) to land into the
wind. I released my undercarriage about 100 feet
above the ground and rocked my wings as much as I
dared so the wheels would lock down. By this time my
gas gauge read empty. At about ten feet off the ground
Lt. Brown was screaming on the radio, "Pull up your
wheels, only one of them is down!" With no hydraulic
system, I had no choice; but they locked just before I
touched down.

A shell had blown a tire, and the plane was swinging
off to the right toward a group of B-26s. I quickly
turned off all switches, unlocked the tail wheel and
ground-looped violently to the left. The plane went
halfway around and stopped. The hole in my left wing
was now blazing, so I jumped out of the airplane and
ordered the fast-assembling ground crew to get a fire
extinguisher and put the fire out.

An ambulance drove me to the hospital and the medical officer sterilized the five holes at the back of my
scalp. The next day, our own flight surgeon dug one
piece of shrapnel out of my scalp.

"Look at that crazy guy!" said Johnston that afternoon,
pointing to Fid wrestling with another pilot. "This morning,
Doc Fontenot digs a chunk of shrapnel out his thick skull—
and he's in a scrap already!"

Fid's airplane was riddled with holes large and small.

Had he been flying a Mustang instead of the rugged Thunderbolt, I doubt he would have made it back.

Charlie Sweat's loss was a shocker. We had been together since the early days at Zephyrhills, Florida, and he was well liked by everyone in the squadron. He was the first 354th pilot to get an air victory and the first to destroy an enemy airplane on the ground, which he accomplished on that ill-fated mission. He was an excellent pilot, well on his way to becoming an outstanding leader, but flak does not take such things into account.

On March 11, 1944, I flew my first mission in a P-51B. The other two squadrons each put twenty Mustangs into the air; we had only enough to provide two flights of four, two spares, and two relays. We escorted two combat wings of B-17s attacking targets in Münster. An unbroken layer of low clouds obscured the ground and probably kept the Luftwaffe grounded, but it didn't silence the flak batteries. As we approached Münster, flak became intense and uncomfortably accurate. We took violent evasive action, but it was all around—and close.

As the bombers left the target area and headed home, Pop Allard, flying in the no. 4 slot in the lead flight, reported that his oil pressure had fallen to zero. Captain Kucheman maneuvered to check Pop's engine for signs of oil leak, but before he could get into position, Pop said in a very calm voice, "I gotta get out. Good luck, fellas." He fell clear of the airplane, and his chute opened just before he entered the overcast. Apparently a piece of shrapnel from the heavy flak barrage had severed an oil line. He was later reported a POW.

On March 12, the engine fell out of a Mustang at another base as the pilot was warming it up. The pilot was killed. VIII Fighter Command grounded all Mustangs until a thorough inspection of the engine mounts was performed. The four bolts holding the engine had to be removed and tested.

Since there weren't enough cranes and hoists to suspend the engines with the bolts removed, it was often necessary to remove one bolt at a time, have it tested, replace it, and then remove another bolt. Captain Walt Randall and his group worked around the clock to get the Mustangs back in service. By March 16, all VIII Fighter Command P-51s had been checked and were back in business.

"What are you trying to do, commit suicide?" asked Burt.

"Yeah, are you out of your mind?" seconded Duff.

It was March 14. We were sitting at the bar in the officers' club; I had just told them that I had volunteered to join an experimental group organized by Col. Glenn Duncan, commanding officer of the 353rd Fighter Group stationed at Metfield. I was leaving the next morning.

In spite of Fighter Command's recent change in fighter tactics, permitting escort fighters to pursue enemy aircraft away from the bomber stream—under certain conditions—and even destroy them on the ground, most of the groups seemed reluctant to venture below fifteen thousand feet. It was still considered dangerous for P-47s to tangle with Me-109s and FW-190s below twenty thousand feet. Duncan tried to convince Major General Kepner that strafing attacks against German airfields were not only practical but also necessary if we were to attain air superiority over Germany. "If they don't come up to challenge us," he argued, "we have to go down and destroy them on their airfields."

General Kepner was always willing to listen to new ideas. He had been the driving force behind the addition of an 85-gallon fuel tank behind the cockpit to give the P-51 greater range, enough to take the bombers wherever they went. There were strong arguments against it at the time—the center of gravity would be moved too far back, and so on—but Kepner persisted. The important modification was made, giving the P-51 enough internal fuel to go all the way, take on the German fighters, and still get back home.

He listened to Duncan's arguments and agreed to let him

form a volunteer group of P-47 pilots to develop low-level tactics and to try them out on German airfields. Duncan dubbed the group "Bill's Buzz Boys" in honor of General Kepner and probably with tongue in cheek.

"Why are you doing this?" Burt persisted.

"Look," I said, "I've been here over six months, I've flown about thirty-five missions, and I've been scheduled to fly element leader just once. You've flown at least as many missions as I have, Duff, and you shot down one aircraft. How many times have you led a flight or an element?"

"Once."

"Right! And we both have just as much combat experience as those guys who do. We were in Class 43-A, same as Jeeter, Chuck, Perry, Woody, and Bob Kurtz. They're leading elements and flights, but we're flying wing!"

"Did it ever occur to you," said Burt, "that it's because you're damn good at it?"

"They're just as good at it as we are, Burt. I think it all goes back to that stupid barrel roll I did around Stimson's airplane at Philly. That branded me as a screwball, and because Jim was with me, he was tarred with the same brush."

"Maybe it's a matter of rank?" offered Burt.

"We're all first lieutenants, Burt."

"Maybe flying time?"

"Hell, I went into the cadet program with eighty hours flying time and a pilot's license. I probably have more flying time than any of them. It's my image! Anyway, I feel like I'm in a rut. I've gotta do something, even if it's wrong."

"I don't know about wrong," said Duff, "but it's damn foolish!"

"You know damn well we're at least as good as those guys and better than most. We just don't get a chance to prove it. Do you want to fly wing the rest of the war, Duff?" He didn't answer.

A wingman's role was carefully circumscribed in our tactical doctrine. His function was to keep an enemy pilot from getting behind the leader and shooting him down. In our spread-out "finger" formation, the no. 2 and no. 4 men were supposed to scan the area to the rear of flight while the flight leader and element leader searched for enemy fighters ahead of the formation. The wingman's role was strictly defensive; the leaders were the hunter-killers of the formation. Inevitably, very few kills were made by wingmen. When a wingman was doing his job, he seldom got a chance to fire at an enemy airplane.

Duff and Burt kept trying to talk me out of going, but it was no use. I knew it would be exciting, and it might change my image.

When I volunteered, I had no idea that others in the squadron also had, but I soon learned that there were three others: Capt. Stud Starr, 1st Lt. Kenny Williams, and 2d Lt. Gil Wright. On March 15 we flew our Thunderbolts to the 353d Fighter Group air base in Metfield, about sixty miles from Steeple Morden as the crow flies, and reported to Col. Glenn Duncan. Our crew chiefs, assistant crew chiefs, and armorers followed by road. We were assigned quarters and given a tour of the base, which was not much different from other Eighth Air Force fighter bases. As long as we could find the officers' mess (and bar) and find a way to the flight line, we had no complaints.

Glenn Duncan was one of those colorful characters who inspire the rest of us to exceed our perceived limitations. Like all good leaders, he led by example, never expecting others to take risks he didn't take himself. A dove of peace was painted on the nose of his airplane. "I'm determined to have peace," he was quoted as saying, "even if I have to kill every #%@&ing German to do it!" His ground crew told me that he seldom came back from a mission with ammunition still in his trays. He always found something to shoot at.

Though known as "Bill's Buzz Boys," our official designation was the 353C Group. Our P-47s were equipped with new paddle-blade propellers, nearly a foot longer, with wider blades; they dramatically improved the plane's low-altitude performance, especially its rate of climb.

For ten days we were given intensive training in aircraft identification, antiaircraft gun ranges and capabilities, and strafing tactics. We also were given free rein in our training flights. Our simulated attacks on the airfield at Metfield were great sport for us but hell for the people on the ground, who often had to lie prone to avoid decapitation.

Finally, on March 26, it was time to test the theory. Colonel Duncan led twelve P-47s on a bombing and strafing mission to airfields in the Chartres-Châteaudun area, about sixty miles southwest of Paris. Four P-47s carried two fragmentation bomb clusters. The only thing I remember about this mission is that Kenny Williams was shot down. We inflicted a lot of damage, according to the mission reports, including one aircraft destroyed and four others damaged. Two of the returning P-47s had moderate damage and three others had slight damage from the flak encountered.

Our next strafing mission was on March 29. We attacked two airfields near Dümmer Lake, then another in Holland on our way home. I flew Duncan's wing—to his left—on this mission. His encounter report, which reflects the pugnacious—almost frenzied—nature of his leadership, is quoted in part:

I was leading a Squadron of 12 ships whose sole purpose was to attack ground installations and destroy any aircraft or enemy installations. As planned, the three flights went to designated airdromes previously picked for their importance. I took my flight of four down on Bramsche airdrome.

We began our dive from about 10,000 feet from out of the sun and hit zero feet about two miles from the field. I pulled up to about 150 feet as I crossed my checkpoint on the edge of the drome and began squirting a few bursts. No matter how hard I looked I could not see any aircraft parked or hidden. The only thing of interest was a light flak tower on the northeast side of the field that shot to beat hell but couldn't figure the correct deflection for 400 mph on a P-47. We four pulled up to about 5,000 feet on the far side of the field and surveyed the situation. A little bit of flak followed us but was not too great a bother.

There were no aircraft in view, so I poured a long burst into a blister hangar, though I couldn't see what was in it. To my surprise, there was a huge explosion and the entire hangar was engulfed in flames. I then saw a train moving east adjacent to the airfield, so I put a burst into the locomotive and punctured the boiler, causing the usual tall plume of steam to erupt.

As I was looking for a suitable target on our first pass, I saw a machine-gun emplacement to my right. Two gunners in a circular sandbagged revetment were blazing away. Their guns were pointed straight at me, but I was doing better than four hundred miles per hour, so I knew the bullets were passing well behind me. On our next pass across the field, I put that gun emplacement out of business. Duncan's report continues:

We had turned left trying to pick up another available target when we saw an airdrome [Vechta] off to the right. Due to the close proximity of the drome and our position, I called to the rest of the flight and told them to stay up and go on around to the edge of the field as I was going down. I passed across the front of the hangar line and saw many twin-engine and single-engine aircraft parked on the drome. I lined up two of the twin engines and let go. The first one lit up quite well but never did blow up or catch fire while I was coming on it. The second one took quite a number of strikes and consequently caught fire. . . .

I pulled up from this and joined the flight dodging the various bursts of flak that were coming up.

Duncan then noticed a B-17 sitting on its belly in a nearby open field. He told us to circle while he set fire to it. We could see flak bursting around him, but we couldn't see where it was coming from. Duncan continues:

I again assembled the four ships and pulled up to about 5,000 feet heading out. I looked back and the B-17 was burning fiercely and left a great column of smoke up to about 3,000 to 4,000 feet. It only took a short while for us to pick up another airdrome [Twente/Enschede], and this seemed to present a very likely target as a staff car was speeding across one end of it and there were several twin-engine and single-engine aircraft parked, clearly visible from our great range. I called for the flight to go down and, believe me, the boys were really flying good this day. They stayed together very well. We dove down to the deck and came across the drome in good four-ship line abreast, each individual picking a likely target. The staff car caught quite a lot of .50 cal. from both the man on my left [Fortier] and myself, at which time my guns ran dry.

I had picked out a twin-engine aircraft and poured a long burst into it before it blew up. Then I spotted the staff car and was firing away at that when I noticed Colonel Duncan sliding toward me on my right. I eased to the left and fired a burst into a small hangar but didn't see any results because I had to pull up to avoid flying into it. Duncan continues:

The four ships came out of this in good order but when we pulled up, one of the boys [Lieutenant Edwards] said he had been hit. I throttled back and got all of us together so that we could lick our wounds and see how the trip home would be. One boy [Chetwood] had received a 20mm in the left wheel, but this did not alter his flying characteristics other than leaving him with no speed indicator or altimeter, and a little shaky feeling. Edwards had been hit in his gas tanks and said the gauges were going down like a minute sand clock.

This boy went all out so as to get the most from his gas supply and consequently ran out of gas about 40 miles off the English Coast.

Edwards bailed out and was picked up by air/sea rescue. Chetwood managed to land the airplane safely even though the tire had been blown away from his left wheel. The plane was damaged but was repaired within two days.

Colonel Duncan claimed one Me-110 and one B-17 destroyed, one twin-engine airplane probably destroyed, and one Me-410 and five unidentified aircraft damaged. He was a one-man wrecking crew. I destroyed one Me-110, and damaged one blister hangar and one locomotive that had the misfortune to be near the airfield. The total claims for this mission were seven aircraft destroyed, five probably destroyed, and nine damaged, plus eight locomotives, three hangars, one staff car, one barge, and six flak towers either destroyed or severely damaged. In short, we raised hell.

We lost one airplane, but the pilot bailed out, and air/sea rescue plucked him out of the cold North Sea. Four other aircraft were damaged by flak. Colonel Duncan was jubilant. "We keep this up and Kepner will be a believer!"

There was no mission scheduled the next day; ground crews were still patching up damage from the previous missions. My plane wasn't damaged, so I received permission to visit my "family" at Steeple Morden.

The 355th was no longer flying P-47s; the transition to Mustangs had been completed. The paddle-blade prop on my P-47 fascinated the pilots. "Where were these when we needed them?" asked Brady.

I told Burt about the previous day's mission, including my claim of one Me-110 destroyed. It was not officially credited to me because I was technically part of a different group at the time. It didn't matter to me then, nor does it now.

This short visit with my "family" made me realize how closely knit our squadron had become. It was indeed like a family, with a few petty squabbles, but it was held together by mutual respect, camaraderie, and the knowledge that our lives often depended on others in the squadron.

"Bill's Buzz Boys" flew eight missions, two were bomber escorts; I flew five of them, one of which was an escort mission—no strafing. Ironically, I flew someone's wing on each mission. I was shot at plenty in those few missions and miraculously escaped being hit by flak. My plane was damaged on one occasion. Coming off a strafing run, I was flying just inches above the treetops to avoid the flak. Suddenly I noticed red-hot tracers just a few feet above my canopy. Instinctively, I nudged the stick forward and flew right through the top of a tall pine tree. The tree snapped like a toothpick, and the plane swiveled sharply to the right. For a few moments I felt like I was flying sideways, but I quickly regained control and pulled up above treetop level. There was a dent in the leading edge of my right wing, just outboard of the four machine guns. It was about eight inches deep, but the Jug could take a lot more punishment than that and still keep flying.

In the six strafing missions, we lost three planes, and thirteen others were damaged by flak. Claims were fourteen aircraft destroyed, six probably destroyed, and fourteen damaged. In addition, thirty-two locomotives, ten boats, ten hangars, and nine flak towers were either destroyed or heavily damaged.

On April 12 General Kepner sent this message to Colonel Duncan: "Upon completion of this day's mission the flying unit known as Bill's Buzz Boys will be dissolved and pilots and planes returned to their proper station. The Commanding General expresses his sincere appreciation to each pilot and to those supervisory personnel contributing to the successful development of new fighter tactics."

Meanwhile, back at Steeple:

On the day I left, the 354th Squadron had its best day to date. Flying Mustangs, they intercepted a gaggle of Me-109s heading for the bombers. Jeeter Neal shot down two and shared in the destruction of another with Chuck Lenfest. Korky, Duff, and Silky Morris each got one. The group shot down sixteen Me-109s for a loss of two 358th Squadron Mustangs.

On March 18, Jeeter and Henry Brown each nailed a 109 while Chuck and Mendy were sharing another.

Photo taken the day I left home. January 1942.

Aviation Cadet Norman J. Fortier, 11038879. February 1942.

Bob Damico and Bud Fortier, Dorr Field, Florida. July 1942.

Ready for my first flight in the P-39. January 1943.

P-51B and P-47B.

Emil Perry, Korky, Bud Fortier, and Jim Duffy. A Flight, Philadelphia.

Lt. Col. "Speed" Hubbard, Lt. Col. Gerald Dix, Lt. Col. William Cummings. July 1943.

Officers' club bar and lounge. Early 1944.

Control tower at Steeple Morden.

Art DeCosta working on a mural in the officers' mess. Late 1943.

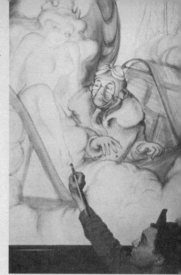

DeCosta's nose art on *Miss Thunder,* Korky's P-47. "Pop" Allard with Koraleski.

Duff and I shared this room for eighteen months. I slept in the top bunk.

On the wing of my P-51B.
Note the RAF helmet and
flight "boots." June 1944.

Jim Duffy looking
pensive.

Jim Duffy in his *Dragon Wagon*, WR-Y.

My P-51B with two 75-gallon wing tanks. May 1944.

Bert Marshall in his P-51C Mustang with the Malcom Hood modification. July 1944.

Clay Kinnard and Burt Sims in front of Kinnard's P-51B *Man o' War.* (Major Kinnard was the number 1 Bulldog.) May 1944.

The 355th Fighter Group forming up and heading out. Late 1944.

Bud and Duff, WR-N and WR-Y, in formation. Early 1945.

The 354th Fighter Squadron pilots. Back row (l. to r.): Stan Silva, Joe Mellen, Al White, Jack Fletcher, Jim Duffy, and Jim Jabara. Front row: C. G. Todd, Bud Fortier, Ace Graham, Bob Heaton, and "Long Jawn" Stanton. April 1945.

Bud and Duff.
November 1943.

Gordon M. "Ace" Graham
with Yank, the 354th Squadron
mascot. February 1945.

SSgt. Herbert McKibbin on the right, Sgt. Richard Dawe on
the left—crew chief and assistant on WR-N. Early 1945.

Hal Culp married an English girl on March 19 and was generously allowed a whole week off for his honeymoon.

On March 29 Korky got credit for destroying a Focke-Wulf 190 without firing a shot. His encounter report is quoted in part:

> There were Me-109s and FW-190s all over the place. We were milling around like mad. I squirted at three or four, then chased one off my wingman's tail. I picked out another one and stayed with him, waiting to get in a good shot. He started to do snap-rolls, and the next thing I knew we were both spinning down through the clouds. We broke out at about 2,000 feet, with me about 300 yards behind him, still spinning. Boy, I thought, it's too late. I stopped my ship from spinning and started my pullout.
>
> The ground was staring me right in the face. I had grabbed the stick with both hands and hauled back as hard as I could, and the pressure caused me to black out. I remember thinking, "Well, at least you'll be unconscious when you hit."
>
> When I recovered a few moments later the ship was cocked up on one wing, about fifty feet above the ground, and had just slid between two trees. I looked back and could see what was left of the Focke-Wulf 190 I had been chasing. Pieces of it still were bouncing along the ground, and flames were all over the wreckage. I was plenty lucky!

On the same mission, Henry Brown got his fifth when he shot the wing off of a FW-190, and Kinnard nailed another. Happy-go-lucky Henry was well on his way to becoming a tiger.

On April 5 the 355th strafed German airfields in the area southwest of Munich and destroyed a record fifty-one aircraft, seven of which were air victories. At least ten were Luftwaffe training aircraft, and three hapless trainees were

shot down while trying desperately to land. All this occurred while I was in a volunteer group supposedly developing tactics for strafing German airfields. This was the first
"strafing only" mission for the 355th. General Kepner had
become a believer before he disbanded "Bill's Buzz Boys."

Three pilots were killed on this mission, one in our
squadron. Hal Culp, married less than a month, struck a
power line on a strafing run and crashed. Major Kinnard and
Chaplain Zeigler had the unpleasant and difficult task of no-
tifying his bride.

During the twenty-nine days that I served with "Bill's
Buzz Boys" and destroyed one German aircraft on the
ground, the 355th Fighter Group destroyed sixty aircraft in
the air and ninety-six on the ground. Most other VIII Fighter
Command groups had similar records during that period.

Had General Kepner already decided, I wondered, to ex-
pand the fighter mission to include the strafing of airfields
even before the first Buzz Boy mission left the ground? Was
he just patronizing a gung-ho combat leader, Colonel
Duncan, to make him feel that he was an innovator for a tactic that Kepner had already decided on? The "successful development of new fighter tactics" that Kepner mentioned in
his farewell message to the Buzz Boys—the tactics and
techniques that the Buzz Boys had developed—were never
summarized in any report nor disseminated to other fighter
groups. Had I been part of an "experiment" in which the
outcome had been predetermined? I had an uneasy feeling
that I had been used.

April 1944

Early in April, pilots throughout VIII Fighter Command were issued G suits. More accurately, they were anti-G suits, designed to minimize the effect of high-G forces on pilot performance. In any maneuver involving high-G forces, such as a sharp pullout from a steep dive, the blood tended to drain from the upper part of the body toward the legs and thighs, resulting in a gradual deterioration of vision called grayout, followed by total loss of vision, called blackout. Sustained blackout could cause the pilot to lose consciousness. The G suits had inflatable air bladders in the lower abdomen, thigh, and calf areas. As G forces increased, the bladders inflated, squeezing the pilot's leg and abdomen to keep blood from draining from the upper body. Pilots were skeptical at first, but we soon learned to appreciate the edge that the G suit provided in combat situations involving high-G forces.

Norm Olson, the 355th's first ace, was killed on April 8 while strafing the airdrome at Gifhorn after escorting the bombers to Braunschweig. He was on his third strafing run after destroying one Me-109 on the ground when he was hit by flak. His wingman saw Norm slump forward in his shoulder harness; then his Mustang made a slow 180-degree turn and spiraled into the ground. Olson was the only 355th air ace killed in action during the entire war. Some were shot down by flak and became POWs, but the group did not lose a single air ace in air-to-air combat.

On April 11, flak claimed another victim, this time

another veteran, Curtis Johnston. It was the group's deepest penetration yet into German territory, escorting B-17s attacking aircraft engine factories near Sorau (now Żary, in Poland), 113 miles southeast of Berlin. The relief escort took over as the bombers were withdrawing on a northerly heading east of Berlin. Johnston and his flight spotted aircraft on the ground at Strausberg airfield and made three passes, during which he destroyed three Ju-88s. There was no flak at the airfield, but as they skirted the southern side of Berlin, they got the full treatment. About five minutes later, Johnny announced that his oil pressure was near zero. Five minutes after that he reported that he was bailing out.

Later, Chuck Lenfest's microphone button became stuck in the on position and he began a long monologue. Since his transmitter was on, no one else could use that channel. Of course, Chuck didn't realize that he was transmitting.

"Look at those poor #@$%& bombers!" was his first observation. "I wonder if they know where the #$&%@ they're going. I sure as hell don't."

There was no mistaking Chuck's slow Idaho drawl. It was useless to try to transmit to him, so Mendy eased in close and tried to signal with his hands that the mike button was stuck. Chuck looked at him and said, "Look at old Mendy! What does that silly sonofabitch think he's doing?" Mendy gave up.

The group was next treated to a few bawdy songs and more comments on the progress of the mission. "Why are we headed back? I don't want to go home yet!" and "Where in hell is Jeeter? I hope they didn't shoot his ass off back there." And "What a long #%$@ing mission this is! My old ass is plenty sore!

"I think I'll drop down to ten thousand so I can light up my old pipe."

He kept up his running commentary of the mission, his fellow pilots, the bombers, the Germans, and the weather, and he had a captive audience throughout the performance, which went on for more than thirty minutes. When Chuck finally realized there was something wrong with his radio, he stopped talking. But the damage had already been done.

Jeeter's comment after the mission was typical. "I was laughing so hard, even the flak didn't bother me."

When Chuck entered Gremlin Villa, red-faced and smiling sheepishly, he was greeted with a storm of good-natured heckling. For once he was speechless.

Jim Duffy's Irish luck got him out of another tight squeeze on April 13. Kinnard was leading the group with our squadron, providing penetration and target support to bombers attacking Lechfeld and Oberpfaffenhofen. The plan was to strafe both airfields immediately after the bombing attack, in the hope of catching the antiaircraft gunners still in their air-raid shelters.

Bob Woody led the second section into the strafing run just as the last pattern of bombs appeared across the field— or so he thought. Just as Blue Flight spread across the field to strafe, the ground under them erupted in yellow and red geysers.

"They're setting off land mines!" someone yelled.

"Those aren't land mines, those are bombs!" someone else yelled, "We didn't wait long enough!"

The strafing run, well organized until then, came unglued as fighters scrambled to get clear of the exploding bombs. Kinnard got the troops back together and worked the field over thoroughly, destroying nineteen aircraft on the ground. Most of Blue Flight got out of harm's way, but not Duff.

When Duff got back to base, Sgt. Bob Baldwin showed him two large holes, one underneath each wing. In each hole was a large, jagged bomb splinter. "Lieutenant," Bob said, "you're going to have to learn to take better care of my airplane!"

I returned to Steeple Morden that same day. There were a few changes. Instead of the stubby eight-gun Thunderbolts, sleek Mustangs were dispersed on hardstands. These were the B models with the "birdcage" cockpits and two .50-caliber machine guns in each wing—a radical departure from the roomy cockpit of the P-47, its eight-gun firepower, and the smooth, powerful roar of that big engine.

It didn't take long to become attached to the raspy-sounding four-gun Mustang. It was a sweet-flying airplane with a two-stage supercharger that gave it excellent performance at all altitudes. Best of all, it had range! For the first time, we could escort bombers wherever they went and still have plenty of fuel to tangle with Luftwaffe pilots over their own turf. And it was more than a match for the Me-109 and the FW-190 at any altitude.

Kinnard's reputation had changed while I was away. He had firmly established himself as an aggressive and capable leader. On the day I returned, he destroyed four German aircraft on the ground and now led the group in scoring. He still spent many hours poring over the German order of battle, Luftwaffe techniques, and all the intelligence reports he could lay his hands on. He often led the group, and his briefings reflected those hours of study. "Their people," he'd say in his slow Tennessee drawl, "will be coming at us from these three places"—his pointer jabbed the location of three German airfields—"and I'll be leading our people from here"—the pointer jabbed again—"to intercept them before they get to our bomber folks." In Kinnard's briefings, the participants in this war were always "people" or "folks," or sometimes "potatoes" when referring to Germans. The group pilots smiled, but they had learned to respect his expertise and leadership.

Something else had changed. I flew a thirty-minute refresher hop on April 14, and my second P-51 combat mission the next day. Korky led the flight, and I led his second element. I never flew wingman again. Maybe my *image* had changed.

It was a fouled-up mission from the beginning. We were awakened at 7:30 A.M. and told to get to the mess hall and eat because a field order had been received, but it mentioned no times. On our way to the mess hall, we got the word that briefing was at eight-fifteen! We scrambled to the group briefing room, but briefing was delayed because many of the pilots couldn't make it. We were to sweep an area west of Berlin—no bomber escort.

Korky wasn't scheduled to fly that day, but he filled in when the scheduled squadron leader couldn't make it. Bill Boulet was flying his wing; I was leading the second element, with 1st Lt. Bob Taylor on my wing. Yellow Flight, right behind us, consisted of Williamson, Don Jacobson, R. C. Brown, and Bob Harness. Captain Starr was leading the second section of eight ships.

Shortly after takeoff, Harness had to abort because of radio trouble; R. C. Brown came back with landing gear problems; and Bill Boulet returned with radio problems; escorted by Williamson. Jacobson filled Boulet's slot in Red Flight. Yellow Flight had disintegrated. About five minutes past the Zuider Zee, Korky reported that his oil pressure had gone to zero and he was heading home. "Blue Leader, take over the squadron," he radioed. "Bud, you stay with them." I slid over to Blue Flight, with Taylor to my right.

Jacobson stayed with Korky. When the coolant boiled over, Korky knew he had no chance of making it to England, nor even to the North Sea for an Air/Sea Rescue pickup. He bailed out over Holland, and his chute was seen to open. He spent the rest of the war in a POW camp.

There were layers upon layers of overcast, and Starr tried to maneuver the squadron through this maze but eventually turned around and came home. The other two squadrons dropped down to strafe a couple of airfields and lost three pilots to heavy flak.

Korky's loss was a staggering blow to the squadron. An outstanding pilot and recognized leader, he had long been looked upon as a tower of strength and role model for incoming replacements. He was the first 354th Squadron ace and seemed destined to be among our top aces. He was just two missions away from completing his first combat tour.

All in all, it was a miserable day for the squadron and the group.

RAF Squadron Leader Niblett, a Typhoon pilot, was visiting our group for a few days. He got a quickie checkout in the Mustang and was eager to fly a mission with us. On

April 19, he got his chance. Major Rosenblatt led our squadron that day, and Niblett was on his wing. Bob Woody, who had been promoted to captain earlier in April—along with Bob Kurtz, Chuck Lenfest, and Jeeter Neal—was leading Yellow Flight, and I led his second element. We were to provide area support for bombers attacking an aircraft assembly plant at Kassel.

On climbout over the North Sea, Fid Barger radioed that his engine was running rough, so he turned back, taking Jacobson with him. Red Flight now consisted of Rosenblatt and Niblett. Shortly after landfall just north of The Hague, Rosey reported that *his* engine was running rough and he turned back, taking a "brassed-off" Squadron Leader Niblett with him. Rosey told Woody to take over the squadron. We were now Red Flight. (It should be mentioned that the Merlin engine had a tendency to foul up spark plugs, causing the engine to run rough. It may have been "macho" to ignore the roughness of the engine, but it wasn't smart. The fouled plugs could cause the engine to quit at the most inopportune times.)

As we approached the bombers in the target area at sixteen thousand feet, we saw a large number of contrails at least ten thousand feet above us. We tried to climb up to intercept them, but before we could get anywhere near, they had swooped down on the bombers, pressed their attack, and headed for the deck as we watched helplessly from a distance. At least one bomber went down, and a few others were trailing smoke.

Suddenly, a lone Me-109 straggler came down from ten o'clock high right in front of Red Flight. Bob immediately turned in behind him, but the 109 pulled away in a wide spiral dive. That allowed Woody to cut inside of him and make up some of the distance, with the rest of Red Flight strung out behind him. I took a quick look at my airspeed indicator and saw that it was passing the red line. I quit looking at it.

The 109 was slipping, sliding, bobbing, and weaving, but Bob was gaining fast. He started shooting at about two hundred fifty yards, and got hits in the wing-root area. He kept closing and shooting down to about fifty yards, when the

109 suddenly exploded in a ball of fire. Woody couldn't avoid flying through the explosion. From my vantage point about 500 yards back, I thought he and the 109 had collided.

Then I saw Woody's airplane pop out on the other side of all the debris, still intact and under control. We were at 3,000 feet; no other enemy aircraft was in sight, so we headed back up to the bomber stream.

The rest of the flight was uneventful. When we got back to Steeple, we looked over Woody's plane. The paint on his right wing was blistered and peeling, and there were several holes and pockmarks all over the wing. The intense heat had scorched the tail section so badly that the elevator had to be replaced. In his encounter report Woody wrote, "I really thought I had had it!"

I made a little mental note to myself: "Don't allow your plane to get so close to the enemy that you'll either overrun him or get caught up in his explosion. You can hit him just as hard from 100 yards out."

April 21 was "big wheels" day at Steeple. Undersecretary of State Edward R. Stettinius Jr.; Lieutenant General Carl A. Spaatz, commander of Theater Air Forces; Lieutenant General James H. Doolittle, commander of the Eighth Air Force; Major General William Kepner, commander of VIII Fighter Command; Brigadier General Jesse Auton, commander of the 65th Fighter Wing; and a sizable entourage arrived by C-47, just in time to attend a briefing for the scheduled mission. The briefing turned into a long session, because each step along the way had to be explained in minute detail for the benefit of the visiting dignitaries.

The wheels were then shown some of our combat films. Finally they moved to the officers' mess for a belated lunch. Henry Brown, Jeeter Neal, and high-scoring pilots from the other two squadrons were seated with the wheels, while the station orchestra—the Fighter Comets—provided the music. Major John DeWitt of the 358th, who was about fifty years old when he joined us in Philadelphia, also sat with the big wheels. He had flown combat missions with

General Spaatz in World War I. It crossed my mind that Spaatz may have picked Steeple Morden to visit because he wanted to see DeWitt again.

After lunch, the party toured the base, then moved to the flight line to view a P-47, a P-38, two Mustangs, and four pilots in full flying gear and G suits. There also was a dinghy, fully inflated and with its sail set, occupied by Sergeant Fred Estabrook. They proceeded to "DeWitt Acres"—the 358th dispersal area, complete with its miniature golf course. As the planes taxied out to the runway, Mr. Stettinius and his party went to the control tower to watch the group take off and assemble.

Kinnard led the group with our squadron. I was element leader in Woody's Blue Flight. We took off, assembled over the field, and climbed out on course. Halfway across the North Sea at twenty thousand feet, we were advised that the mission had been scrubbed because of bad weather over the Continent. When we returned to base, the wheels had departed.

"You don't believe there really *was* a mission today, do you?" Perry asked sarcastically as we trudged up the slope to Gremlin Villa, our parachutes slung over our shoulders.

"Nah!" said Duff. "This was just a big show for the big wheels."

"How often do we get a briefing five hours before scheduled takeoff?" added Woody.

Kenny Williams, who was shot down on the first mission with Bill's Buzz Boys, returned to Steeple on April 22. He had lost a little weight—he was pretty skinny to begin with—but was otherwise in good condition. We were all glad to see him, but he was so happy to be "home" that he was almost jumping for joy.

Late that evening, the Luftwaffe managed to sneak several Me-110s and Me-410s into East Anglia, on the deck to avoid radar detection. In the semidarkness they joined the landing pattern of returning 2d Bomb Division bombers and shot down nine unsuspecting B-24s.

On April 22 our squadron call sign was changed from the

bland "Haywood" to the more aggressive "Falcon." I've often wondered if that call-sign change influenced the attitude of our pilots. The call signs of the other two squadrons in the group were now Custard and Bentley. The Falcons destroyed more enemy aircraft than either the Bentleys or the Custards—by substantial margins. Coincidence?

April 23 was a beautiful day—unusually warm sun, unusually clear sky—so naturally there was no mission scheduled. As Brady put it, "Hell, you know we're not supposed to fly unless the ceiling is fifty feet and the overcast goes up to forty thousand feet!"

The pilots met at the briefing room to hear Kenny Williams describe, within some tight bounds of security, his evasion trip through France and Spain back to England. He couldn't divulge much of the activities and techniques of the French Underground, but he stressed how valuable had been the lessons he had learned from the escape-and-evasion lectures before he was shot down.

Most of us spent the rest of that day developing an epidemic of spring fever.

The weather next day was nowhere near perfect, so there was a mission scheduled. We were to escort bombers targeting airfields immediately west of Munich. The English weather was back to normal, but he Continent was basking in the glorious sunshine we had enjoyed the day before. It was perfect weather for flying, and the Luftwaffe thought so, too.

Major Kucheman led the squadron. Bob Woody was leading Yellow Flight, with Bill Boulet on his wing. I was leading the second element with newly assigned 2d Lt. Dick Cross on my wing. It was Dick's second mission. Chuck Lenfest led the eight ships of Blue Section.

Just as we picked up our assigned task force, I spotted a smaller box of bombers to the south of the main formation, and it looked like they were catching hell from a bunch of fighters. I called Woody, and at about the same time, Bill Boulet, who was monitoring the bomber channel, chimed in with the same report. Woody immediately turned toward them and jammed his throttle to the firewall. Kucheman's Red Flight was climbing to intercept about twenty Me-109s at thirty thousand feet; Blue Section was told to stay with the bombers.

Yellow Flight was strung out in trail formation, trying to catch up with Woody as he reached the five Me-109s headed for the bombers. They were in a loose echelon formation to their leader's right, and stepped back. Woody got behind the trailing German, climbed up his tail, and blew him out of the sky. Apparently the others in that formation were concentrating on the B-17s and had no inkling of what was happening behind them, because they kept flying straight ahead toward the bombers. Woody moved up to the next one in line and with well-placed bursts knocked him out of the sky. On to the next, with the same result. And the next.

At this point the rest of Yellow Flight caught up with Bob. Boulet had lined up on the leader of the formation and was firing as he closed. He got some good hits but noticed that Woody, who hadn't seen Bill closing in, was sliding over in front of him and firing at the same airplane. Bill backed off. Woody was less than a hundred yards behind the 109, pouring deadly fire into it. Pieces fell off as the engine blew up, spewing oil all over Woody's windshield. The 109 fell into an uncontrolled spiral toward the ground, trailing smoke and flames.

"Bud, I've got oil all over my canopy," called Woody. "Take over the flight and I'll fly your wing." That caused a little confusion because Cross was already flying my wing. But we had no time for confusion. Cross moved to Boulet's wing.

I spotted a lone Me-109 below me, headed for the deck. I got on his tail, closed to about two hundred yards, and started firing. I observed many hits and his engine started smoking. I was then too close and had to pull up to avoid overrunning him. Bill Boulet had latched on to me, so he got behind the 109 and got some good hits before he also overran him.

We were at treetop level. I slid back behind the 109 and

opened fire again. I saw plenty of hits all over the plane. He jettisoned his canopy and looked behind him—I was close enough to see him clearly—then pulled his plane straight up, hoping to get enough altitude to bail out. I swung out of his way and watched as the plane reached about seven hundred feet. The pilot bailed out just as his airplane stalled and headed down. When he got to about three hundred feet, his parachute began to stream out behind him, but it was too late. A wave of nausea swept over me as I saw him hit the ground, bounce a few inches, and settle in the dust. Until that moment, this had been machine against machine—his against mine—but now he was dead, and I had killed him. His Me-109 was burning a hundred yards away.

As I started to climb back toward the bomber stream, I looked behind me. I was alone. At about eight thousand feet, I spotted another Me-109 below me, so I went after it. I had closed to about three hundred yards when the pilot saw me and turned sharply into me. I stayed right with him and opened fire. I saw several hits just aft of the canopy; then the 109 straightened and dove for the deck. I climbed right up his butt, firing all the way. He never recovered from his dive. I had to pull up sharply to avoid hitting the 109 as it struck the ground and exploded.

I started to climb back up. I looked around and saw no one near me; I thought I was alone, but just then Woody called in another 109 circling the crash I had just left. I found that 109 quickly enough and bounced him. He was in a tight turn when I opened fire. I observed hits around the wing roots; then I swung wide as I overran him. I took a quick look behind me—there was another Me-109 sitting on my tail, guns winking as he fired away. With my adrenaline pump working overtime, I racked it in tight and after a few Lufbery circles—we were too low for aerobatics—it became apparent to the 109 pilot that I was gaining position on him and that this fight was one he was probably destined to lose, so he dove away and headed east, hoping to outrun me.

I started after him, but he was nearly half a mile ahead of me; I had too much catching up to do. I was low on fuel, and tracers had already alerted me that I was running out of ammunition, so I broke off in a sharp climbing turn and headed home. He kept going east, probably happy to call it a draw.

The bombers, the Mustangs, and the Me-109s were all gone. I was alone. I climbed to twenty-five thousand feet, hoping to find a flight of Mustangs to join. Twenty minutes later, I saw twelve fighters about two thousand feet above and slightly ahead of me, to my right. They were flying on a heading roughly twenty degrees west of mine. Hoping to see friendly markings, I eased over in their direction. They were FW-190s.

If I headed away from them, I'd be easy pickings, so I headed toward them and throttled back to stay behind them, hoping they wouldn't see me. Apparently they didn't—or maybe they had more important targets in mind. I kept an eye on them as they gradually outdistanced me. My pulse rate slowly returned to normal.

It was a long, lonely ride home. I kept my head on a swivel to avoid unpleasant surprises. Somewhere along the way, I pulled up the relief tube from under the seat and started to ease the pressure on my bladder. To my disgust, the relief tube cone filled up and started to spill over. In the freezing temperature at twenty-five thousand feet, the relief tube discharge line had frozen shut. I sat there for a while, holding a tube full of urine in my left hand, wondering what to do with it. Just then, the engine quit! I had run out of gas on the selected tank. To add to the confusion, several bursts of flak appeared just off my right wing, close enough that I could hear them.

I was suddenly doing several things at once. I reached for the fuel selector and switched to another tank, flipped the booster pumps on, and started a climbing turn to the left. The engine came to life and I jammed the throttle and prop control to the firewall.

The relief tube was on the floor. McKibbin and Dawe had an unpleasant task ahead of them.

It had been quite a day. Our flight had destroyed nine airplanes and damaged three others.

———

Two days later, Bill Boulet was shot down by an overeager B-17 gunner. There were no enemy fighters in the area, and our group had been providing close escort for the bombers for nearly an hour. Major Kucheman led the squadron; Dick Cross was on his wing, and Woody led the second element, with Boulet on his wing. When they took up escort duty, Kucheman eased close to the bombers, on a parallel track, to identify the tail markings. Woody called out, "Falcon leader, the bombers are shooting at us!" Kucheman immediately turned away from them.

Forty-five minutes later, the bombers turned away from the target, and another group came in to take up the escort chores. The Mission Summary Report for Field Order 313 included these comments: "Lt. Boulet believed shot down at 1001 in target area by bombers on port side of second box. . . . Capt. Woody observed puffs of smoke from bombers firing. No bombers were under attack. Not a single e/a [enemy aircraft] observed or reported on entire route." The Mission Summary Report then added this caustic parenthetical remark: "Attack on Lt. Boulet is considered extremely gross carelessness in light of the fact that we had been escorting the 'big alleged friends' for more than forty-five minutes. At time of attack he was flying parallel to bomber track, and had not turned his nose toward the formation."

When his coolant boiled over and the engine overheated, it was obvious Bill had to bail out. He did it by the book. He released his seat and shoulder harness, disconnected his oxygen hose and headphone, and jettisoned the canopy. He then rolled the plane over on its back and jammed the stick forward, which popped him out clear of the tail section. He delayed opening his chute until he was just above the cloud layer that extended to eight thousand feet. He was captured within twenty-four hours near Braunschweig and spent the rest of the war in a POW camp.

Chuck Lenfest and Bob Kurtz finished their tours of duty on April 27. At that time, combat tours were two hundred hours. Chuck and Bob needed only a couple of hours each, so they were assigned relay duty as the bombers hit railroad marshaling yards in France—targeting that had become grist for the invasion rumor mill. They were orbiting in the Pas-de-Calais area, and Bob was incensed that "those damn German flak gunners were shooting at a couple of harmless relays—and coming awful damn close!" They left a few days later for thirty days' R&R in the States. Both had signed up for another tour with the 355th.

The squadron suffered another tough blow on April 29 when Jeeter Neal failed to return from an escort mission to Berlin. On the way to the rendezvous, Jeeter spotted four FW-190s. He and Herb Fritts, his wingman, went after them. The 190s dove for the cloud cover below, with Jeeter and Herb in hot pursuit. At well over four hundred miles per hour, the 190s entered the top of what appeared to be a thin cloud layer at seven thousand feet, and Jeeter followed. Fritts lost sight of Jeeter in the overcast and hauled back hard on the stick to recover from the dive. He broke out in the clear below the clouds at about a hundred feet and managed to just clear the treetops as his Mustang zoomed back into the overcast. His G suit kept him from blacking out, but "it was getting pretty gray" by the time he popped out of the overcast, with his plane seemingly hanging on its prop. Herb regained control and tried to raise Jeeter on the R/T radio but got no response. No other planes were in sight; he headed home alone.

Jeeter was never seen again. He was within two missions of finishing his tour. Everyone in the squadron mourned his loss, not only because of his ability and leadership but also because of his sense of humor and good nature. Everyone liked Jeeter.

April closed with what the newspapers were calling the "invasion blitz" as the bombers hit German airfields in France. The Luftwaffe took the day off, and the mission was uneventful. April, however, was our squadron's most eventful month to date. The war was heating up.

May 1944

"Takeoff at four-fifteen!" I said to Burt, "They can't do that! It's only fifteen minutes to happy hour at the club!"

"Yeah," he replied, "and you might miss chow, too. War is hell!"

In spite of my objections, we took off on time that afternoon of May 1. For the first time, I was leading a flight. Lieutenant Colonel Dix led the group with our squadron; I led Yellow Flight with Bob Taylor, Emil Perry, and Dick Cross; Stud Starr led Blue Flight. Bombers were pasting airfields throughout France, and we were assigned to escort three boxes of B-17s. We picked them up at Dinant, a tiny dot on the map south of Namur, Belgium; and escorted them to the target at Metz, a slightly larger dot on the map south of Luxembourg; then back to a point five miles north of Namur. The bombers were stacked from twenty thousand to twenty-three thousand feet, below a thick layer of clouds.

Mustangs and Thunderbolts were approaching to relieve us as we finished our escort stint. We were slightly ahead of the rear box of bombers when I saw fifteen to twenty FW-190s coming in fast behind them. I called them in to the group leader, and racked around to head them off. The Germans were using the roller-coaster attack: swooping down below the bomber stream to build up speed, climbing to attack the bombers from below, then split-essing to the deck. That tactic usually began from the front of the bomber stream, but this time they came from the rear. Six of them were already diving away after striking the bombers; the rest broke for the deck when they spotted us coming. We went after them.

I latched onto a 190 but lost it as we dove through layers of clouds and haze. I continued diving toward the deck, where I could see a lot of airplanes milling around. It was very hazy below the clouds—visibility less than two miles—but I managed to get behind another 190, and following a quick check to see that Taylor was still with me, I opened fire from about two hundred yards. I saw strikes immediately around the 190's tail section.

I expected him to turn, but to my surprise he firewalled it and flattened out at treetop level. Black smoke poured from his engine, and I knew he had his throttle as far forward as it would go. This was a late-model long-nosed FW-190 with a top speed close to that of a Mustang. He was ducking behind trees and hills, skidding and turning just a few feet above the ground.

I managed to get a few more hits, but he was slowly pulling away from me because of his tactics. When he scooted over a hill, he turned sharply to a different heading, and when I followed him over those hills, I had to look around in the haze to see which way he went. It was a deadly cat-and-mouse game, and the mouse was getting away.

Two thoughts then occurred to me: He was leading me into Germany, and I was running low on fuel. I alerted Taylor, and the next time the 190 ducked behind a hill, I racked the Mustang into a tight left turn and we headed back toward England. I could almost hear Bob's sigh of relief.

By the time we got back to Steeple and finished debriefing, it was after nine, and the officers' club dining room had closed, but the club officer knew better than to antagonize thirty-plus fighter pilots. He reopened the dining room.

May 2. "Your attention, gentlemen, please!" Burt's voice always had the drill sergeant's authoritarian quality that commands attention. The Ping-Pong match stopped, and conversations ceased in midsentence in Gremlin Villa.

"Major Kinnard is now Lieutenant Colonel Kinnard, as of today!" Cheers and applause greeted the announcement.

"Couldn't happen to a nicer guy!" shouted Henry Brown. That sentiment echoed throughout the room.

"Just a few months ago, we were wondering if he'd ever fly a mission," said Perry. "I guess he showed us!"

When Kinnard entered half an hour later, he was greeted with a rousing reception and a number of hands to shake. "If y'all aren't doing anything this evenin'," he said with a grin, "I might buy you a drink." Louder cheers.

"Trouble is," Duff murmured in my ear, "now he'll get moved up to Group and we'll lose him."

On May 4 we were supposed to sweep the Berlin area twenty minutes ahead of the bombers, then take up escort duty as they approached the target. It didn't happen. As we neared Dümmer Lake, well short of Berlin, our wing controller sent the recall signal. Nasty weather had made a shambles of the bomber formations, and their mission was called off.

Duff was leading the flight for the first time, and I led his second element. Right after the recall, someone in another flight called, "Bandits at six o'clock low!" so we turned and spotted a number of fighters diving away below us. We peeled off after them. They entered a cloud layer, and we followed. They were nowhere in sight when we broke through the overcast.

"Anybody see where they went?" asked Duff. No answer.

"There's a train at two o'clock. I'm heading down."

We followed. It was a long freight train coming to a stop at a small village. "Bud," Duff said, "stay up and check for flak cars. If you see any, take 'em out." Since the episode with the flak barges, Duff had become wary of hidden flak batteries.

Bob Taylor and I watched as Duff and Dick Cross worked the locomotive over, producing the usual high geyser of steam. There were no flak cars, and on one of Dick's passes, the freight car he shot at nearly blew him out of the sky when it exploded. Bob and I joined in strafing the rest of the cars. We put a lot of holes in them, but there were no more fireworks.

Shortly after we took off, Lieutenant General Doolittle, the Eighth Air Force commander, brought a distinguished visitor to our base. I sometimes wondered why they chose Steeple to show to visitors, and not permanent installations such as Debden, home of the famous 4th Fighter Group and its cadre of former Eagle Squadron veterans. Maybe they wanted to elicit sympathy for the military people who lived in relatively seedy conditions while fighting the war. That would be difficult to do at Debden, where pilots lived in comfortable permanent quarters with batmen at their service and a cozy officers' club for their leisure hours.

General Doolittle's guest was Viscount Hugh Trenchard, G.C.B., G.C.V.O., D.S.O., D.C.L., L.L.D., and marshal of the Royal Air Force. Lord Trenchard, known as the Father of the Royal Air Force, held a rank equivalent to a five-star general. Brigadier General Jesse Auton, who was also in the visiting party, explained the ongoing mission to him in detail. Combat films were shown to the dignitaries and to a group of pilots and intelligence officers.

Lord Trenchard chatted with several pilots for over half an hour, intensely interested in their accounts of combat. He spent another half hour looking over a P-47 and a P-38 that had been flown in for his visit, and one of our P-51s. The visitors left before we returned from the mission.

Henry Brown was impressed. "That was a very sharp old gentleman," he told us later. "He didn't miss a trick!"

Burt Sims was promoted to captain on May 6. He was grinning broadly all day and into the evening, even as his bar bill shot skyward. Late in the party, he called "Attention!" in his drill-sergeant voice and announced that all lieutenants would from now on have to call him "sir." He was immediately told where to go and what he could do when he got there. He was still grinning.

A flight didn't look good on May 8. The mission was to sweep the Berlin area in advance of the bombers, then escort them partway back. Stewart led the group with the 357th, and Dix was leading the 354th. Duff was leading Falcon Yellow Flight, with Perry on his wing; I was his element leader, with Bob Taylor on my wing. I felt my engine running a little rough after takeoff, but I thought it would smooth out during the climbout. As we were passing through fifteen thousand feet, it started to skip. I told Duff what was happening and turned back. By the time I got to Steeple, the instruments in the cockpit were vibrating and the engine was still skipping an occasional beat. McKibbin and Dawe were not happy to see me.

Pilots didn't like to abort a mission—we had put in a lot of effort getting mentally and physically ready. We also knew that the crew chief would be in trouble with the line chief if it turned out to be his fault. A crew chief took proprietary pride in the reliability of *his* airplane, and an aborted mission was a black mark on his reputation. Sergeant Julius Mosely, crew chief of WR-C, had the best record in the squadron—only two aborts in nearly two years of combat missions. But fighters were complicated machines, with complicated systems to keep them flying: fuel and oil systems, radio equipment, electrical and hydraulic systems, and engine components. All had to be working at optimum levels to keep the airplane flying. All it took was one little item—like fouled spark plugs—to trigger an abort. The pilot's pride was wrapped up in these events—too many aborted missions reflected adversely on his intestinal fortitude, even though much of it was beyond his control. Except for the squadron commander, a pilot's assigned airplane was not exclusively his to fly; when he wasn't on the schedule, another pilot—often newly assigned—flew his plane.

A few minutes after I left, Perry's engine began to cough and sputter, and he aborted. That left Duff and Taylor, but not for long. Taylor couldn't get his external tanks to feed, so he had to return. Duff was Yellow Flight all by himself.

When Swede Benson aborted because of radio failure, Duff filled the vacated element leader slot in Starr's Blue Flight, and Yellow Flight disappeared.

On the way in, a large gaggle of German fighters was sighted north of Braunschweig at about five thousand feet, but Stewart reluctantly passed them up, because that would leave our assigned bombers without escort. Later, the 352d Fighter Group lit into the gaggle, scattered them, and shot down twenty-nine.

In spite of its occasional cantankerous disposition, I was now completely comfortable in the P-51B. I had become accustomed to its raspy sound, four-gun armament, and even its tendency to foul up spark plugs—partly because of the fuel used, and partly because of the reduced power settings necessary to conserve fuel on long-range missions.

A few pilots experienced gun stoppages in one or more of the .50-caliber machine guns—sometimes all four. Most of the time these stoppages occurred in steep turns, in high-G-force situations. The guns were positioned at an angle in the laminar-flow wings, and the ammunition feed trays sometimes became jammed. An ammo-belt-motor booster helped alleviate the problem, but it didn't eliminate it completely.

The fuselage tank was behind the pilot's seat and below the radio. Though called a 75-gallon tank, its actual capacity was 85 gallons, and it weighed more than five hundred pounds. When filled with fuel, that weight moved the center of gravity (CG) aft and made the airplane unstable. We had a standing order to use fuel from this tank after takeoff until it was down to about twenty-five gallons, which moved the CG forward to its optimum position.

Some pilots—usually replacement pilots with little P-51 experience—claimed that it didn't give any warning of an approaching stall, especially a high-speed stall. I never understood what they were talking about. I could always sense—in the control column and in the seat of my pants— an approaching stall. It wasn't a rattle-and-shake warning; it was subtle—a slight tremor in the stick or an almost imper-

ceptible shudder of the airplane. The Mustang was telling
me to ease up on that back pressure just a hair, or add
power, or both.

We missed the P-47's dependable eight-gun firepower
and its ability to absorb considerable damage and still bring
us back home. "A kid with a rifle could bring that Mustang
down," said Perry, aiming an imaginary rifle at a P-51 flying
by, "but not the Jug." The coolant system plumbing was the
most vulnerable element in the Mustang's power package—
even a small hole was enough to stop the engine.

Sometimes the coolant boiled over even without a bullet
hole. The air scoop door control switch, just above the rudder trim control, had three positions: closed, open, and automatic; its normal setting was automatic. The coolant
temperature gauge was just below the manifold pressure
gauge on the instrument panel. If the automatic cooler door
system malfunctioned, the door was driven to the fully
closed position, blocking the airflow through the radiator. It
didn't take long for the coolant temperature to rise rapidly
when that happened. Unless the pilot happened to be watching that gauge, he'd have no inkling of a problem until the
pressure relief plug blew and the coolant started boiling
over. If he *did* happen to notice the temperature rising on the
gauge, he could avoid disaster by moving the control switch
to the "open" position. Otherwise his options were limited:
Bail out or belly in. Fortunately, those malfunctions seldom
happened.

In spite of its little eccentricities, we grew to love the
Mustang. It took us to Berlin and beyond, where we could
tangle on even terms—or better—with 109s and 190s. And
it took us back to England. The Jug couldn't do that.

Back from a restful week at the Flak Home, Woody led
the flight and I led his second element as B-24s hit German
airfields and marshaling yards in France on May 9, adding
more fuel to the invasion-rumor factory. We were at the target, St.-Trond airfield, fifteen minutes before the bombers
appeared. We swept the area, looking for German fighters,

but none appeared. After the bombing, the 358th Squadron strafed the airfield, but the smoke from the bombing was so thick they couldn't find anything to shoot at.

We escorted the bombers back to the Chànnel through occasional inaccurate flak.

Luftwaffe airfields were once again targeted the next day, this time in the Bremen/Oldenburg area in Germany. Foggy Schmucker was pessimistic. "It looks bad over the Continent," he said. "Layered clouds all the way up to at least twenty-five thousand. If you're lucky, you'll find the bombers." The cloud base over Steeple was at three thousand feet. Lieutenant Colonel Dix led the group with the 358th Squadron. We were to sweep the target area prior to the arrival of the bombers, then escort them back to the North Sea.

Major Kucheman led our squadron, and I led his second element. Duff led Yellow Flight, just behind us. On climbout we encountered thick, multilayered clouds that soon became solid overcast. The group broke up into flights, flying close formation on instruments. At twenty-two thousand feet, Duff radioed that his supercharger hadn't cut in and he was headed back, but rather than try to break up the flight in the thick overcast, he was taking the whole flight back.

"Uncle, this is Colgate," the radio crackled. "The Big Friends are running an hour late." We were between layers and knew we had just made landfall over Holland by the flak barrage that greeted our passage. We continued our climb, trying to get above the overcast. Thirty minutes later Colgate told us the bomber mission had been scrubbed. We were to sweep the area, then return to base.

I took a quick peek at the altimeter—twenty-nine thousand feet—and we were still on instruments. "Falcon leader here. We're turning back." Kucheman had had enough. He had no idea where the other flights were, and we could only hope that they weren't in the same piece of sky we were in.

I had seen nothing but Kucheman's right wing for nearly an hour, so I was not unhappy with his decision.

The 357th Squadron had turned back ten minutes earlier. Dix led the 358th on a southerly heading and topped the overcast at twenty-five thousand feet. They swept the area well south of the target but found no one to play with.

The ceiling at Steeple was still three thousand feet, so we had no problem getting back in. When I climbed out of the cockpit, my muscles and joints felt like they were a hundred years old. It had been a long, exhausting trip. Flying tight formation in thick clouds for a long stretch was hard on the eyes and nerves. When Kucheman came dragging in to Gremlin Villa, he said to me with a tired smile, "You did a nice job, Bud."

"So did you, Major," I replied, surprised and pleased by his compliment. Since the incident in the billeting area when Duff lit into him and the CO, he had been a little cool and aloof toward both of us—not unfriendly, but distant.

Doc Fontenot greeted us at Gremlin Villa with a shot of medicinal whiskey to calm us down.

May 12 marked the beginning of the Eighth Air Force campaign against the German oil industry—a campaign that had begun a month earlier with the low-level bombing of the Ploesti oil fields in Romania by Fifteenth Air Force B-24s based in Italy.

We escorted B-17s against oil targets in the Zwickau area. As we approached the targets, I saw two Me-109s at three o'clock high, heading our way. I called Woody, and Blue Flight turned into them. They lost interest and dove away. The rest was a milk run.

"We made history again today. Our group took part in the longest flight ever made by fighter aircraft. We went to Poland."

That's the way Burt Sims began his squadron history narrative for May 13, 1944. I can't vouch for the accuracy of that second sentence, but I know it was the longest flight I had made until then.

Briefing was at 10:15 A.M. Nearly every pilot made some kind of wisecrack when he entered the briefing room and saw that red string stretched almost off the map. "Is that in Europe?" "Won't the Russians get mad?" "Where do we refuel? In Berlin?"

Our assignment was to cover B-17s attacking a Focke-Wulf assembly plant at Poznan, 150 miles east of Berlin and only about 200 miles from Soviet-occupied territory. Another Mustang group escorted B-24s that attacked a synthetic oil plant at nearby Politz.

Lieutenant Colonel Dix, the group air executive officer, led our squadron and the group. I was leading Blue Flight, with Davis on my wing, Perry in the no. 3 slot, and Taylor on his wing. We took off just before noon and made rendezvous with the bombers east of Berlin more than two and a half hours later. Soon after crossing the Polish border, someone in the 357th Squadron called in a large number of bogeys approaching the head of the bomber stream, so we hustled over that way.

Dix spotted about a dozen Me-410s—the destroyers—toward the rear of the first box of bombers and went after them, followed by Yellow Flight. At the same time, I saw eight Ju-88s heading for the front of the box, so I went after them. At that time, Ju-88s were used primarily as night fighters against RAF bombers. Ju-88s were relatively slow and their crews had little experience attacking bombers in the daytime, so they looked for straggling, crippled bombers. They avoided escort fighters whenever possible. When the 88s saw us coming, they dove for the clouds below.

One of them crossed about a thousand yards ahead of me, and I cut him off. I was in a diving right turn and closing fast. The 88 tried to dive straightaway, but I opened fire and saw hits all over the right side of the fuselage and tail. Pieces fell off and flames erupted from the wing section. I pulled up to avoid overrunning and looked back. The Ju-88 was burning and coming apart.

The other 88s had disappeared in the cloud bank below,

so I led Blue Flight back up to where I thought the bomber stream was. The bombers and escort fighters were nowhere in view.

"Falcon Blue leader, this is Blue 4. I'm getting low on fuel." Bob Taylor could have added, "and a long way from home." I called the group leader and told him I was heading back.

"Roger," he replied, "and you'd better go north a little to stay away from Big B." Berlin was a good place to stay away from, so we flew well to the north of it.

We were cruising at twenty-three thousand feet with reduced power settings to conserve fuel. Through a few breaks in the clouds below us, I was able to pick out Bremen before we blundered over it. We made another little detour to the north to go around it.

About fifteen miles northwest of Bremen, I spotted five Focke-Wulf 190s at two o'clock, heading southwest at about fifteen thousand feet. We were above them and up-sun, so they didn't see us. "Let's get 'em!" I radioed to the flight, "Everybody take one." My plan was to make one pass and keep going because we were all getting low on fuel, especially Taylor. We didn't have enough for a prolonged dogfight.

Back up to full power, I started the dive toward the two 190s on the left. Perry went after the three on the right. My speed built up considerably as I closed on the one at the far left of the formation. I started firing at about three hundred yards, closing to a hundred yards, firing all the way from dead astern and slightly above.

He never knew what hit him. There were strikes all over the airplane, concentrated on the cockpit area and wing roots. Pieces fell off as I pulled up into a power climb. I looked back and saw the 190 in a slow, steep spiral dive, trailing black smoke and debris. I was quite sure the pilot was unconscious or dead. The 190 was in a near-vertical dive when it entered the cloud layer at ten thousand feet, still trailing smoke.

The other 190s split-essed for the clouds below. Perry nailed two, and the other two found cloud cover.

I throttled back to let Perry catch up; then we climbed to twenty-five thousand feet and returned to England. Taylor landed at Manston RAF Station to refuel, but the rest of us made it home. We got back to Steeple a little after 6:00 P.M. As usual, low, thick clouds and rain greeted us. This was our seventh mission in seven days.

The other two squadrons didn't find any Luftwaffe activity, and stayed with the bombers.

When we got back to Gremlin Villa, Burt told us that the 8th Fighter Command had released us from operations all the next day. The bar did a robust business that evening.

It had been a long day, but longer ones lay ahead.

Mendenhall left for his thirty-day R&R leave in the States on May 15, and I took over D Flight. For the first time since I joined the squadron, I was no longer in A Flight. I had mixed feelings—glad to be a flight leader, but sad to leave A Flight.

On May 15, word trickled down from the 65th Fighter Wing that Korky had been awarded the Silver Star for gallantry in action on the March 6 mission.

"Do you suppose they'll tell him about it in the POW camp?" asked Duff.

"If they do, it'll be small comfort to him," said Burt.

Lieutenant Colonel Edward W. Szaniawski was the colorful and popular commander of the 357th Fighter Squadron. He adopted the nickname "Jonesy" because he tired of having people ask him how he pronounced his name. Whenever he said "Shah NESS key" some wiseacre would invariably say *"Gesundheit!"* or "God bless you!," so when asked how to pronounce it, he'd reply "Jonesy." He bore a superficial resemblance to Jimmy Durante; even his speech had that Durante rasp. Pilots in all three squadrons liked and respected him.

On May 19 he was Uncle, leading the group with his squadron. Kinnard led our squadron, and I led the second element in Red Flight. We made landfall north of Ijmuiden, stayed well north of the Amsterdam flak batteries, and headed east toward Potsdam. Part of our group was to escort bombers to Berlin; the rest of the group was supposed to escort other bombers, to Braunschweig. At Potsdam, though we could see the incoming bomber stream headed for Berlin, we were directed by Fighter Control to abandon the Berlin mission and concentrate on the Braunschweig attack.

The weather was lousy. Banks of heavy clouds made it difficult to keep the group intact.

When someone reported fifty-plus enemy aircraft on a parallel course to the bombers and about three thousand feet above them, Jonesy and his squadron raced to intercept, and we followed. The enemy fighters were too far ahead for us to catch, and with all the maneuvering in and out of clouds, Jonesy became separated from his squadron, and I lost Kinnard. My wingman, Bill Martin, was still with me, and we found Jonesy. When I checked in with Kinnard he said, "Stay with Uncle."

After about fifteen minutes of trying to locate the bombers, Jonesy said, "To hell with it! Let's head back!" Then he asked us how our fuel supply was. We said it was okay, and he said, "Good! Let's go down and see if we can drum up some business." We headed for the deck. He spotted an airfield near Dümmer Lake, and we made a pass at it. There was nothing worthwhile to shoot at, but plenty of flak. We kept going and soon came to the airfield at Diepholz.

Bill Martin had moved over to Jonesy's left wing, so we were flying in a vee formation. As we started our strafing run, I didn't see any prime targets, but the whole airfield seemed to erupt with flak—20mm and 40mm cannon shells and tracers from machine guns. About halfway across the field, Bill saw Jonesy's plane take a couple of hard hits in the left wing and engine section by what appeared to be 40mm shells.

"I've been hit," Jonesy said calmly. "There's a big hole in my left wing. I'm going to try to make it back."

About three miles beyond the airfield, his coolant started to boil over and he knew he had no chance of getting back to England. He climbed to about two thousand feet to bail out or find a suitable field to belly in. Directly in front of us was a long, level field between two rows of trees in what appeared to be a military training area. "I'm going to belly it in here," he said. "When I get out of the plane, set it on fire."

We circled above him as he eased down toward the ground. As I completed the first circle, I saw an armored car headed in Jonesy's direction. I thought that if I could delay them, it might give him a better chance to escape. I made a pass, firing at the armored car and a row of four or five tanks in front of a two-story brick barracks building. The armored car stopped, and there was dust and smoke all around it. The soldiers ran hell-bent for the barracks.

In the meantime, Jonesy bellied in, and announced to us that he was okay, and had entered a heavily wooded area at the edge of the field. I made a firing pass at his P-51 and saw strikes all around the cockpit area; then smoke curled from the wing roots. Bill Martin followed, put the finishing touches to the airplane, and left it burning. I circled the area a couple of times and shot up a few more of their tanks. I saw soldiers firing their rifles at me from the barracks windows. Perry's remark about a kid with a rifle bringing down a Mustang flashed through my mind. I knew that if they managed to shoot me down, I'd be in for a rough afternoon. I kept the German soldiers inside the barracks for about five minutes, hoping that Jonesy would have time to put a few miles between them and him, but then I had to leave because of a dwindling fuel supply.

As it was, Jonesy was in for a rough afternoon. As soon as Bill and I left, the soldiers were out in force and soon captured him. They might have treated him more kindly had I not sprayed them with .50-caliber ammunition. Though I didn't know it, and intended only to keep them at bay until Jonesy could hide in the surrounding woods, some soldiers were wounded, and a few were killed in my attack. They had great fun making Jonesy's life miserable until a German colonel arrived on the scene and called a halt to their fun and games. Jonesy spent the rest of the war as a POW.

When the war ended, a few of our POWs came back to Steeple Morden before being shipped back to the States. Jonesy was one of them. We were all gathered around listening to the story of his capture and the rough treatment he had received until the German colonel arrived. He looked around at us and said, "And who was that dumb sonofabitch who shot up those soldiers?"

I was a major then and could have exercised my Constitutional right to remain silent, but I said, "That was me, Jonesy."

He glared at me for about five seconds, then his expression softened. "Well," he said, "I guess you were only doing what you thought was right."

On May 20 we escorted bombers hitting airfields and railway marshaling yards in France. Invasion fever was rampant, and we were required to have four aircraft on alert status from dawn to dusk. Colonel Cummings led the group with the 358th; Major Rosenblatt led our squadron, Duff led Yellow Flight behind Rosenblatt, and I led the second section with Blue Flight. Rich Brown, who was finishing his tour on this mission, led Green Flight.

When we reached the bombers, Cummings saw that two of the boxes were without escort, so he sent the 357th to cover them. He then sent the 354th to investigate fighter contrails about five thousand feet above and ahead of the bomber stream, but he told our Green Flight to stay with the last box of bombers.

It took us quite a while to catch up with the contrails above us, but as we got within a thousand feet of them, we saw six FW-190s. They saw us at about the same time and split for the deck. We chased them, but lost them in the clouds at five thousand feet.

In the meantime, Green Flight spotted about a dozen enemy planes above them. As they climbed to intercept them, four FW-190s and two Me-109s bounced them from the rear and shot down First Lieutenant Jacobson and Second

Lieutenant Donaldson before diving for the deck. Both were later reported KIA.

It had been a frustrating morning. No one in our group scored, but no bombers were lost.

That afternoon, Kinnard called a meeting of squadron pilots to discuss tactics. He sketched a new formation he believed would solve the problem posed by changes in Luftwaffe tactics. Kinnard's plan was to have two sections of eight planes, each section flying line abreast—eight trailing eight as shown:

T   T   T   T   T   T   T   T

T   T   T   T   T   T   T   T

"This formation will present an intimidating front to their people and give us plenty of cross cover." He gave several other "advantages" of such a formation. We sat quietly and respectfully, but each of us had serious doubts about the "advantages" he was describing.

"Kinnard is a helluva nice guy and a great leader," said Duff after the meeting, "but where in hell does he get these goofy ideas?"

"Doesn't he have any idea how hard it is to keep a long line-abreast formation like that?" Perry chimed in. "That's a full-time job! We wouldn't have time to look for Krauts."

"You know how he is," I said. "We might try this once, then we'll go back to business as usual. Like it was before."

There was a party in the officers' club that night, and as the party wore on, Kinnard probably got a few earfuls about that formation. It was never tried or even mentioned after that.

The 354th was saying farewell to Bob Woody, who had completed his tour of duty and was being transferred to VIII Fighter Command headquarters.

The loss of Lieutenants Jacobson and Donaldson, plus the fact that many of the "old hands" had completed their tours and were no longer on operational status, meant that there were fewer pilots to carry the load. Since May 1, seven of our veteran pilots had finished their combat stints and left. Two-day passes to London were few and far between.

The mission on May 21 was another indication that the invasion was getting closer. The bombers got a day of rest, but VIII Fighter Command unleashed a large number of fighter groups to attack trains, airfields, and any other military targets they could find. Cummings led our squadron, and I led Blue Flight. The 357th found and destroyed five German aircraft on the ground; the rest of us destroyed eight trains, four trucks, several radio stations, and one flak tower. A few of our aircraft collected assorted holes from flak, but all returned safely to base.

There was no mention of the line-abreast formation. It was as if the meeting of squadron pilots had never happened.

The May 24 briefing was at 7:00 A.M. It was Berlin again. Our group was assigned to protect the 2d Task Force, six boxes of B-17s.

There was a change in the usual routine. Colonel Don Blakeslee, commander of the 4th Fighter Group, with an eight-ship section above the bomber penetration route, would control four fighter groups, including the rest of the 4th Group covering the first three wings, the 355th Group covering the last three boxes, and two other fighter groups. Blakeslee's call sign was Quarterback. If the Luftwaffe showed up with a large group of fighters, he could direct a large force to intercept.

Kinnard was leading the three flights of our squadron to provide top cover; I was leading Blue Flight, with Herb Fritts on my wing, and Gil Wright and Bill Martin in my second element. Lieutenant Colonel Ray Myers was leading the group with the 358th, and Captain Colson was leading the 357th in the low position.

That's the way it was supposed to be.

Shortly after switching to my 75-gallon external fuel tanks on climbout, I knew I had a problem. The ever-increasing aileron trim changes made it obvious that I wasn't getting fuel from the right tank. I checked circuit breakers, tried flicking the switches on and off, but nothing worked—no fuel from the right tank. A quick mental calculation convinced me I could get by without that fuel. I'd simply use all the fuel from the left tank, then drop them both. I'd have to keep adding aileron trim, but that should pose no great control problem.

Halfway across the North Sea, Kinnard had trouble with *his* fuel tanks. The selector switch was stuck on a tank that had been siphoning since takeoff and was now empty. Deprived of fuel, the engine quit. For a few anxious moments, he thought he'd have to bail out—not the ideal choice over the cold waters of the North Sea. He managed to jar the switch loose by "kicking hell out it" and selected another tank. The engine came to life, but Kinnard had by then lost confidence in his fuel control system.

"Falcon Leader here. I'm returning to base. Blue Leader, take over. The spare can escort me back." Silky Morris, spare no. 1, joined him.

I took over the lead. A few minutes later, 1st Lt. Bob Harness reported that his engine was acting up and he was returning to base. Fid Barger escorted him, and Walt Christensen, the only one left from Kinnard's flight, tagged along. That left eight of us in the high squadron.

Then the weather got into the act. As we made landfall on schedule, we encountered thick layers of clouds, with smaller patches between layers. If I had stayed above the lead squadron, I'd have been in or above a thick layer, and there would have been no way to keep visual contact. The 357th had the same problem. As a result, all three squadrons were squeezed between layers, trying to stay in visual contact with each other.

"Uncle here. Turning forty-five degrees right." I couldn't believe my ears. The group leader was turning his squadron right into us. He probably believed that we were well above him, where we would have been had it not been for the clouds.

What was left of the 354th came apart at the seams.

There was a wild scramble as we tried frantically to avoid collisions. Flights became separated in cloud layers, and when things settled down, Perry's flight was alone, with no bombers or fighters in sight. He saw no point in milling around in the cloud layers looking for us, so he set course for England. My second element, Lieutenants Wright and Martin, found Perry's flight but not mine. They joined him.

I was now leading a squadron of two aircraft—Herb Fritts and me. We found the rest of the group and finally rendezvoused with the bombers. They were not on time nor at the altitude they were supposed to have been.

"A bunch of 109s at twelve o'clock low, climbing toward the bombers!" came from an unidentified source.

The radio chatter confirmed that a large gaggle of Me-109s and FW-190s was climbing toward the head of the bomber stream, and Uncle called for us to drop external tanks. By this time I had cranked in almost full aileron trim to maintain control. I pressed the tank release button on top of the stick with my thumb. I had left enough fuel in the left tank to help keep the wings level. It dropped off but the full right tank did not. Now I needed full left aileron trim, and the stick nearly full left, to keep the wings level.

"Uncle, this is Quarterback. Keep one squadron with the bombers, and take the rest up front!"

"Roger," replied Myers. "Falcon Leader, this is Uncle. Stay with this box of bombers." He obviously didn't know that the 354th Fighter Squadron consisted of two first lieutenants, and one of them had a problem.

"Falcon Leader here. Roger." I felt like saying, "You mean both of us?" I was still trying to get rid of that full external tank. I skidded the plane right and left, bobbed up and down, and flipped every bomb and tank release and salvo switch I could find—all to no avail. The tank seemed welded to the shackle.

"Falcon Leader, bogies at four o'clock high!" Fritts radioed. I looked over my right shoulder and saw two Me-109s in a slanting dive toward us.

"Roger. We'll break into them, but wait for my call."

I didn't want to call the break too soon, because they would simply break off the attack and keep going. I wanted them to commit themselves so we could get them turning with us. I was confident that we could outturn them, and we'd have them for sure. I had completely forgotten about that tank. If this sounds like I was a cool, ice-in-my-veins pro, I can assure you that my blood pressure and pulse rate were considerably elevated, and the pit of my stomach felt that familiar twinge.

When they got into shooting range, I called, "Break right . . . *now!*" As soon as I released stick pressure from its full left position, the ship rolled rapidly to the right, and I pulled back sharply. The Mustang shuddered, snap-rolled viciously to the right, and started spinning toward a layer of clouds. That damned tank!

It was a thin layer. By the time I got through it, I had the plane just barely under control, but it wasn't easy. I quickly looked around and saw a fighter right on my tail about two hundred yards behind me, in perfect position for a kill. I was already rolling to the right because of the tank, so I pulled the stick hard back—with the same result I had achieved the first time. For an instant, I thought I should bail out, but early in the spin I felt a thump as the wing tank finally let go.

I recovered from the spin and immediately went into a sharp left turn because of the full aileron trim I had cranked in to compensate for the full tank. I started to crank the aileron trim back to normal and looked back. There was that fighter still directly behind me! I tightened the turn as much as I could.

"Relax, Bud. It's only me," Herb Fritts announced in a calm voice. I don't know how he managed to stay with me during those wild gyrations.

We had no chance of finding the bombers or rejoining the group. We were below ten thousand feet after my spin exercises; I could see the ground through breaks in the clouds. "Might as well see if there's anything moving down there," I thought.

We descended in a shallow high-speed dive and turned

to a westerly heading. As we approached two thousand feet, I spotted a freight train a few miles south of us. At that stage of the war, it was open season on all German trains and trucks. With Fritts about three hundred yards behind me, I made a low pass over the locomotive to give the engineer a chance to bail out and to check for flak, then came around on a firing run. The locomotive was almost completely stopped, and I suspect that the engineer had jumped into the nearest ditch. I lined up the gunsight on the boiler and squeezed the trigger on the stick. I watched the flashes from the API shells crawl across the boiler, and a huge column of steam erupted straight up from the locomotive.

I pulled into a tight left turn to avoid the column of steam and to see how Fritts was doing. I saw his plane streaking toward the train, firing as he came. As he flew through the geyser of steam, his airplane seemed to lurch; then it crashed to the ground in a ball of yellow-orange flame just beyond the locomotive. I knew there was no way he could have survived that crash. I flew over and around the train, looking for any gun emplacements that might have accounted for the crash. There was none. The only explanation I could think of was that his airplane had struck a piece of the exploding boiler as Herb flew through the steaming geyser.

Through the shock, I felt a great weariness descend on me. I was tired. Tired of flying. Tired of the war. And tired of seeing young lives snuffed out in balls of fire.

Alone and shaken, I started a climb through the layer of clouds. I leveled off at twenty-three thousand feet, still in the overcast, and headed for England. I thought it safer to stay in the overcast, where I wouldn't have to keep wondering if anyone was behind me, looking through a gunsight.

The thick stratus cloud layer provided smooth flying. The silent gloom of the clouds and the purring of the engine were a soothing balm for my frayed nerves.

Sudden flashes of red-orange light shattered my reverie as the jarring thumps of antiaircraft shells bursting too close jolted me back to reality. I jammed the throttle full and started a climbing turn to the right, straightened out for about thirty seconds, then turned left, still climbing. It was all I could do: change headings and altitude—and pray.

After about a minute that seemed more like an hour, the flak subsided. I was at twenty-eight thousand feet and still in the overcast. I throttled back and resumed my original heading. I later learned that I had blundered over Bremen, a large, well-defended German city.

England was socked in, as usual. After an instrument approach, I landed in a drizzling rain. The sopping English countryside seemed dreary and dark, matching my mood.

After the debriefing, Doc Fontenot greeted me with a shot of medicinal whiskey. "You look like you could use a little rest," he said. "I'm grounding you for two days. Check with me before you fly another mission." I didn't argue. I went to London that afternoon with Rich Brown, who was still waiting for orders to the States for R&R. I wasn't sure that two days in London was what Doc Fontenot meant by "a little rest," but it was a change of scenery.

I had been flying combat missions for nine months, with only occasional two-day passes to London to ease the strain—and there is considerable doubt in my mind about the therapeutic value of a two-day pass to London. It was a lively city, and we often came back to base sorely in need of rest and recuperation, but it was different, and it served as a pressure relief valve.

Occasionally, we went elsewhere on pass. Brighton, on the southern coast, and the picturesque city of Torquay, near Portsmouth, were favorite alternatives to hectic London. Except for these occasional diversions, our lives were limited to the humdrum routine of the base and the not-so-humdrum routine of combat missions.

On base there was the usually bustling activity in the officers' club game room and Gremlin Villa; the Comet Theater showed old movies two or three times a week; and the Red Cross Aero Club, which was open to all ranks.

I was back at Steeple on May 26. Seven replacement pilots—all second lieutenants—had reported for duty on May
25: Robert Bradley, Floyd Taylor, Robert Couture, Robert
Hulderman, Sumner Williams, Clarence Graham, and
Garlyn Hoffman. They were, as Burt put it, "welcome as
money from home." I checked in with Doc Fontenot and he
cleared me—reluctantly, I thought—to operational status.

On May 27 we were to provide area support for bombers
hitting a number of marshaling yards at Strasbourg,
Saarbrücken, Karlsruhe, and a few other places. Kinnard
was slated to lead the group with our squadron. As usual, he
was up early, poring over intelligence reports and trying to
figure out where the Luftwaffe would show up. At the group
briefing he gave us a little pep talk: "Those potatoes," he
said, referring to the Germans, "will come steaming in right
around Strasbourg, trying to get at the bombers. They have
a lot of people down there, so it looks like our chance to
clean house. But we've got to stick together! I want the
whole group to be together when we see these monkeys! If
we can go at 'em in one big bunch, and tear right into 'em,
we'll all get some. What we want to do is cut right at 'em—
and start shootin'. Break 'em up! Go at 'em head-on!"

He poked the map at the Strasbourg area with his
wooden pointer. "Right there," he said, "is where they'll be
tryin' to break through."

He called the shot exactly right. The Germans were
there, trying to break through, twenty minutes before we got
there. The 4th Fighter Group *was* there, however. When we
arrived on the scene, that little war was over—a field day for
the 4th, a milk run for us.

Duff finished his combat tour with this mission.
Originally 200 hours of combat time was a full tour of duty.
It soon became 250 hours, then 275 hours. Duff finished
275 hours two days before the tour became 300 hours. He
opted to return to the 355th for another tour after his thirty-
day R&R leave. "If you go back to the States, I won't have
anybody to play chess with," I told him. "Why don't you

spend your thirty-day leave right here in sunny England?"
He didn't bother to answer. The look was enough. Perry
took over A Flight.

I wasn't on the May 28 mission to the Leipzig area.
Kinnard was group leader, and again he predicted German
tactics exactly as they later played out. Again he stressed
"Stay together!" Unfortunately, he had to return early because of radio problems and a faulty ignition harness that
was causing his engine to misfire. He told 1st Lt. Jim Austin
to take over the squadron, and Captain Colson to lead the
group with the 357th. Captain Blair was leading the 358th.

There were sixteen early returns in the group—five from
the 354th, including Captain Blair. That left the 354th and
358th squadrons manned entirely by first and second lieutenants. Fid Barger took over Kinnard's flight and dropped
back behind Austin's flight in the Green Flight position.
There were not many combat veterans in the group when it
rendezvoused with the bombers. Somehow, the group became widely scattered, the very thing Kinnard had warned
against.

From the tail end of the bomber stream, at twenty-six
thousand feet, Jim Austin spotted a large gaggle of FW-
190s ahead of and above his two flights. As he climbed to
intercept, he noticed eight Me-109s behind them and well
above thirty thousand feet. "Fid!" he called. "Watch out for
those 109s at four o'clock high!"

"Got 'em," replied Fid. Just then, four of the 109s came
streaking down toward Green Flight, followed closely by
the second four. "Here they come," said Fid. He called the
break as the 109s neared shooting range. He and his wingman, Walt Christensen, broke into the oncoming 109s.
Austin turned sharply to bring his flight into the fray but
didn't get back in time. From that point, the situation broke
into wild confusion, with German fighters all over the place.
The other two squadrons were far ahead with the bombers
and unable to help. Barger and Christensen were never seen
again; both were later reported KIA.

Kinnard was shaken. "Damn, damn, damn!" he kept saying. "If I'd been there, it might have been different!"

"You'd have never gotten there," said Captain Randall, our engineering officer. "Not with that ignition harness."

The 357th shot down two Me-109s on the way home.

"Where were they when we needed 'em?" said Austin.

May 29. Poland again! It was our second trip to Poznan. Every pilot entering the briefing room had a remark—mostly caustic—about the long haul.

"Are they issuing pillows for my ass?"

"Do they know how far that is?"

"I'll tell you how far it is," said Danny Lewis. "From here to Poznan is about the same distance as New York to Chicago—and you're making a round trip, nonstop!"

"Yeah," said Perry, "but they wouldn't shoot at us there."

For the first time, we carried two 108-gallon external wing tanks. Another innovation—one of Kinnard's experiments—was in the ammunition trays of the four .50-caliber machine guns. In the first twenty rounds of each gun, a tracer shell was placed between each of regular API bullets. "If we stick together like we're supposed to," he explained, "when we tear into those gaggles with guns blazing, it'll make 'em nervous seeing a whole bunch of tracers coming at 'em, and maybe break 'em up."

Colonel Cummings led this one. Kucheman led our squadron, Perry led Yellow Flight, and I led Blue Flight. There was more combat experience in our squadron this time but not much rank. Except for Major Kucheman, we were all lieutenants. We flew a straight line to a point about fifteen miles southwest of Berlin, then to a point just a few miles northwest of Poznan, where we rendezvoused with the bombers. Huge columns of black smoke from the target area rose nearly to our altitude. The bombers headed northwest, toward the Baltic. It was the long way home for them, but it bypassed the heavy flak areas.

It turned out to be a 1,500-mile milk run—six and a half

hours strapped in that small cockpit, no Luftwaffe, occasional flak, and lots of sore butts.

From a standpoint of hours, it was my longest flight so far.

"Burt," I said, "this is my birthday! May 30! Memorial Day! Surely you don't expect me to go strike fear in the heart of the wily Hun on my twenty-second birthday?"

"You're on the schedule! Happy birthday!"

Kinnard led the group to Halberstadt, where we picked up the bombers on their withdrawal. Soon after rendezvous, the 358th sailed into a gaggle of FW-190s and Me-109s and shot down four. There was so much excited chatter from the 358th pilots that the rest of us couldn't figure out where all the action was. Kinnard was furious, trying to get a word in edgewise, only to be blocked by the constant yelling on the channel: "There goes one!" "Go get 'em!" "Break right!" "Look out behind you!" The inexperience of the newcomers was obvious.

Kinnard kept trying to say, "Where in hell are you?" but couldn't get through the bedlam.

After the mission, Kinnard called a meeting of all pilots on the mission and really tore into the 358th for poor radio discipline. "You guys got four," he said. "If we'd known where you were, we could have had twenty!" He was livid.

McKibbin, ever the entrepreneur, started to raise rabbits in a pen behind the hardstand, intending to make "lots of money" by selling them to neighboring farmers. His "starter" twosome turned out to be males, so they wound up in a rabbit stew.

Next day, I had a rabbit's foot dangling from a small chain from the instrument panel. "It wasn't lucky for the rabbit," said Mac, "but it'll bring you lots of luck!"

A very busy May closed out with another milk run, on May 31. No hits, no runs, no errors.

The group flew twenty-one missions in May. I flew fifteen of them.

June 1944

The first day of June featured lousy weather and the addition of five replacement pilots to our roster: Capt. Bert W. Marshall Jr., and Victor Denti, Heber Huish, Gilbert Patterson, and Royce Priest, all second lieutenants.

Captain Marshall brought a wealth of flying experience with him, having earned his wings in January 1941. He also brought an outstanding record of fortitude and leadership that was to stand him—and the 354th Squadron—in good stead in the coming months.

He was born in Royse City, Texas, in November 1919, the second of four sons. The Marshall family had its share of hard luck in the Depression. Bert's father's business failed, his older brother died in 1930 from a brain injury after being kicked by a horse, and his youngest brother became deaf from meningitis at age ten.

Bert attended high school at Greenville, about ten miles from home, and soon became the star quarterback of its football team while working a nearly full-time job. He was all-state quarterback as a sophomore in 1934 and in each of the next two years. In 1935, he led the Greenville Lions to a state championship, but Greenville lost the 1936 championship game to Amarillo. Bert played that entire game with a separated shoulder. He was a charter member of the Texas High School Hall of Fame as the only high school quarterback to win all-state honors three years in a row.

He was All-American quarterback at Vanderbilt University, Tennessee, in 1937. Vanderbilt lost the final game for a Rose Bowl berth to Alabama, 9–7. Bert tore up his knee during that game, an injury that ended his football career.

To put all this in perspective, Bert Marshall was about 5 feet, 6 inches tall and never weighed more than 160 pounds in his life.

While at Vanderbilt, he and Clay Kinnard became friends when both were dating the same girl: Dinah Shore.

He entered the Army Air Corps after graduating from Vanderbilt and received his wings and second lieutenant's gold bars in January 1941.

He was assigned to the Training Command and performed instructor duties at various locations, all the while trying as hard as he could to get transferred to a tactical outfit. In March 1943 he was assigned to a B-26 medium bomber group but was sent to fighters when he argued that the rudder pedals were "too far away" for him to reach.

When Bert's name showed up in a replacement pool in England in May 1944, Kinnard pulled a few strings to get him assigned to the 355th Group. When he arrived at Steeple, Kinnard made sure he was assigned to the 354th Squadron.

We knew nothing of Bert's history when he joined the squadron. As far as we were concerned, he was just another captain from Training Command. He was soft-spoken, unpretentious, and unfailingly courteous to everybody, down to the lowest buck private.

The June 2 mission had all tongues wagging, "The invasion! A matter of days, maybe hours!" Under radar control, we were to patrol an area south of the bomber strikes against gun emplacements along the French coast and especially in the Pas-de-Calais area, the shortest distance between England and France. Kinnard led the squadron, but a strange set of circumstances forced him to drop out, and I wound up leading.

Kinnard's left wing tank dropped off early on his takeoff roll. He managed to turn off into the 357th dispersal area, where he rounded up a lot of help in a hurry. A new tank

was hastily attached, and a refueling truck driver slipped the
hose into the tank, then withdrew it with the announcement
that seventy-five gallons had been pumped. Kinnard taxied
out and took off again in the wake of the group. Spectators
at Gremlin Villa noticed that immediately after becoming
airborne, his right wing dipped down sharply, dangerously
close to the runway.

He caught up with us and managed to get everyone
formed up and on course, but all the while he had to crank in
full left aileron trim and hold the stick as far left as it would
go. He told me to take over and returned to base, where he
dropped both tanks before landing. The right tank broke
open on impact and spewed fuel over a wide patch of
ground. The left tank, the replacement tank, did not break
open—it just bounced along the ground. As soon as he
landed, he inspected the tank and found fewer than two gallons of fuel in it. He had a few words with the fuel truck
driver, but it turned out that the truck's gas gauge was not
operating properly.

The Continent was socked in. We didn't see any German
fighters, and didn't even see the ground until we crossed the
Channel on the way home. The 65th Fighter Wing controller kept saying, "Sorry. No business." A boring overture
to an exciting month.

Part of the entry for June 3 in Bill Marshall's book:
"Lieutenant Browning of the 354FS went down west of
Paris with engine coolant trouble at 1425 hours to become
POW. Nothing else exciting happened. . . ."

Browning was my wingman that day. We had been flying low and looking for targets of opportunity, so his engine
coolant trouble could have resulted from that activity—
some "kid with a rifle," maybe? A more likely scenario was
that the automatic air-scoop door control malfunctioned and
drove the door to the fully closed position. For whatever
reason, Browning's engine coolant boiled over and he decided to belly in.

He was having trouble seeing through the boiling coolant

from the engine, and I guided him toward a large, open field. I made wide S-turns and slowed down to avoid over-running him. As Browning belly-landed successfully and radioed that he was okay, my S-turn took me far to his right, at about 200 feet and 180 miles per hour.

I was watching him, but I saw some activity out of the corner of my eye off to my right. I looked over and saw what seemed at the time to be acres of antiaircraft guns. The Germans were apparently as surprised to see me as vice versa, and I could see them scrambling to reach the guns.

I saw machine-gun emplacements and antiaircraft guns ranging from 20mm and 40mm to the big 88mm stuff. Some of the guns were already depressed to my level, swiveling around to my direction. With four .50-caliber machine guns at my disposal, it didn't seem like an even match, so I promptly executed that age-old military maneuver known as "hauling ass." As the air behind me suddenly filled with white puffs from the 20mm cannons and black puffs from the 40mm stuff, I bent the throttle forward to full power and rapidly put a bunch of trees between me and those guns.

"Nothing else exciting happened. . . ." Indeed!

During the debriefing after the mission, Burt was trying to help me pinpoint the location of all those guns. I probably wasn't much help. "What do you think all those guns were doing there?" I asked.

"I've seen intelligence reports lately about the Krauts getting ready to launch some kind of robot bomb. That might be one of their sites."

"Robot bomb?"

"Yeah, like a pilotless plane, or a flying bomb. They've been working on it. Maybe you stumbled onto one of the sites they're building."

" 'Stumbled' isn't the right word."

"True enough. By the way, you may not have heard about it yet, but your roomie is now a captain—like me!" There was that grin again.

I was pleasantly surprised. Since Jim's promotion to first lieutenant had been unfairly delayed back in September, I thought his promotion to captain might be similarly set back. I was glad that Duff's name was on the list, but a little surprised and disappointed that my name wasn't. That didn't dampen the big celebration at the club that .night, however.

The following day, we flew a patrol in the Abbeville-Amiens area, trying to get a reaction from the Luftwaffe. The patrol was uneventful until Flight Officer Henry Davis, newly assigned and flying his first mission in my flight, reported that his coolant was boiling over. "Damn!" I thought. "This is yesterday all over again." We had encountered no flak, and were too high for the "kid-with-a-rifle" scenario, so the coolant door control was the most likely cause.

"What do you want to do?" asked Lieutenant Colonel Dix, who was leading the squadron. "Bail out or find a field for a belly-landing?"

"I'm going to try to get to the Channel and bail out there. With a little luck, Air/Sea Rescue will find me."

We were above twenty thousand feet over Abbeville and could see the Channel. I told Dix I would escort Davis and call Air/Sea Rescue. I switched to the emergency channel after telling Davis to do the same. I called a Mayday message and described our intentions, location, heading, and airspeed.

"Roger. This is Dumbo. Keep transmitting so we can get bearings on you."

Davis had throttled back to try to keep the coolant from draining out too quickly, and we were losing altitude. I kept giving Dumbo a long count periodically so they could keep track of us. It occurred to me that the Germans were also able to keep track of us.

We were crossing out at Cayeux-sur-Mer at six thousand feet, and I thought his chances looked good. He might be able to get at least five or six miles past the coast before bailing out at a minimum of fifteen hundred feet. Just then the sky erupted in 20mm and 40mm flak, most of it zeroed in on Davis's crippled ship.

"Dumbo, Falcon Blue Leader. We're crossing out and

being shot at!" I was able to take evasive action, but he couldn't. I could see that he was taking heavy hits. His Mustang suddenly nosed over into a steep dive, then crashed and exploded on the beach. There was no parachute. I pulled into full-power climbing turns and left the flak behind. "Dumbo, Blue Leader here. Cancel the Mayday. Blue Two was shot down on the beach."

Another wingman lost—three in such a short time—and another young life snuffed out. Feelings of doubt, fear, sorrow, and even guilt whirled in my brain as I headed home. Was I becoming a jinx?

"That whole French coastline is one huge gun emplacement," said Mike Glantz at debriefing. "The Germans know the invasion's coming. They just don't know when or where."

Kinnard led another patrol the next morning, June 5, with his old friend Bert Marshall leading his second element. Bombers pounded the coastal gun emplacements again. Bert had joined the squadron just two days earlier, but in view of his flight experience, he needed no extended precombat training. The mission was uneventful. After we landed, a number of unusual activities indicated that the invasion was about to begin.

All afternoon and into the night, ground crews were busily painting large black and white stripes around the fuselage and wings of the fighters. We found out later that all Allied fighters—and even most of the medium bombers—were getting the same paint job to aid in recognition during the early phases of the assault. At 7:00 P.M., the group intelligence section was hosting a number of the local "wheels." First, Colonel Cummings arrived with a bulging brown envelope; then came the intelligence troops: Major Lewis, Captain Nicholson, and Captain Mason. A little later, the squadron commanders arrived, then Capt. Foggy Schmucker, the weather officer, and Capt. Bill Rush, the tower officer. It didn't take long for the rumor mill to put all the pieces together, but the biggest piece came when the

bars at the officers' club and the NCO club were closed at
7:00 P.M. Pilots were advised to go to bed and get some
sleep.

. I went to bed early that night. A few short hours later,
Mike was shaking me. "Briefing at midnight in the group
briefing room." It had to be D day.

The briefing room door was locked, and the large reading
room next to it was jammed with pilots. High-spirited chatter filled the room. As pilots filed in, they were greeted by
"This is it!" Major Rosenblatt arrived and called the roll—a
most unusual procedure that somehow injected a note of
gravity into the proceedings. Then the briefing door room
was unlocked and the pilots swarmed in, laughing and
jostling each other, exclaiming about the display on the
large mission map. It showed more than the usual information. Bold black and red arrows pointed to the landing areas,
labeled GOLD, JUNO, OMAHA, and UTAH.

At nine minutes after midnight, we were called to attention as Colonel Cummings strode to the stage.

He began quietly in his usual unhurried voice: "The general told me this afternoon that the biggest show in history
has started—namely the invasion of France." To give us an
idea of the scope of this operation, he read parts of the docu-
ments he was holding in his hand: ". . . a five-divisional
front fifty miles wide . . . four thousand transport and naval
vessels . . . five hundred B-26 bombers hit the beach area
from twelve thousand feet . . . three hundred C-47s with
gliders . . . one thousand RAF heavy bombers . . . Eighth
Air Force heavy bombers hitting beach targets . . . P-38s
over the shipping routes and beachhead. . . ."

He went on and on, smoothly and calmly, while we listened with intense concentration, reading the details of the
operation. He reminded us that we were about to take part in
a historic battle, and that we had an important role to play.
"We're going to do our part," he said, "and we're going to
do it well!"

"Only the 354th and 357th will fly the first mission,

taking off at 0230, but there will be at least three missions today, so you squadron commanders be sure to spread the experienced people around evenly."

Colonel Dix would be leading the first mission. "We'll be taking off at 0234," he said and smiled. "Yes, it's dark then. We'll fly a patrol pattern over an area behind the invasion beaches to make sure the Luftwaffe can't get near them. Other fighter groups will be doing the same thing all around us, and we'd better make damn sure we stay in our assigned area and at our assigned altitude. It could get real crowded up there."

"Do we keep our running lights on?" asked Kucheman.

"The runway lights will be on, and we'll keep our running lights on until we make landfall. After that you'll have to line yourself up on the flare of your leader's exhaust stack. But we'll be at twenty-five thousand feet, and it'll be getting light up there by the time we arrive."

Foggy Schmucker wasn't happy about the weather outlook. "As you approach the Channel and the Continent," he said, "you'll run into layered clouds all the way up to thirty thousand feet. You might be able to stay between layers, but I don't think you'll see much. You won't see the beach-heads on your way home, either."

After the weather and intelligence briefings, Colonel Cummings came back onstage. "On the way out this morning, you'll see the largest fleet in history in the Channel. We stay at our assigned altitude. The P-38s will be on the deck supporting the landings, because they're not likely to be mistaken for German aircraft."

"Just one more thing," he said with a slight smile. "If you have to bail out over that fleet, try to land on a ship that's heading back to England." We laughed, and the tension was broken.

I was scheduled to fly that mission, but when I got back to Gremlin Villa, my name wasn't on the board. "We're scheduled to fly three missions today," Major Kucheman explained, "and Group wants us to spread our experienced people around." He smiled at me. "You, Bud, are experienced. You're going on the next two."

I can't say that I was disappointed. I couldn't figure out what we would accomplish milling around southeast of Paris in semidarkness at twenty-five thousand feet. It seemed to me that if the Luftwaffe wanted to get into the action, it would use a more direct approach. Our next mission wasn't scheduled until afternoon, so I went back to bed and didn't even wake up when the Mustangs took off on schedule.

From Burt's narrative history: "Finally, in the darkness, they went to their planes. All of the ground personnel gathered at the hardstands and in front of the various buildings to watch the takeoff. The red and green lights glowed unwinkingly, and the sharp, high-pitched roar of the engines rolled across the quiet countryside. Clouds drooped low, but through a jagged wound a path of moonlight streamed to give an eerie touch to the scene."

I was back at the flight line for an 11:00 A.M. briefing. Ground crews were hanging 250-pound bombs on the wing shackles; this mission would be a bit more exciting than milling around between cloud layers southeast of Paris. Pilots who had flown the first mission reported that the assembly and climbout, which were accomplished in the dark, in and out of clouds, had been quite hairy. Foggy had called it right: They were between layers at twenty-five thousand feet. Daylight had come early at that altitude, and the rest of the mission was a boring, back-and-forth patrol. And they didn't see the beachheads on their way home. What they did see was lots of flak. Dick Cross picked up a few large holes in his tail section, but all returned safely.

Led by Colonel Cummings, sixteen 357th Mustangs took off as we were entering the briefing room. Eight of them carried two 250-pound bombs. Our second mission was an exact duplicate of theirs. Kinnard's Red Flight and my Yellow Flight carried 250-pound bombs. Our mission, simply stated, was "find suitable targets, bomb and strafe them."

We took off at 1:15 P.M. We crossed the Channel at twenty thousand feet. Through breaks in the clouds beneath us, we caught glimpses of the gigantic battle being waged below. Along the beaches and just inland, the signs of battle were plain. We could see columns of black smoke, bright orange flashes, the pattern of shells falling beyond the beachheads, shells fired by heavy cruisers a few miles out in the Channel, Ninth Air Force fighter-bombers swooping down on German defensive positions, and the beaches swarming with men and machines.

About ten miles beyond the battle lines, we dropped to about two thousand feet, looking for "targets of opportunity," as they were called: trains, trucks, railroad marshaling yards, and all military vehicles.

We were flying slightly behind and to the left of Red Flight, along a tree-lined road running north and south. Suddenly we were directly over a column of about twelve German tanks heading north. I pressed my mike button: "Falcon Leader from Yellow Leader. There's a bunch of tanks at nine o'clock!" There was no reply from Kinnard. I knew his hearing was deteriorating and I assumed that he hadn't heard me, but there was no time for further radio chatter.

Caught by surprise, the tanks scattered off the road into the wooded area on each side. A steep climbing turn put me in position for a bomb run.

I couldn't see the tanks as I started my dive, but they had to be in those woods, so I aimed at a spot just off the road and fired the guns as I approached. There was plenty of return fire from both sides of the road.

A five-second delay had been set into the fusing of the bombs, so I dove almost to treetop level before releasing both bombs. I pulled into a steep climbing turn and looked back. Twin geysers of red-orange flame sprouted from the woods, and a few seconds later I felt rather than heard the explosion.

My wingman's bombs hit on the other side of the road. Then the second element came in and dropped. One bomb hit the road, but the other three dropped in the woods. Thick black smoke poured from the woods, so I knew we had hit

some tanks. Occasional explosions still shook the trees, and
a few fires could be seen through the leaves. I looked around
for the rest of the squadron, but we were alone. Kinnard had
not heard my call. He and the rest of the squadron were
many miles south of us by now. Having done all the damage
we could do to the tanks, we went looking for targets to
strafe.

We found a freight train in a marshaling yard, blew up
the locomotive, and set fire to some of the boxcars. We were
getting shot at but couldn't see where it was coming from.
Low on ammunition, we headed home. We climbed to
twenty thousand feet before crossing the invasion area.

Through broken clouds we could see the huge number of
naval vessels engaged in the operation. As some reporter
later put it, "It looked as if you could walk across the
Channel, from ship to ship, and not get your feet wet."

We were back by three o'clock. Ground crews again
swarmed all over the planes, readying them for another mission. When I got back to Gremlin Villa, I found out that the
next mission was set for a 6:00 P.M. takeoff—time enough
for a quick nap on one of the ready-room cots.

Summer days are long in England. Even though we took
off in the evening, there was plenty of daylight left. We flew
over the beachheads at twenty thousand feet, high enough to
keep the troops below from getting nervous about us, then
down to the deck. A low-level patrol, without bombs this
time.

We found three trains and shot up the locomotives. We
were trying to stop the Germans from using any transportation—ground or air—in support of their troops in the invasion area.

We were flying at or below fifty feet, having a great time
watching French farmers and their families waving at us
and smiling. They knew, of course, that the invasion had begun, and they were cheering us on.

We climbed to about two thousand feet to have a better
look around. Almost immediately we spotted about twenty
Ju-87s, the infamous Stuka dive bombers, heading north

toward the beachheads at treetop level. We could hardly believe our luck.

Ju-87s were old and slow, with a crew of two: the pilot, and a rear gunner who had one machine gun (about .30-caliber), hardly a match for the Mustang and its four .50-caliber machine guns. The 357th Squadron also was in that area, eager to get in on the turkey shoot. Our biggest problem was avoiding collisions with other P-51s scrambling to get at the Stukas.

I got one in my gunsight and came straight up its tail. I could see the tracers from that rear machine gun sliding past me, but I wasn't the least bit concerned. It never occurred to me that I might get hit.

The Stuka pilot was trying desperately to get the plane on the ground and run for it. Others were trying the same thing. They were much too low to bail out.

I squeezed the trigger and heard and felt the hammering of the four .50s in the wings. Through the gunsight, I saw the API shells lighting up the fuselage of the Ju-87, then half a dozen hits around the tail section, which stopped the flow of tracers coming my way.

The Stuka hurtled to the ground, out of control, and crashed with a huge explosion as its bombs went off. All around me I could see other Stukas crashing and burning. A few managed to crash-land, and their crews raced for cover. None of those Ju-87s reached the beachheads.

Low on ammunition, we headed home. French farmers and their families were still outside watching and waving as we sped by just a few hundred feet over their heads.

The sun was setting as we arrived back at the base. By the time I landed, taxied to the dispersal area, and shut the engine down, it was dusk. A cool mist was beginning to blanket the peaceful English countryside. The ground crews clustered around the planes again, but there was no sense of urgency this time.

I looked around for transportation to the ready room but there was none, so I slung my parachute over my shoulder and started walking. The rest of my flight joined me. One of them, newly assigned, had flown all three missions that day and was dog-weary. "Long day!" he said to me. "Is it always like this?"

I couldn't resist. "No," I said. "Some days it gets rough."

Bert Marshall flew in the lead flight with Colonel Dix and got his first air victory when he nailed a Ju-87 on his second combat mission. "There were so many of us trying to get at those poor guys," he commented, "it's a wonder we didn't have a few collisions."

"Yeah," said Dix. "The guys storming those beaches wouldn't have been happy to see those Stukas, but we were delighted."

The 355th came through D day with claims of fifteen aircraft destroyed and considerable damage inflicted on enemy targets for the loss of two aircraft to flak—both from the 357th Fighter Squadron. One pilot was killed and the other taken prisoner.

Later that day we were stunned by the news that FW-190s had bounced the veteran 4th Fighter Group from above while it was in the middle of a strafing run. The 4th lost seven pilots, including two of its aces. Six were killed; one managed to evade. It was a stern reminder that we could not afford to get careless—ever.

After D day, June found us flying more bombing and strafing missions. Eighth Air Force fighters patrolled the areas surrounding the invasion beachhead. Our mission was to clobber anything that moved by road, rail, river, or air. German troops and supplies moved only during the brief hours of darkness. Ninth Air Force P-47s gave close tactical support to the ground troops and interdicted all enemy traffic closer to the front lines. The Luftwaffe made only sporadic attempts to break through the shield of Allied fighters, but few reached the beachhead. Allied airpower owned the skies.

The 358th Squadron flew the first strafing mission on June 7. They took off at 5:05 A.M., found a few targets and plenty of flak, and were back by 8:00 A.M.

The 357th Squadron took off on a bombing-strafing mission at 6:53 A.M. and had a rough day. They bombed and strafed a convoy and a train near Châteaudun. One pilot was hit by flak and bellied in, but managed to evade capture. Lieutenant Thomas Foster was killed when one of his bombs hit a freight car full of munitions. He was caught up in the huge explosion and crashed. A few miles away, about a dozen FW-190s caught Yellow Flight by surprise as they were strafing and shot down three Mustangs. Two of the pilots became POWs, and one was killed. The 357th had its worst day of the war.

The 354th Squadron took off at 9:30 A.M.—giving us a chance to catch up on some sleep—to patrol the Évreux area, about fifty miles northwest of Paris. Kinnard led the squadron, and I led Blue Flight. We shot up a few trucks and tanks; I was wishing we had brought a couple of bombs for those tanks. Our .50-caliber bullets were bouncing off them, and they were giving us plenty of return fire. I enjoyed flying low and fast, but not when a lot of people were shooting at me.

We had better luck with the trucks and a couple of freight trains in a marshaling yard at Évreux. There was plenty of flak there also, mostly the 20mm and 40mm variety. Lieutenant Bob Couture was hit and bailed out, but he evaded capture and returned to England within a month.

We were back shortly after noon. We had time for a leisurely lunch and a short rest before the next 354th mission, which was scheduled for takeoff at 5:20 P.M. Colonel Cummings led the squadron and I led Blue Flight again; Bert Marshall led my second element. For a change, we were escorting B-17s and B-24s attacking targets in the Angers–Tours area, about 160 miles southwest of Paris. There was no Luftwaffe reaction—just the usual flak. We landed at 9:30 P.M. in the middle of a rain squall that dropped the visibility to about half a mile.

"Landing in this kind of weather makes my ass pucker," said Bert on the way back to Gremlin Villa in Kinnard's jeep.

"Welcome to the club," I said.

I wasn't on the June 8 mission when the group visited the
Bordeaux–Poitiers area. While strafing a train, Lt. Col.
Gerald Dix's airplane was hit by flak. A few minutes later,
his coolant boiled over. He bailed out near Bordeaux and
was quickly captured. Flight Officer Edward Williams of
the 358th was hammered by flak but managed to get back to
the English coast. He was killed while attempting to crash-
land his severely damaged airplane.

The low-level, high-speed bombing and strafing missions
were exciting, but they were taking their toll in men and machines. The strain was beginning to show on a few faces.

The loss of Gerald Dix was a heavy blow to the group.
He had been with us since the beginning and was a well-
liked and respected leader. With Colonel Stewart home on
leave, there were vacancies to fill. Kinnard was moved upstairs to become the group executive officer, Kucheman assumed command of the 354th Squadron, and Bert Marshall
became the squadron operations officer.

Also on June 8, I became a captain, which accounts for
the fact that I didn't fly the next day—that and the fact the
weather was lousy and nobody else flew either. Just as
well—my head was hurting most of the morning.

On June 9 we received three more replacement pilots: 1st
Lts. Warren Schwab and Alvin White, and 2d Lt. James
Kilmer. As far as I knew, Al White was the only pilot in the
squadron, maybe the group, with an aeronautical engineering degree.

The 354th flew three missions on June 10. I was scheduled for the first one, but shortly after takeoff I found that
my radio was no longer working, so I had to return. I was
then scheduled for the third one. Two accidents, one minor
and one deadly, occurred while our planes were returning
from the first mission.

Lieutenant John Ellison, Perry's wingman, had brake
trouble on his landing roll, ran off Runway 22, and hit the
mobile control unit. He cleared the runway in time for Dick
Cross, the element leader, to land. No one was injured, and

a cletrac—a tractor-type vehicle used to tow airplanes—was dispatched from the tower area to the scene of Ellison's accident. The cletrac dashed across the taxiway directly in the path of Dick Cross's P-51 that was taxiing over a small rise in front of the tower. The men on the cletrac—Cpl. Everett Harvey and Cpl. Harold Spevak—were both killed instantly in the collision with the Mustang's whirling propeller. It was a sickening, blood-stained scene.

Dick was shaken to the core. Back in Gremlin Villa, he sat with his head in his hands, staring straight ahead blankly, and muttering over and over, "I'll never fly another airplane! So help me God, I'll never fly again!" Doc Fontenot gave him a few pills to calm him down. Major Kucheman, Bert Marshall, and I tried to talk to him, but he wasn't listening. After a while the pills took effect and he fell asleep on one of the cots.

We took off at 6:30 P.M. on the third mission of the day, eight Mustangs carrying two 250-pound bombs apiece. Kucheman led the squadron and I led the second flight. The target area was Rennes, and our objective was anything that deprived the Germans of the means of transportation—bridges, railroads, highways, and anything that moved along those conduits. The weather was terrible, as it had been for most of the month so far, but we found a break in the overcast and slipped down below the clouds. The visibility was limited and there seemed to be no worthwhile targets, but we finally found a railroad track and dropped our eggs on it, leaving a few craters for the Germans to repair before they could use it again. Low on fuel, we headed home. It was nearly 10:00 P.M. when we landed. Burt, Mike, and Doc were the reception committee. Everyone else was either in bed or at the bar.

"Burt! It's only four o'clock!" I muttered. "It's probably still dark outside!"

Burt opened the blackout curtain. "It's not dark outside! And you'll be taking off at 0620. And you're going on a bombing mission. Get up!"

"Do I look like a bomber pilot?"

"You don't look like *any* kind of pilot right now. Get up!"

Duff stirred in his bunk. "Why don't you guys shut up and let me get my beauty rest? And close that damn curtain!"

It was June 11. Briefing was at 5:00 A.M. Our Gremlin Villa snack bar had the usual Spam and eggs—fresh eggs, not the powdered kind featured at the officers' mess, thanks to enterprising noncoms who knew how to trade with the local farmers—and good, strong coffee, so we were all reasonably awake by then. I sat next to Silky Morris. Kinnard was leading the group again. "This time we'll be carrying two 500-pound bombs," he announced with a wide grin.

Silky leaned over to me and whispered, "Does he think those are B-17s out there?"

Almost as if he had heard that remark, Kinnard continued, "They're not even as heavy as the full 108-gallon fuel tanks we've been carrying, and they'll raise a lot more hell." The usual mission: Find targets that will do the most damage to the German transportation system in the Châteauroux area. The bombs had a five-second-delay fuse, presumably to keep us from blowing ourselves up.

The weather was more of the same—lots of clouds and lousy visibility underneath. Kinnard and his flight found a juicy target—a fuel storage area with six fat trucks in plain view. In very short order, that area was a flaming inferno. I found a long bridge and dropped both bombs on it. One of my bombs struck the bridge, but because of the delayed fusing, the bomb bounced and exploded a few feet above the road surface. The other bomb missed the bridge and exploded in the water beneath it. Two bombs from my flight managed to hit the bridge with the right timing and put a few gaping holes in it. We strafed a couple of barges, a transformer station, and a few freight cars, but poor visibility limited our activities. We didn't raise quite as much hell as Kinnard would have liked.

While we were away, Major Kucheman and Bert Marshall had a long talk with Dick Cross. Both were low-key but stern: That was a terrible tragedy, but he was not to blame himself. There was a war to win, and he was needed. At the end of the long session, Bert said, "I have two airplanes out there ready for us to fly. You and I are going to go up together. You'll fly my wing. Let's go!" Dick followed. After the flight, Kucheman said, "Now take a forty-eight-hour pass to London and go see a couple of plays, or whatever you do in London. And when you get back, you'll be on the schedule. Who would you like to have with you?" Dick and one of his friends left for London that afternoon.

On June 12 I drew the early mission again, taking off at 6:36 A.M. Each of the squadrons had a different area to patrol. Kucheman led our squadron, and I was Blue leader. It was a routine patrol in the Lille–Cambrai area—the kind of thing we had been doing all month—looking in vain for the Luftwaffe.

The second mission had us escorting B-26s, a different kind of assignment. Kinnard took his brand-new P-51D, *Man o' War,* on its maiden flight on this mission. The B-26s were fast, medium-altitude twin-engine bombers, so we didn't have to weave above or around them; we could cruise right along with them. They *did* attract a lot of flak at twelve thousand feet, but we took evasive action, and the bombers came through unscathed. We changed our group formation to prevent Luftwaffe attacks from above—one squadron was at twelve thousand feet, right with the B-26s; the second was at fourteen thousand feet; and the third was at twenty thousand feet.

There had been rumors of a "red hot" Me-109 group in the target area. The flight leaders' aircraft reportedly sported a bright yellow band around the nose. I was reminded of the same kind of rumors when we became operational. The "Abbeville Boys" with the yellow-nosed FW-190s were supposedly the top guns in the Luftwaffe. We never encountered any of them. This 109 group had bounced the 353d Fighter Group a few days earlier and shot down eight for the loss of three. The 353d commander, Colonel Glenn Duncan, led his group back to the area the next day and they knocked down nine of the "red hots" without loss. Knowing Colonel Duncan from my Buzz Boy experience, I could just imagine the pep talk he had given to his troops before that mission.

None of the "red hots" appeared. It was another milk run. The Luftwaffe seemed to be picking its fights carefully.

Five new pilots joined the 354th on July 12, all second lieutenants, raising our total number of assigned pilots to thirty-seven, not counting the five who were on leave in the States. The squadron now had plenty of pilots but not much experience. All the incoming pilots came from operational training units, where they learned some of the tactical skills they would need. The rest of what they needed to know would come only on combat missions.

The Luftwaffe was facing a serious shortage of experienced pilots. Many of their veteran leaders had been killed, and the flight schools were hard-pressed to produce trained replacements. Some replacements reported to Luftwaffe units right out of flying school, with no operational training at all.

Oft-bombed German aircraft factories were desperately striving to produce enough fighter aircraft to replace those lost in the air and on the ground. Our factories were sending us an increasing number of improved versions of fighters and bombers.

We had high-powered visitors on July 13: General George C. Marshall, Army chief of staff; General Henry H. (Hap) Arnold, chief of the Army Air Forces; Lieutenant General James H. Doolittle, commander of the Eighth Air Force; Major General William Kepner, commander of VIII Fighter Command; and Brigadier General Jesse Auton, commander of the 65th Fighter Wing.

"That's our whole chain of command," noted Mike Glantz, "right from the top!"

There was no advance warning of their visit; Colonel Cummings was advised after lunch to expect them in two hours. There was time to do a quick clean-up job, park four shiny new P-51Ds in front of the control tower, set up the usual dinghy display—this time featuring our own Bill Martin buttoned in the fully inflated dinghy with sail hoisted—and alert the photo lab to have the gun-camera show ready. The photo lab kept a file of the group's best combat films just for this purpose. The visitors arrived at 4:30 P.M. with about a dozen staff people. By then we all looked as if we were doing something constructive.

General Marshall found the dinghy display quite interesting. "Do you have rations in there?" he asked Bill.

"Yes, sir!" replied Bill as he fumbled around beneath the dinghy canopy, trying to locate the package, his face getting redder and redder. Finally he said with a groan, "I can't find the goddamn thing!"

"Never mind," said Marshall with a smile, as Arnold tried to keep from laughing out loud.

They trooped into the briefing room in time for the briefing for our second mission, on which I was scheduled. They had to sit through ten minutes of combat film first. I wondered if they had to see combat films at every fighter base they visited. If so, it must have seemed like they were seeing the same film over and over again.

Kinnard conducted the briefing and did a professional job. He didn't refer to "our people" or "those potatoes" or "our folks" even once. I sat there thinking the visitors would have preferred his usual style. At the conclusion of the briefing, General Arnold spoke a few words of encouragement, then said, "I wish the chief of staff would get up here and say something, so you could at least get a look at him."

General Marshall smiled and came onstage. He spoke briefly about how the armed forces had grown from "the ragged edge of nothing" to the powerful force that was preparing to destroy our enemies throughout the world. He then reminisced about his role in World War I, in the same area we were to fly over today. We were all more than a bit awed by these legendary figures.

The visiting dignitaries left in a light rain at 6:30 P.M., just before we taxied out.

We were to patrol the Rouen–Beauvais area under Type 16 Radar Control. Because the Luftwaffe had been bouncing outfits lately from very high altitudes, Kinnard directed that the 354th, with Kucheman leading, would be at twenty-two thousand feet; the 357th at twenty-four thousand feet; and the 358th at twenty-six thousand feet or higher if clouds permitted.

We formed up between layers at five thousand feet, and from that point we didn't see the ground for three hours. We were above the clouds or between layers as our radar controller—call sign Snackbar—vectored us from one phantom gaggle to another. We had no idea where we were until Snackbar released us from control and gave us a heading home. We broke out of the clouds five minutes later and saw that we were over the large islands southwest of Rotterdam, far to the northeast of our assigned area. "Snackbar," an unidentified voice called, "is this your first day on the job?" There was no response.

Amazingly, the weather on our arrival was excellent—ceiling and visibility unlimited.

June 13 marked the first appearance over London of the German V-1 pilotless bombs. The "V" was from the German *Vergeltungswaffen* (vengeance weapon). Hitler assured his field marshals that the V-1 would soon have a decisive effect on the war. His generals begged him to use it against the invasion beaches or the invasion ports in the south of England, but he decreed that the bombs be concentrated on London to "convert the English to peace."

The V-1 was a flying bomb. It had short, stubby wings, was powered by a pulse-jet engine, and it carried a two-thousand-pound warhead. It flew at low altitudes—usually below twenty-five hundred feet—and its top speed was about four hundred miles per hour. The jet engine made a pulsing, buzzing noise—hence the nickname "buzz bomb." They were launched in the general direction of London, with just enough fuel to get there. When the fuel ran out, the engine stopped, the V-1 dove into the city, and the bomb exploded on impact. RAF fighters were able to intercept and shoot down a few along the way, but this was no cause for celebration for the people living along "buzz-bomb alley" below—the bombs still exploded on contact.

Captain Mike Glantz banged on my door next morning and barged in. "Rise and shine! Briefing at 0515!"

"C'mon, Mike, you guys are pickin' on me! I'm not scheduled today, am I?"

"You are not only scheduled, Captain, you are leading the squadron!"

That woke me up. I wasn't sure he was serious until I saw the schedule at Gremlin Villa. There it was, Captain Fortier leading. It wasn't the first time I led the squadron, but the first time I was *scheduled* to lead.

Lieutenant Colonel Ray Myers, commander of the 358th, led the group. For a welcome change, the weather was fine. We were assigned to patrol an area near Paris while the bombers plastered a number of airfields from Twente-Enschede in Holland to Le Bourget, just outside the French capital. There were patchy clouds in our patrol area and plenty of flak from the Paris batteries, but the mission was just another ho-hummer.

Jim Duffy and Rich Brown finally left for their thirty-day R&R leave on June 15. After waiting nearly three weeks, they were given a one-hour notice to be ready to depart via courier plane that would take them to Prestwick, Scotland. They made it.

The next three days featured grinding milk runs. The Luftwaffe was showing up now and then, but not where we were.

The mission on June 18 indicated that we were getting back to our normal routine. We were to escort bombers to Hannover, our first incursion of Germany in nearly a month. It was another of those "briefing at 0515" wake-up calls that had been all too common lately. Kinnard led the group and our squadron; I led his second element. We were to rendezvous with the bombers near Bremen, take them to the target and back "to the limit of endurance." While we were still climbing over the North Sea, we got a message from the bombers, via the bomber/fighter intercom C channel, saying that their feet were dry, meaning they were already over land. Since they were approaching the rendezvous point from the north, that would mean they were way ahead of schedule and were flying unescorted.

Kinnard ordered the group to drop tanks and "pour the coal on" to get to the bombers quickly. It later developed that the message had either been erroneous in the first place or had been misunderstood. The bombers were not over land at the time, and we were way too early at the rendezvous point. Kinnard told the other two squadrons to wait for the assigned bombers while the 354th picked up three boxes of unescorted B-17s at Cuxhaven and took them to Hamburg.

The Continent was completely covered with clouds. No German fighters appeared, but there was the usual heavy flak over the cities.

When I entered Gremlin Villa after the mission, Doc Fontenot said, "Bud, I'm sending you to the Flak Home."

"Why now, Doc? I only need a few more missions to finish my tour." The number of hours in a combat tour had risen to three hundred.

"I just got news of one opening there this week. And you need it. You'll even get a nice, comfortable jeep ride to the place in the morning."

There was no arguing with the flight surgeon. Besides, I was looking forward to a week away from the war—in the quiet English countryside. The rest of my combat tour could wait.

The Flak Home was a rambling old estate almost hidden in a peaceful valley a few miles outside of Exeter, in southwestern England. Flight crews could unwind in the informal and distinctly unmilitary atmosphere—no uniforms, no rank, and no shoptalk about the war. For those without civilian clothing, an assortment of informal attire was available in most sizes; and if it didn't fit, no one cared. Aircraft were seldom seen or heard. For one week, the war ceased to exist.

The kitchen and housekeeping staff lived in a small cottage on the estate grounds. The hostess was a pleasant, attractive young lady in her midtwenties. Her function was to arrange fishing trips, rounds of golf, horseback riding, and any other activity (within reason) for the temporary residents of the estate. She lived in an apartment above a small pub about a mile down the road and worked at the estate every morning. "Come knock me up sometime," she'd say, then laugh when she saw the expression on our faces. "Around here, that means come visit me—come knock on my door."

Most residents just lazed around the estate, reading, or playing chess or checkers or snooker—the English version of billiards—or card games. The first two days, the rain and fog discouraged outdoor activities. The rest of the week was warm and sunny. Some went fishing or horseback riding. I played a little tennis, a round of golf, and a lot of chess; and I read a few books. I visited the pub down the road, but I didn't knock up the hostess. It was a pleasant, relaxing hiatus from combat.

I was back at Steeple on Monday, June 26, and found myself scheduled for the next day's mission. While I was away, the squadron had a great day on June 20, knocking down eleven and damaging two. Bert Marshall demonstrated his skill as he picked off a 109 that had already put about a dozen holes in Clarence Graham's Mustang, then did the same thing to another 109 on Gil Wright's tail. Characteristically, Bert said it was "pure luck." In his halfdozen missions he had already shot down three German aircraft.

On June 24 the 354th and 357th squadrons returned to a well-camouflaged grass airfield that had been spotted the

day before near Angers, France. After systematically silencing the airfield's antiaircraft defenses, they destroyed
twenty-nine aircraft on the ground with no losses.

The mission on June 27 had a few strange turns in it. All
twelve ships in each squadron would be carrying two 250-
pound bombs, so there was no high cover. The mission was
first to patrol the area just west of Laon, under radar control,
then travel up the rail line running northeast from Laon to
Hirson, looking for targets to bomb. Soft-spoken Jim Austin
murmured to me, "Isn't that bass-ackward? Shouldn't we
bomb first?" I agreed it looked that way. Major Rosenblatt,
group operations officer, led the group with the 357th
Squadron; I was leading the 354th, and Jim was leading
Blue Flight in our squadron.

The patrol proceeded without incident until Snackbar directed Uncle to send a flight east of Paris to escort two
straggling bombers in need of protection. That surprised
me. Why would Snackbar call for only one flight? Then another surprise: "Uncle here. Falcon Blue Flight, drop bombs
on the airfield right below us, then go help the stragglers."

I almost broke in with, "Why don't you send one of your
own flights?" but knew I couldn't win that one. I was frustrated. Something about this situation didn't feel right, but I
was not in a position to countermand Uncle's decision.

Jim's flight streaked down in trail formation and dropped
their bombs on the airfield. One bomb exploded on a runway; the others in a nearby dispersal area. There didn't appear to be any aircraft on the field. Jim started to climb, and
the rest of the flight was trying to catch up. At that point
Uncle announced that we were heading up the railroad line
to look for targets.

As we headed northeast, Austin's flight was still trying to
get together. Jim was circling at ten thousand feet, and the
other three, still widely scattered, were climbing to meet
him. Jim started a right turn to head toward Paris, slowing
down to let the rest of the flight catch up. As he swung
around a large cloud, about twenty aircraft came streaming

toward him from about two thousand feet above. "Falcon Blue Leader from Blue Three. Bogeys at nine o'clock high!"

"I see them," said Jim. "Look like Spitfires."

"They don't have invasion stripes! And they're coming right at us!" an unidentified voice called out. The Spitfires turned out to be Me-109s.

Blue Flight, greatly outnumbered and still far apart, was in no position to put up any organized resistance. It was every man for himself. Austin racked around in a tight left turn. Hulderman split-essed for the deck. Folger tried to out-turn them but wound up with nine of them on his tail, so he ducked into the nearest cloud. Ruark was seen trying to out-climb them; he was jamming the radio channel with "Falcon Blue Leader . . . Falcon Blue 2! Falcon Blue Leader . . . Falcon Blue 2!" He kept transmitting that—and nothing else—and thereby jammed the channel, so no one else could transmit. Suddenly his transmission stopped and nothing was heard from him from that point. It was later determined that he bailed out and evaded capture.

The rest of Blue Flight straggled back to England.

In the meantime, we had dropped down to two thousand feet and were bombing the railroad track, concentrating on intersections with major highways. We managed to cut the track at several places but also inadvertently planted a few bombs in various cornfields.

There was some lively discussion of this mission back at Gremlin Villa. Major Kucheman, without placing the blame on anyone, pointed out that it would have been better to re-form Blue Flight immediately after the bombing, rather than try to do it on the way to the straggling bombers. Then there was a discussion about the wisdom of sending one flight into an area known to contain significant forces of German fighters. "Maybe that transmission wasn't Snackbar at all," suggested Austin. "Could it possibly have been the Germans transmitting those directions?"

"Yeah!" agreed Gil Wright. "Like that message we got a few missions ago about the bombers being way ahead of schedule. That turned out to be phony." Our misgivings about that decision were relayed to Group headquarters and to Snackbar.

Speed Hubbard came by Steeple Morden for a visit on June 29, after evading through the occupied countries to Spain. Since he had knowledge of the Underground pipeline, he was barred from further combat in the ETO, and was on his way back to the States. There had been much speculation about how his engine came loose when he bailed out on November 13—speculation that German fighters were in the area and may have caused the damage—but he cleared it all up. He was hit by flak around the engine before it dropped out—no fighters.

He recognized me and came over to shake hands. "Done any barrel rolls lately?" he asked with a grin. He had been the only one in the chain of command at Philly to put in a good word for me.

The V-1 attacks on London continued unabated. Though wildly inaccurate (an estimated 57 percent reached the target), these two-thousand-pound flying bombs were destroying and damaging thousands of houses a day in the Greater London area. There was mounting political pressure on the military to "put a stop to this." Easier said than done: The V-1s were launched from short catapults that were hard to find from the air, and they were heavily defended with anti-aircraft guns.

A couple of milk runs closed out June, our busiest month to date. The group flew forty-four missions. I flew fifteen of them, even with a week off.

July 1944

"Just a year ago today," said Burt on July 1, "we were waving good-bye to Miss Liberty in New York Harbor."

"Yeah, and we thought we'd be home by Christmas," I said.

"Well, it might be over by this Christmas."

"It doesn't look like it right now."

By the end of June, the Allied armies in the invasion area had linked up but were making slow progress moving inland. The expansion was insufficient to make room for Patton's Third Army, which was still waiting in England. The British and the Canadians were at a standstill outside Caen, one of the key D day objectives; they were unable to move in the face of overwhelming German tank forces. The Americans were mired in the so-called hedgerow war, taking heavy casualties but gaining little ground. Fighting through thick hedgerows against determined defenders had not been part of the GIs' training, and they were slow in developing successful tactics.

The weather was terrible on this first day of July, and the scheduled mission was scrubbed shortly after takeoff. The next day, three task forces of heavy bombers pounded the V-1 launch sites in the Pas-de-Calais area. We provided area support, but the Luftwaffe pilots were taking Sunday off. The bombers took heavy doses of flak; I saw two going down in flames and three others headed for England trailing smoke.

July 3 featured heavy, sustained, almost tropical rain. A scheduled mission was abandoned in midmorning. "Good thing," said Burt. "You'd have had to paddle out to the airplanes in your dinghies."

The Fourth of July. No flag-waving. No bands playing. No parades. Just Mike Glantz and Burt Sims racing through the pilot quarters shortly after 4:00 A.M. announcing that the briefing was at four-thirty. The panic was on. We managed to get there by four-thirty and then had to wait until four fifty-five before the briefing began. "Why do they do this to us?" I asked Burt. He shrugged.

It was just an escort job, taking the Big Friends to a dot on the map called Gien, about seventy-five miles south of Paris, so they could destroy a couple of railroad bridges. We were to pick up the bombers a few miles northeast of Caen, then escort them all around. It didn't quite happen that way.

Cummings led the group with our squadron, I was to his left with Yellow Flight, Ralph Schutt was leading Blue Flight on the other side of Cummings, and Silky Morris led Green Flight to Ralph's right. We were in our loose combat formation, weaving above the bomber stream. I saw Paris ahead and thought that Colonel Cummings was cutting it a bit close—Paris had quite a few flak batteries. As if he read my mind, he started a slow starboard turn.

"Uncle, this is Falcon Green leader. Bogeys coming at us at seven o'clock!" I swiveled my head around and saw a large group of fighters coming right at us at our altitude. I started to break into them.

"They're P-47s! Don't shoot!" an unidentified voice warned.

In a very few seconds the Jugs—in a loose combat formation also—were whistling through our formation. Planes were going every which way, trying to avoid collisions. My left turn into the P-47 formation had put me over the outskirts of Paris, and heavy flak was blossoming all around, adding to the confusion.

When things settled down, our squadron was scattered all over the area. I couldn't find Cummings and his flight.

Ralph Schutt, leading Blue Flight, joined me; Silky Morris found himself alone with his flight.

I found the bomber stream and latched onto a box of bombers with my two flights. Cummings and Morris each found a bomber box to escort, though we did not see each other until we got back to Steeple. Clouds hid the target area, and I couldn't tell if the bombers dropped their bombs. We escorted them back to the English Channel without incident.

It was just another milk run, made much more exciting by a bunch of Jugs.

By July 1 we had pretty much gone back to our routine of escort duty for the Eighth Air Force heavy bombers, but every now and then we were given area patrol and interdiction missions to help the ground troops. Such was the case on July 8, when we were assigned to patrol the area between Provins and Montmirail, about forty miles east-southeast of Paris. Our job, as usual, was to hit everything that moved and some things that were parked. We shot up a locomotive a little south of Montmirail but left the passenger cars intact because there was no indication that this was a troop train.

"Uncle, this is Custard Blue Four. There's a bunch of airplanes parked at the edge of the woods near that open field!" Kucheman, who was leading the group, couldn't see the planes, nor could anyone else in our squadron, so he told the 357th to look. They reported about thirty planes, carefully camouflaged, among the trees surrounding a large open field. They made two firing passes, then Kucheman told them to fly top cover for the other two squadrons. This didn't sit well with the 357th, but they had no choice. They circled above us as we set up a traffic pattern and proceeded to destroy airplanes.

On my first pass I couldn't see anything in that wooded area. The airplanes were indeed well camouflaged, practically covered with leafy branches. On my second pass I shot at a single-engine plane, probably an Me-109. I saw a number of hits, but it didn't burn. On my third pass I lined up on another single-engine aircraft and bored in, firing all the way. I saw hits around the cockpit area and wings, then noticed that the number of hits suddenly increased dramatically. Out of the corner of my eye I saw a P-51 fewer than a hundred feet to my left and sliding toward me, firing away. I realized that this guy was shooting at the same airplane I was, and we were on a collision course. I broke away to my right just as the camouflaged airplane exploded and burned. The other pilot saw me at nearly the same time and broke to his left. I noted his identification letters: WR-O.

I didn't see any flak, but one of the 358th pilots crashed into some trees after he had made his pass, and his plane blew up. There must have been some machine-gun fire coming from those woods, but no 20mm stuff.

After three passes, Kucheman called for us to regroup, and we headed home. When we got back, he caught a lot of flak from the 357th pilots. "We saw those airplanes first!" they griped, "and you made us fly top cover while you shot them all up!"

Kucheman maintained that he had called the 357th off because some of them had turned left after the first pass and others had turned right, setting up a likely midair collision or two. He also said he had intended to tell the 357th to "mop up" after we made three passes, but his radio had failed. The 357th pilots were not convinced. "You didn't have any trouble calling the homing station for a steer!" they reminded him. They were steaming!

The pilot of WR-O was Dick Cross. We talked it over and decided that we'd share credit for that one.

The bombers pounded the V-1 launch areas again on July 9 while we provided area support in case the Luftwaffe showed up. The V-1 launch pads were short, heavy steel catapults, widely scattered, and well camouflaged. Saturation bombing of the entire area was the only option for the heavy bombers. The flak was heavy and accurate, and the bombers, flying lower than their usual bombing altitude of twenty-five thousand feet, paid a heavy price.

V-1s rained down on London day and night, sometimes more than one every hour. Hundreds of barrage balloons, held in place by strong steel cables, floated about three thousand feet above the city. Originally deployed to discourage low-level attacks by the Luftwaffe, they were no help against the V-1s. Whenever one hit a steel cable anchoring the balloon, it crashed into the city and exploded on contact. Antiaircraft guns and RAF fighters shot down some of them, but that often meant that the V-1 damaged some other community. Ninth Air Force medium bombers and fighters, responding to political pressure to "do something" about the attacks, were taking heavy losses trying to destroy the launch platforms.

Billy Hovde, the first pilot in the group to earn a thirty-day R&R leave to the States, returned on July 10 and took command of the 358th. Billy was a likable gung-ho West Pointer who had joined us at Philadelphia. He was warmly greeted on his return to the group.

More than a thousand bombers headed for Munich on July 11 to bomb industrial targets. We took off with a full fuel load, including two 108-gallon external wing tanks. We were to make landfall at Gravelines, about halfway between Dunkerque and Calais; sweep down to Verdun; then pick up our escort chores with the last task force of B-17s at Strasbourg. Kucheman was leading the group with our squadron; I was leading the eight-ship Blue Section. In view of recent Luftwaffe reactions, we expected a warm reception and a busy day.

As we approached Gravelines, Kucheman's receiver went out. "Falcon Blue Leader, waggle your wings if you read me." His transmitter was fine. I waggled my wings. "Okay, Bud," he said, "I'm returning to base. You take the lead of the squadron and the group. Have fun!" He peeled up and away toward England. Bert Marshall took over Kucheman's flight; Floyd Taylor, the spare, filled in. Bert became Blue leader, and my flight was now Red Flight.

Suddenly I was Uncle! For the first time, I was leading the whole group of forty-eight Mustangs, and I had mixed feelings that I didn't have time to analyze. A thick cloud cover made map-reading impossible, so I set course on a southeasterly heading for Verdun. Time-and-distance navigation was the only available option. The radio was silent, and there seemed to be no one in the huge, empty sky besides us. I had written the headings and times on the back of my hand at the briefing, as had all the other pilots, and I was hoping I had copied correctly.

Over Verdun—I hoped—I turned about twenty degrees left to the compass heading to Strasbourg. We were at twenty-nine thousand feet, and clouds seemed to cover the entire Continent below us; there was not a break to be seen. We droned on.

Suddenly I saw contrails dead ahead—heavy contrails, the kind that a bomber stream leaves in its wake. As we overtook them, the bombers came into view, with fighters weaving all around them. I couldn't believe my luck. I had found our bomber task force, just as if I knew what I was doing. I was elated.

The escorting fighters checked us out, then headed home as we took up our assigned positions. Strasbourg put up a little flak, but none of the bombers appeared to be in trouble, and we were above them.

Munich, though, was a different story. From the initial point to the target, the bombers plowed through heavy, intense, and accurate flak. We stayed above and to the sides of the bomber stream, knowing that German fighters would not attack through such a heavy flak barrage. The flak batteries didn't entirely ignore us; we had a few close calls, but no one was hit. The bombers dropped their eggs through the overcast.

Our C channel pilot (who maintained contact with the bombers and relayed information to us) reported several bombers in distress. One had three engines out, one B-24 in the target area had two engines shot out, and one B-17 was seen heading across Lake Constance toward Switzerland with one engine feathered and another trailing smoke. At least two were seen going down in the target area. There were no German fighters in the area, and we were frustrated by our inability to help.

Once we left the Munich area, the flak stopped and the bombers headed back toward Strasbourg. We kept a close watch on stragglers trying to keep up on three engines or with parts of wings or tails shot off, but no enemy fighters appeared. At Strasbourg the 479th Fighter Group came in and took over our escort duties, and we headed home.

We crossed out just northeast of Calais; we could tell by the flak blossoming just to the left of our formation. The weather over England was no better, so we took spacing for our instrument approach to Steeple and landed without further incident.

It turned out to be a milk run, except for John Folger and Floyd Tremberth, who had drawn the radio-relay assignment. When they became separated in thick clouds, the controller told them to find their way home. Floyd let down through the clouds and broke out of the overcast just above the barrage balloons over London. He jammed the throttle to the firewall and started a 180-degree climbing turn to avoid the balloons. He was back in the overcast, his gyro instruments tumbled, and he became totally disoriented. He knew he was in an uncontrolled spin, so he bailed out. He landed in a potato patch just outside of London. His P-51 crashed in an open field north of the city.

Back at Gremlin Villa, Bert Marshall patted me on the back. "Nice job, Bud," he said. I smiled. I didn't dare speak—I was afraid my voice would crack.

Later that evening, Major Kucheman called a meeting of pilots to explain the activity we had noticed at Steeple Morden, the apparent training of pilots in AT-6s and their transition into brand-new P-51Ds with a streamlined canopy and six machine guns. Kinnard had already latched on to one of those. He declared it his own *Man o' War* and found no one to dispute his claim.

All this activity had to do with the formation of a new fighter unit that included experienced bomber pilots who had completed their tours of combat duty. The Scouting Force, as it was named, would consist of formations of four or eight Mustangs to precede the bomber strike force, report on weather conditions and possible enemy activity in the target area, and recommend alternate targets when necessary. The scouting force was looking for "some damn good fighter pilots" to fly with the converted bomber pilots until they became thoroughly competent.

"Are you interested, Bud?" Kucheman asked me with a big smile.

"No, thanks!" I replied with a smile of my own. "I've done enough volunteering for one tour."

Lieutenants Carl Hull, Sumner Williams, and James Kilmer expressed an interest in joining such a group. It was still in the experimental stage, but it had the backing of higher headquarters.

The Scouting Force was the brainchild of two people: Col. Budd J. Peaslee, commander of the 384th Bomb Group, and Lt. Col. John A. Brooks, a staff officer at Eighth Air Force headquarters. Each had completed a combat tour in heavy bombers and was looking for an answer to one of the more vexing problems facing bomber crews—inaccurate weather information at the target area and en route. One early proposal envisioned sending a lone bomber ahead of the strike force to report on weather conditions and possible Luftwaffe activity, but that option was quickly ruled out because a lone bomber could easily be shot down.

Next, the RAF twin-engine Mosquito was considered. It was fast, but there were questions about its vulnerability and availability. Assigning the mission to a fighter group also was rejected because fighter pilots were not familiar with bomber operations. Thunderbolts didn't have enough range at that time, so it came down to the Mustang.

One obvious problem was that Mustang pilots were not familiar with bomber formations and tactics. Bomber pilots could be taught to fly the Mustang, but training them to become combat-ready fighter pilots would take time. The solution: Train certain experienced bomber pilots who had flown a combat tour in heavy bombers to lead the P-51 flights, and fill out the flights with experienced fighter pilots.

In June 1944 Colonel Peaslee was given the task of activating and training the Scouting Force (Experimental) at Steeple Morden. He selected his scout pilots from volunteer bomber pilots who had completed their combat tours. The fighter pilots were selected volunteers from various fighter groups throughout the Eighth Air Force. The bomber pilots flew twenty hours in the 355th Fighter Group AT-6 trainer, then at least twenty hours in Mustangs before they were considered ready.

On July 16 the Scouting Force, led by Colonel Peaslee, flew its first mission—flying ahead of a bomber attack on Munich. The experiment was a success; the Scouting Force flew thirty-five missions in the next two months.

Scouting Force pilots flew brand-new P-51Ds drawn from 355th Fighter Group resources. Fighter pilots were on detached service to the Scouting Force, and assigned to the 355th Fighter Group for administrative and subsistence purposes. Maintenance support, including mechanics and armament personnel, also was drawn from 355th resources. Scouting Force Mustangs retained the 355th squadron letter designations (WR-A, OS-B, etc.) but added a black horizontal bar above the letters.

In September 1944 the three bomb divisions were redesignated air divisions, and each air division acquired a fighter wing. Peaslee's scouting force had been working with the 1st Bomb Division, so it moved to Honington, because Steeple Morden was now in the 2d Air Division. Lieutenant Colonel John Brooks was assigned to activate and train the 2d Scouting Force at Steeple Morden, drawing fighter pilot volunteers from the 65th Fighter Wing.

The 2d Scouting Force flew the first of its 136 missions on September 26, with eight Mustangs led by Maj. Frank Elliott. Their primary mission was weather reconnaissance,

preceding the bombers by about thirty minutes. They also provided bomb-damage assessments, secondary-target information, and even engaged German fighters when necessary.

The 2d Scouting Force was a small unit—only twenty-
eight men, including twelve fighter pilots, ten bomber pilots, and six enlisted men—but it contributed significantly
to bomber effectiveness and to our role as escorts.

On July 14 we received six more replacement pilots:
Capt. Norman McDonald from Training Command, 1st Lts.
Herbert Mann and Thomas Wood, and 2d Lts. Charles
Hauver, Peter Sawchuk, and Joseph Horvath. For a pleasant
change, we had plenty of pilots, all of them eager to mix it
up with the Krauts and get a few victories. The Luftwaffe
had a different problem. The number of pilots and airplanes
dwindled daily, and severe fuel shortages limited training
and the number of sorties they could launch.

Ground fog shrouded the airfield as we entered the briefing room at 5:30 A.M. on July 16. The target was Munich
again. Kinnard was leading the group with our squadron; I
was leading Blue Flight. We were to rendezvous with second
task force B-17s just west of Brussels and escort them to
Munich. When the 339th Fighter Group joined us, we were
to drop back and escort the four rear boxes to the limit of endurance.

Takeoff was scheduled for 6:54 A.M., but the fog delayed
us until seven twenty-two. By then our mission had
changed. We were now to escort the four rear boxes of the
first task force, all of which was quite confusing. I hoped
Kinnard knew what we were supposed to be doing.

The weather was great over England but not over the
Continent. We were climbing through twenty thousand feet
when Kinnard reported that his ears were giving him plenty
of grief and he had to return to base. He told me to take over
the squadron and the group. Bert Marshall took over
Kinnard's flight and became Blue Flight, and I took over the
squadron and became Red Flight.

Déjà vu! I was Uncle again, but this time I wasn't quite sure what we were expected to do. The writing on the back of my hand told me what the original plan was, but it had no information about the changes that had been given to Kinnard. I headed for Brussels.

When I spotted 2d Air Division B-24s south of Brussels, I remembered they were part of the *third* task force—also headed for targets in the Munich area. I headed east to try to catch the B-17 task forces. About ten minutes later, the heavy contrails again showed where the main bomber stream was, and I set course to intercept them. I caught up with the B-17s near Luxembourg. There were eleven boxes of them—the first and second task forces were intermingled—stacked down from twenty-nine thousand feet. No other escort fighters were in sight. The bombers were flying a southeasterly course toward Munich.

I told the other two squadrons to follow in a loose trail formation and began weaving toward the lead boxes far ahead. I caught up with the front of the train just as the lead bombers started a right turn to a northwesterly heading. Clouds towering to at least thirty-five thousand feet had walled off Munich, so the bombers were now heading northwest to their secondary target: Mannheim.

Since there was no sign of the 339th or any other escort fighters, we stayed with the B-17s as they bombed what we believed to be Mannheim through the clouds.

Except for plenty of flak along the way, it was just another long milk run.

Back at Gremlin Villa, Bert Marshall said, "You did it again, Bud!"

"Next time, you can be Uncle!" I replied. "It's tough on my nerves."

After the fog lifted, for the first time in a long while, the weather at Steeple was summerlike. Some of the newly assigned pilots took advantage of that to go up on training missions in the afternoon. As he peeled off over the field for landing, Lieutenant Sawchuck was caught in someone's prop-wash and skidded directly in front of Captain McDonald's

Mustang. McDonald's wingtip broke off as it tore part of the rudder from Sawchuck's plane. Both managed to land safely, but it was a close call.

The next day, July 17, I led the 354th and followed Captain Billy Hovde, who was leading the group, to the Orléans–Auxerre area, where we watched the bombers destroy bridges and railroad marshaling yards. There was plenty of flak but no Luftwaffe. That afternoon, eager-beaver Hovde led another mission to watch the bombers saturate the Pas-de-Calais area, hoping to knock out some of the V-1 launch sites. I didn't go with him this time. Again, there was plenty of flak but no Luftwaffe.

On July 18 the group escorted bombers to Peenemünde—without my services. The mission was uneventful, except for Lt. Fred Johnston, whose engine quit over the North Sea. He bailed out and became the group's first Air/Sea Rescue customer.

July 20. "We'll see some of those potatoes today for sure!" said Kinnard in his inimitable Tennessee drawl. He jabbed the pointer at Munich. "They'll be coming from here," then jabbing at Leipzig, "and from here. Let's nail 'em!" The B-17s were hammering targets around Munich. Kinnard led the group with the 357th, but his wingman, Dick Cross, was from our squadron. I led the 354th.

Right after takeoff, Dick's right wing tank started streaming fuel from a broken glass elbow. He circled the field and told the control tower to have the 354th get another plane ready for him. As soon as everyone had taken off, he landed, raced to the plane that had been readied for him, and took off. He caught up with the group just as it crossed into Germany, and resumed his position on Kinnard's wing. He had come a long way since his ill-starred accident.

Ten miles east of Leipzig, we caught up with the head of the bomber task force. The bombers were at twenty-five thousand feet, the 358th was high and to the north of them, the 357th was slightly ahead of them, and we were at our assigned position to the south of them at twenty-six thousand feet. "Uncle from Bentley Leader. A bunch of 'em coming in fast from eight o'clock high! We dropped tanks and racked around in time to see about fifty 109s slashing through the 358th and into the bombers. The 358th pilots managed to block some of them, and they shot down three, but there were just too many. Roughly half of the 109s got through to the bombers and shot down eight, then dove for the cloud deck. We were too far away to help.

"Falcon Leader, this is Blue Leader. Looks like a bunch of bandits at eight o'clock low." I turned left and saw about a dozen fighters swarming around a couple of stragglers below the main bomber stream.

"Let's get 'em!" At full power, I racked my Mustang into a diving turn and raced for the stragglers. The fighters were Me-109s, and when they saw us coming, they split-essed for the clouds. All but one. He had just finished a firing pass at a lone B-17 with heavy smoke trailing behind it. Before I could get to the 109, the B-17 blew up. Nothing was left but a large area of dense black smoke.

I was about eight hundred yards away when the German pilot saw me coming. He turned sharply toward me, and led me through a number of aerobatic routines, but I stayed right on his tail, gaining on him all the while. When he straightened out to dive away, I was about two hundred yards behind him, and he was in my gunsight. I closed to about a hundred yards, firing all the way. I saw plenty of hits all around the wing roots and fuselage. Smoke poured out the back, and flames engulfed the engine. Suddenly the 109 flipped over on its back, the canopy flew off, and the pilot bailed out. The plane went into a steep diving spiral, spewing smoke and flames.

When I saw him dangling in his parachute, my first impulse was to kill him. After all, he had just killed ten young men in that B-17. He deserved to die. I started toward him with my finger on the trigger, but I just couldn't do it. I knew that some of our pilots shot German pilots in their parachutes—"I don't want that sonafabitch to come back tomorrow and shoot *my* ass off!" Others didn't shoot the pilot but obtained the same result by shooting holes in his parachute or setting fire to it. I just couldn't do that.

I leveled off and looked behind me. My flight was in a loose trail formation behind me, and the rest of the squadron was not far behind. The whole damn squadron had followed me! Even if I hadn't hit him, he probably would have looked back and seen all those Mustangs on his tail and bailed out from sheer panic. I turned the gun switch down to "sight & camera" to take his picture, but with all those witnesses, I realized I didn't need film backup. I flipped the gun switch back up to "guns, sight & camera."

Of course, I had no idea the whole squadron had followed me, and Burt didn't mention it in his dispatches to my local newspaper back home, but it does detract (in my mind at least) from my fifth victory.

"Why didn't you shoot the bastard?" asked Mike Glantz at the debriefing, after listening to my account of the B-17 that exploded.

"I don't know. I just couldn't. They don't shoot *us* in our parachutes."

"They have orders not to!" said Mike. "German pilots are told not to shoot our guys who bail out because they want to get information from them during interrogation. I'd have shot him!"

"Mike, I doubt that."

On July 21, Fighter Command decided to adopt, at least temporarily, a variation in the way fighter groups were organized. The veteran 56th Fighter Group had devised it, and Fighter Command believed it was worth a try. For this mission we formed two groups, each group consisting of two sections, and each section containing three flights.

Billy Hovde led A Group—as Uncle—with the first section consisting of three flights from the 358th. Lieutenant Robinson of the 358th led Billy's second section, with one flight from the 358th and two flights from the 357th. The two squadrons used their usual call signs: Bentley and Custard.

I led B Group—as Hornpipe—with the first section consisting of three flights from the 354th; Captain Fred Kelley of the 357th led the second section, which consisted of two flights from the 357th and one from the 354th. The 354th flights would use the call sign Chieftain, and the 357th would use Moses.

Flight colors in each group would be red, yellow, blue, green, white, and black. Each group would then consist of twenty-four Mustangs, with the 357th split up between the two groups. Our normal configuration for a maximum-effort mission would also contain forty-eight airplanes, but each squadron would be intact, with the usual flight designations and call signs.

We saw no tactical advantage to the two-group strategy on this mission, since the routes and timings of both groups were virtually identical. The different flight colors and call signs were potential sources of confusion, at least in the beginning.

"What kind of idiots dream up these foolish things?" Billy asked me before the briefing began.

"The 56th supposedly dreamed this one up," I said, "and if it works for them, more power to them. But leave us alone!"

"Do we have to fly it their way?" he asked Kinnard.

"Afraid so, but the 65th Fighter Wing is gonna get an earful from me!"

We flew it their way, and fortunately the mission was uneventful. There was very little radio chatter—probably because no one was quite sure of his call sign. There was the usual cloud cover, the usual flak, and no Luftwaffe.

Kinnard must have given them quite an earful, because the A Group/B Group concept was shelved—at least for a while—as far as our group was concerned.

The 56th Fighter Group continued to use this innovation—with great success. A surplus of pilots and airplanes enabled them to send two different groups to different targets on the same day—in essence, doubling their number of sorties. Whether their success was due to the A Group/B Group concept, or to the skill of their veteran pilots, was the subject of mild debate at our officers' club bar. Either way, they were one helluva good group, and they made it work, in spades!

I pushed aside the blackout curtains and looked out at the dark, gray morning. Light rain was slanting down from low, ragged clouds; the whole English countryside was soggy and dripping. It had been a rain-soaked month so far, and July 24 kept up that pattern.

Duff had completed his combat tour three weeks earlier, and was already back home catching up on home cooking and other things. The tiny room we had shared for a year was a lonely place without him. I had just one more mission to go, and I was on the schedule.

I walked through the cool drizzle to the orderly room to catch a ride to the flight line. The damp, heavy air muffled the spluttering drone of the Mustang engines being readied by ground crews across the field. "What a lousy day for a mission," I thought. Especially the last.

Three hundred hours was the magic number. After three hundred hours of combat flying, I had a choice: Go back to the States for reassignment, or sign up for a second combat tour and go home for a thirty-day "rest and recuperation" leave. I had opted for another tour, but I was looking forward to that R&R.

Six pilots were already waiting in the weapons carrier. I hopped in the back and exchanged the usual ribald observations on the previous evening's activities. A few more pilots got in before we lurched on our way. The drizzle turned to rain again, and the conversation in the weapons carrier ebbed. We sat staring at the rain, wrapped in our own thoughts.

The drive to the flight line led through Litlington, a centuries-old village—a narrow, twisting, cobblestone road lined with thatched-roof cottages. Rumbling through the

ancient rain-washed streets, I felt curiously detached from
this scene, no more a part of village life than the glistening
fighters a few hundred yards away. Our passage broke the
tranquillity of the old village, but only temporarily. I was
here long before you came, it seemed to say, and I'll be here
long after you leave.

By contrast, our ready room bustled with movement and
high spirits. The record player filled the room with Benny
Goodman, and a fast-moving Ping-Pong game drew a loud
and boisterous audience. The aroma of coffee and Spam-
and-eggs revived my sagging spirits. Fresh eggs were a luxury in England, but one of our enterprising noncoms operated
a thriving black market, trading our gum, candy, and cigarettes for eggs and milk. By the time I finished breakfast, the
rain had stopped and the sky seemed a little brighter as we
headed for the group briefing room.

A low hum of conversation filled the room. About half
the chairs were occupied, and more pilots were straggling in
behind me. I looked at the floodlit map and felt that familiar
twinge just below my navel. A thick red string stretched like
a taut nerve from a spot just southwest of Cambridge, England, to a spot just south of Augsburg, in southern
Germany.

The chalkboard on the left side of the stage gave the mission details: start-engine time, takeoff time, headings, time
to different checkpoints, communications information, and
the target—the airfield at Lechfeld, about ten miles south of
Landsberg. No bombers this trip; this was a strafing mission: at high speed, just a few feet above the ground.

The chalkboard to the right of the stage gave the rest of
the story: the weather. The mission profile revealed thick,
unbroken clouds all the way to the target.

I slouched down next to Burt Sims. "How in hell are we
supposed to find it?"

He shrugged. "Maybe they'll scrub it."

The group operations officer opened the briefing with a
weak joke about the weather. *He* wasn't going on this flight.
He spelled out the details of the route, timing, and all the

other items that make up a combat-mission briefing. Pilots wrote the essentials on the backs or palms of their hands.

"The Germans," he went on, "have been developing a jet-propelled fighter, the Me-262. Most of the work has been going on at the Messerschmitt factory at Lechfeld. We know they've been flying experimental models. We believe they are now building production models—operational, combat-ready fighters." He paused and looked around dramatically. "Jet fighters could change the course of this war. Our job is to destroy them!" I half expected to hear a trumpet fanfare.

The intelligence officer was next. He showed sketches of the 262, then recited the types and numbers of guns that would make up our reception committee at Lechfeld. I was only half listening. He didn't have to convince me that it would be no picnic. We all knew that strafing losses were three to four times higher than those in air-to-air combat. On a strafing run, the only thing that mattered was luck—or fate.

It was Foggy Schmucker's turn. Tops of the overcast would be about fifteen thousand feet over England and a little higher over all of Europe. "There's a fifty-fifty chance," he said, "that you'll find breaks in the overcast in the target area or just east of it." "And if we don't," I thought, "this will be a monotonous, five-hour milk run." Somehow I was not dismayed at that prospect.

Finally, Billy Hovde, who would be leading the group on this mission, took over the pointer. Billy's imminent promotion to major had just been announced, and I knew that if there was any way to find the target, he would find it. The 358th was the lead squadron, then the 357th, and I would be leading the 354th, bringing up the rear.

Our tactics were simple: Dive down on an easterly heading, as if headed for Munich, until below radar detection level, then double back at treetop level, in the hope of catching the defenders by surprise. "Well," I thought, "Billy might catch them by surprise, because he would be the first flight across the field, but by the time *we* got there, everybody

would be firing at us—with rifles on up." Our luck could
wear thin.

Back in our ready room, I went over the mission with the
other pilots. My wingman and no. 4 man were newly assigned, so I had to be sure they knew what to expect. "This
is one hell of a mission for newcomers," I thought, "but in
this business there is no easy way to learn." One more quick
trip to the latrine, then into the weapons carriers again for
the ride to the airplanes.

"Easy mission, Cap'n?" asked McKibbin as he helped
me strap in.

"Milk run."

Exactly on time, the lead squadron's engines sputtered
into life across the field, followed by the 357th to the left.
Our turn. Controls set. . . . Energize. . . . Engage. . . . The
prop turned through four blades. . . . Ignition on. The engine
coughed once then settled into a smooth idle. I checked the
engine instruments. Everything looked good. I signaled
the crew chief to pull the chocks. Fifteen red-tailed Mustangs
followed me to the end of the runway.

The last pair of fighters from the first two squadrons began to roll down the runway. I taxied on the runway, and my
wingman rolled into position at my right wing. Leaning forward to signal advancing power, I released the brakes and
eased the throttle full. With full internal fuel and a 108-
gallon tank under each wing, the Mustangs lumbered clum-
sily down the runway the first few hundred yards, then
swiftly gathered speed and lifted off. Gear handle up; I felt
that soft thump beneath me as the door covers closed—like
a nice, reassuring pat on the ass.

After takeoff, I stayed below the ragged clouds in a slow
right turn to let my second element catch up. My wingman
slid into position on my left wing. The second-element
leader eased just inside my right wing, with his wingman
tucked in close to his right. I would be flying instruments
through the overcast, but they would be flying tight formation, close enough to see me in the thickest clouds.

The overcast was a dark gray, gloomy world as we began our climb. All my attention was focused on the instruments, but out of the corner of my eye I could see the other Mustangs in the wispy clouds, wings interlocked, and only a few inches apart. As we climbed, the clouds became brighter, and at sixteen thousand feet we were skimming the silvery cloudtops. And then suddenly we were in the clear. The brilliant sunshine lifted our spirits. Tension eased, and the formation loosened up. High above, stark white against the deep blue, a single contrail streaked toward the southeast, like a huge chalk mark pointing the way to the target.

Hovde saw my flight coming out of the overcast and radioed his position. My other three flights popped out of the clouds, and I circled to pick them up. In a surprisingly short time, forty-eight ships were in formation, climbing toward Germany.

We leveled off at twenty-five thousand feet and spread out in combat formation. The 354th's four flights were high and to the right of the group leader.

We were navigating by dead reckoning, flying an assigned heading for a specified time, but we did get some navigational help from the German flak batteries. We knew when we crossed the enemy-held coast because of the sporadic, almost casual, black puffs from their 88mm guns. It wasn't close and it looked harmless, but we knew better. We set course for Lechfeld.

There was no sound now but for the almost hypnotic drone of the big Merlin engine, nothing but the deep blue of the sky and dazzling white of the clouds below us as far as we could see in all directions. The Mustangs seemed suspended, motionless, in a silent, empty sky.

Suddenly the sky erupted with orange-red flashes and greasy black puffs of smoke. This was heavy stuff—and it was close! Too damn close! We were over Stuttgart, and the flak was so intense and accurate that the flights in my squadron became separated, bobbing and weaving to escape the hot, jagged shrapnel all around us. The radio came alive.

"Flak!" an excited, high-pitched voice. "No kidding," calm and sarcastic. Another voice: "Let's get the hell out of here!"

The group leader's calm voice: "Uncle here. Cut the chatter. We're taking evasive action." He turned left about forty-five degrees, in a slight climb. I could just barely see the lead squadron through the heavy black barrage. I banked into a climbing left turn, hoping to get above the explosions and deadly puffs of black smoke.

"Falcon Leader, this is Yellow 3. I've been hit!" I looked behind me. Yellow 3 looked all right. There was no smoke; the airplane seemed to be under control.

"Yellow Leader here. I'll check him out." I watched as Yellow Leader slid over to no. 3. There was less flak now; we were getting out of range.

"There's a good-size hole in his left wing, just outboard of the guns," reported Yellow Leader. "Looks okay otherwise, but I'd better take him back." Maybe it was my imagination, but I thought he sounded relieved.

I watched Yellow Flight disappear behind me. Blue and Green Flights had become separated in the flak barrage. Green Flight, unable to find the rest of the group, headed home. Blue Flight, about five miles back, was trying to catch up.

The flak stopped, and we returned to our briefed heading. The radio fell silent. Again I had that eerie feeling of hanging motionless between sky and clouds. Below was an unbroken sea of glaring white. Every now and then, bursts of flak jarred us back to reality, but for the most part it was like a dream world—twenty-eight Mustangs, destined to fly forever between earth and sky.

Gradually I became aware of mountain peaks thrusting through the clouds ahead. I snapped back to reality. The Alps. We were getting close. I checked my watch. If our navigation was anywhere near accurate, we should be somewhere near Augsburg.

As if in confirmation, flak mushroomed all around us, just as heavy and accurate as the Stuttgart variety. Again we took vigorous evasive action. Blue Flight, which had just caught up with me, became separated again, and now there were four of us. It probably wouldn't make much difference, but if we *did* manage to find the target in all this lousy weather, we'd be the last flight across the field.

There was still no sign of a break in the overcast. A milk run after all?

"Looks like a big hole to the south," said an unidentified voice. The group leader turned right, and I felt that twinge again. There it was—a break in the overcast about five miles across. As we got closer, I could see the ground and what looked like a slender ribbon running north–south: the Lech River. I switched to internal fuel.

"Uncle here. Drop babies." I pushed the release button and felt the lurch as the tanks dropped off. The Mustang seemed relieved to be rid of the burden and surged ahead— clean, smooth, and responsive.

One after another, six flights of four dove through the opening in the clouds. It was our turn. So much for the element of surprise. Even the lead flight could expect a warm reception. I turned on the windshield defroster, flipped the gun switch on, and followed in a spiraling dive toward that thin ribbon below.

The Mustang seemed to come alive as the airspeed built up rapidly. Gone was the sensation of hanging motionless. We were moving! Streaking down the walls of cloud, my pulse quickened with the excitement of high-speed flight. Below, I could see the lead flight level off above the river and head for the target, which was still hidden by clouds.

We leveled off just above the trees and headed north, straddling the river. Almost immediately, we were beneath the overcast in a light drizzle that sharply restricted visibility.

With the throttle wide open, doing better than four hundred miles per hour, I was straining to find the airfield in the sunless gloom. I knew the field was west of the river, so if I held this heading . . .

A large hangar, dead ahead. Big brick buildings to the left. "There it is!"

I pulled up to about three hundred feet to get a better angle to fire the guns and find a good target. This also made us more vulnerable, because now the gunners could see us, and we had to maintain a steady, shallow dive to the target—no evasive action; just like flying down somebody's gun barrel.

I spotted a row of hangars on the far side of the field and what looked like Me-262s scattered around in sandbagged revetments. Some were burning, the black, oily smoke merging with the low clouds. I picked out an airplane parked at an angle, half inside a small hangar, and lined it up carefully in my gunsight. There would be only one pass. It had to be good.

I was aware of small white puffs from exploding 20mm shells all around my airplane. I could hear the soft pop of near misses. I forced myself to concentrate: Keep that pip steady on that airplane!

I squeezed the trigger on the stick. The four .50-caliber machine guns in the wings hammered, jarring the airplane as if it had been hit. Instantly, like a string of firecrackers, orange flashes appeared on the fuselage of the 262; then a small yellow flame licked up around the cockpit and flashed into a bright red-orange explosion as the fuel tank blew up.

Then I saw another airplane parked next to it. I fired a short burst and saw a few hits, but I realized that I was getting damn close to that hangar.

I was almost too close. I pulled back on the stick and cleared the hangar roof by inches. As I did, a brilliant flash of light reflected off the clouds to my left, lighting up the whole area. Something had exploded. I banked left a few degrees to avoid flying over the airfield at Landsberg and skimmed the trees until well out of range of the airfield guns. I had seen enough of those for one day. Blue Flight finally caught up with us. They hadn't seen the airfield at all. I felt like saying, "You guys missed all the fun!"

I scanned the engine instruments and checked the plane over for damage. That's when I noticed the large chip in the "bulletproof" windshield. Apparently a shell had hit the windshield on a slant and been deflected off. Somewhere on that strafing run I had been only six inches from having my head blown off.

Red 3 and Red 4 both reported that they could see a few holes in their airplanes, but everything seemed to be running all right. I looked to my left. There was no sign of my wingman. "Where's Red 2?" I asked.

"He went in—just off the airfield," answered Red 4 in a faltering voice. I knew they were roommates. I remembered that bright flash.

Of the last four aircraft on that strafing run, the German gunners had shot down one and hit the other three. I signaled both flights into a tight formation, and we started the long climb through the thick overcast.

It was a long and silent trip back to England. I kept staring at that chipped windshield and thinking about Red 2. The difference between life and death had been inches, or perhaps a few miles per hour one way or the other. This was my seventy-fourth mission, and his second.

Last mission for both.

Bob Kurtz and Chuck Lenfest, back from their thirty-day R&R in the States, were on hand to greet us. They had completed their first tours before the magic number changed from 250 to 300 hours. They were given a warm welcome in the bar that night, as they regaled us with tales of their exploits and experiences on their home turf. Their return signaled a steady infusion of experienced leaders as other R&R veterans returned to the squadron.

On July 27, Silky Morris, who finished his 300 hours of combat duty, left for Goxhill to join the staff of replacement pool instructors. Four new pilots were assigned to our squadron that morning, all second lieutenants: Charles McCurry; Theodore Todd Jr.; O. N. (initials only—no first name) Stanton; and Garth Spitler. Lieutenant Spitler had been a crew chief in the 354th Squadron during the early days in Florida. He had applied for flight training and was accepted before the squadron came overseas. Now he was "coming home" to the 354th as a pilot.

Burt joined me at lunch that day at the officers' club. "Bud, how would you like to be on the radio?"

"I'm on the radio almost every day in that Mustang, Burt."

"No, I mean the *radio* radio, like BBC or NBC."

"What are you driving at?"

"There's a well-known Hollywood actor named Ben Lyon—maybe you've heard of him—who's doing radio broadcasts from London. I don't know if he's a war correspondent now or just doing interviews with experienced and interesting servicemen. Anyhow, his stuff is broadcast on one of the networks back home. It's a morale booster for the home front."

"So?"

"So he called me this morning and said he just had a slot open up for tomorrow's session and needed a good interview. I gave him a short bio sketch of you and he said, 'Great!' and could I have you there by ten tomorrow morning. And I said, 'Yes.' "

"Thanks a lot, but I still have to fly a relay mission for at least an hour and a half to reach that three-hundred mark."

"This won't take long. We'll go into London this afternoon and go to the BBC studios in the morning. We'll be all through by noon. I've already given him your name. You can't let me down now!"

I tried to talk him out of it, but to no avail. That afternoon we boarded a London-bound train at Royston. "What in hell am I supposed to say?" The prospect of being "on the radio" in the United States was a bit unnerving, and I was already feeling nervous.

"No problem," said Burt. "He'll ask you some questions and you just answer them."

"What kind of questions?"

"Oh, I don't know. I suppose things like what airplanes you flew, how good are the German pilots, to what do you attribute your success, and so on."

I was still nervous. And I was plenty nervous the next morning when we arrived in the broadcast studio a few minutes before ten.

Ben Lyon was a big, heavyset man with a friendly smile

and manner. He made me feel right at ease. He told me what kind of questions he would ask, like where did you grow up, how did you get into flying, and so forth. "And remember," he said, "this is not a live broadcast. If we screw it up, we'll do it over."

I don't remember exactly what I said, but it was just the kind of thing the folks back home would want to hear—excellent training, great mechanics, superior airplanes—stuff that would make them feel good.

It went well the first time. Lyon thanked us both and showed us to the lobby. Burt and I quickly found the nearest pub.

In the pub, we decided that there was no point hurrying back to Steeple—we'd never make it in time for supper—so we might as well spend the night in London. The V-1s were very much in evidence, but in situations like that, one develops a fatalistic view—"if my time is up," etc.—and that fatalistic view was more and more reassuring as the pub-crawling progressed.

The hangovers were just subsiding as we left the train station at Royston next morning and flagged a jeep for a ride to Steeple.

Since Emil Perry and I both had fewer than two hours left to complete our combat tours, we were assigned to fly radio relay on July 31 as the group escorted bombers to Munich in another milk run. Since we were both from New Hampshire, we requested permission to use "Yankee Purple Flight" as our call sign—the New Hampshire state flower is the purple lilac. "Request denied," said Marshall with a smile. "Now, if you were both from Texas—" He was drowned out by our comments before he got to the Yellow Rose.

A few bursts of flak were aimed in our direction whenever we ventured too close to the Dutch coast. "Well, at least we can say we were shot at on our last so-called mission," said Perry.

Major Kucheman, who had been 354th commander since Kinnard became group exec, was transferred to group headquarters to become group operations officer. Bert Marshall was now our squadron commander. There was a small party for Kucheman at the officers' club that evening. I shook his hand and wished him well. We had established a friendly but not close relationship, and I had come to respect him as a pilot and leader.

Through most of July, the weather in England and on the Continent was terrible, adding to the enormous difficulties of the hedgerow wars. By July 25 the weather had improved. A huge aerial assault by P-47s, B-26s, B-24s, and B-17s, accompanied by a steady artillery barrage, paved the way for Operation COBRA, the American breakout that opened the road to Paris and even to Germany itself. Patton's Third Army was finally in the battle, and he was begging for the chance to encircle and trap most of the German army and end the war in short order. Eisenhower vetoed his plan.

"I'm not sure you'll still have a war going when I get back," I said to Burt.

"If you hurry, we'll save you some."

The group flew only twenty-three missions in July, just over half the number flown in June. Weather was the biggest problem.

Rest and Recuperation

I left Steeple in the early morning hours of August 5, by jeep to the neighboring B-17 base at Bassingbourne. I boarded a C-47 transport later that morning and arrived at Prestwick, Scotland, some three hours later. Prestwick was a Royal Air Force base used by the U.S. Army Air Forces as an arrival and departure point for flights to and from the United States. I thought I would be sent home on a relatively comfortable Military Air Transport System flight, somewhat comparable to commercial airlines. I was to check in with the transportation office each morning for my departure schedule.

The town of Prestwick is on the Firth of Clyde about seventy-five miles south of Greenock, where we had debarked from the *Queen Elizabeth* fourteen months earlier. The base facilities were typically spartan—just the basics, nothing fancy. I shared a room with about twenty company-grade officers, some heading home and others heading to a new assignment in England. We each had a cot, and there were toilet facilities at each end. There was no nightlife in any of the tiny towns nearby. There was a movie theater on base, but movies were shown on an erratic schedule based on availability. Fortunately, the air base did have an officers' club that did a thriving business every night.

For the next eight days I checked in with the transportation office at nine each morning. "Nothing yet," each day. On the ninth day, the transportation officer smiled and said, "You leave tomorrow!"

"Is it a MATS flight?" I asked.

"Not quite. It's a B-17 being sent back to the States for modification and repair. Takeoff is at ten o'clock in the morning. Be here, ready to go, at 0830."

It was not exactly what I had wanted to hear. A war-weary B-17 being sent back for much-needed repairs wasn't the mode of transportation I would have selected, but I had little choice. I was eager to get home.

It was a long, uncomfortable trip. The B-17 was not designed to carry passengers, and I was the only one on this trip. I was given two GI blankets and told to make myself at home. I damn near froze to death. We stopped at Reykjavik, Iceland, for refueling and were stuck there for two days because of weather. We finally made it to the army base at Fort Devens, Massachusetts.

At nearby Camp Miles Standish, "processing in" took another day, but I was back home in Nashua, New Hampshire, by August 20. Fortunately, my thirty-day leave didn't start until I got home, or I would have had to start back immediately.

I was a captain and an ace, and the hometown turned out in spades to welcome me back. My brother Ray also was in the Army Air Forces, about to graduate from navigation school in California, but the rest of the family was on hand to greet me. The local newspaper, *The Nashua Telegraph,* made a big deal of my arrival, with reporters and photographers at our house taking pictures of me with my proud parents.

The first thing I did after a day or two of family welcoming was buy a car. I had sent an allotment home since I was commissioned, so I had a little money in the bank, which I tapped to buy a 1935 Plymouth convertible complete with rumble seat.

With the fancy (I thought) wheels and my summer uniform complete with a few ribbons, I was soon cutting a wide social swath. Even if I remembered all the details, I wouldn't include them here. The one big event of my leave was a testimonial dinner held in my honor at the Nashua Country Club on August 31. Attending the event were city officials, National Guard senior officers, the pastor of my parish—who had served in the Marine Corps in World War I as a chaplain—former teachers from high school and St. Anselm College, and about three hundred friends and neighbors. Ray had just graduated from navigation school and was able to get home just in time.

After the dinner, a few of the guests said some nice things about me, and I was presented with a gold ring with a small diamond inset and a miniature set of wings on the front. It was only later that I noticed that the wings were like those worn by navy pilots, not Army Air Forces wings. Inscribed on the inside was "Captain Bud Fortier, Testimonial Dinner, August 30, 1944." I accepted the ring and the testimonials on behalf of the soldiers, sailors, and marines who were fighting the war and who were unable to be with us that evening.

It was a night to remember. There were a few other nights to remember.

When my leave ended on September 20, I returned to Camp Miles Standish for orders returning me to the 355th Fighter Group. I expected to be back in England within a few weeks. It wasn't that easy. They couldn't just sign an order saying "Go back to England and rejoin the 355th Fighter Group." Two days after signing in, I was ordered to the reassignment center in Atlantic City, New Jersey.

First Lieutenant Rich Brown, who had finished his combat tour in the 354th, arrived in Atlantic City at the same time I did. He was awaiting reassignment in the United States. We shared a room in a plush hotel right on the beach, the fanciest military billets we had ever experienced. We had to check in to the assignment center daily, and each day we received the same answer: "Nothing yet. Check in tomorrow." Supplies and replacements for the ground forces engaged in heavy fighting in France took up most of the available sea transport. I was not high on that priority list, but that did not distress me. Atlantic City was not the worst place in the world to be stranded. There were other hotels nearby and a number of attractive women on the beach each day, so we really didn't mind the delay.

On October 1 I was ordered to report to Camp Kilmer, New Jersey. "That has a familiar ring to it," said Rich. "I almost wish I were going with you."

"Why don't you change your mind and come along with me?" I asked.

"Thanks, but no thanks. Good luck!" We went our separate ways. I headed for Camp Kilmer, hoping the *Queen Elizabeth* was sailing from New York soon. That would be a fast trip.

I was at Camp Kilmer only three days. It was just as confused and disorganized as it had been a year ago. Again they insisted on issuing gas masks, impregnated clothing, mosquito netting, and all sorts of equipment I knew I wouldn't need; and again, I "forgot" to take all this with me when I left. On October 5 I boarded the SS *Nieuw Amsterdam* of the Holland-America Line at the New York pier. She wasn't as big as the *Queen,* but she had been a first-class luxury liner and was fast enough to cross the Atlantic unescorted.

The crossing took about a week and was uneventful. The ship was crowded as expected, and there were rumors that she also carried bombs, ammunition, and fuel in her hold. "Great!" I thought, "A German U-boat could blow us up to at least thirty thousand feet!"

I had a *déjà vu* feeling on debarkation at Greenock. I checked in at the processing center at Prestwick and got my rail ticket to Royston.

Jim Duffy had returned from leave about a month earlier and had a new roommate, a second lieutenant. I was a captain, so I was able to persuade him to move in with someone else. I rejoined Duff in our cozy cell. The chess matches resumed.

Meanwhile, Back at the War . . .

When I left England for home, the Americans were racing across France, driving an exhausted and disorganized Wehrmacht ahead of them. General George Patton's Third Army spearheaded the advance, but the British and the

Canadians were still unable to break through the Panzer divisions facing them. From newspaper accounts at the end of August, it appeared that the war might end before Christmas. By the end of September, however, after the failure of Operation Market Garden to open up the northern route to Berlin, Patton's Third Army and General Courtney Hodges's First Army were at a virtual standstill. I knew that there'd be plenty of war left for me when I got back.

There were many changes and plenty of excitement at Steeple Morden while I was away.

On August 5 Bob Kurtz attacked a gaggle of 109s and in the ensuing dogfight was hit by 20mm shells, one of which severed his throttle linkage. Unable to control the engine power and too low to bail out, he crash-landed his badly damaged Mustang and sustained severe head injuries. Fortunately, he crashed near a German hospital, where he was taken and treated. When fully recovered, he spent the rest of the war in a POW camp.

On August 15, Bert Marshall made it back to Steeple with more than fifty holes in his plane after strafing a German airfield in Holland. "Those guys are serious," he said with a smile. "They were trying to kill me!"

On August 18 Bert was again hit by flak after a strafing attack on a German airfield and had to crash-land in a nearby hayfield. As he was lining up his approach to the field, his element leader, Lt. Royce "Deacon" Priest, radioed that he would land in the same field to pick him up. "Don't be a damn fool," said Bert. "You go on home. Do *not* try to pick me up! And that's an order!"

Priest paid no attention. He landed in the hayfield and taxied to the far end. Marshall ran toward him, and there followed a spirited exchange. "Get the hell out of here!" yelled Marshall.

"Get in the cockpit!" shouted Priest.

"Get out of here, and that's an order!" roared Bert above the sound of the Merlin engine.

Priest climbed out of the cockpit, threw his parachute

and dinghy on the ground, and yelled, "Get in before the damn engine overheats!"

There was a brief discussion as to who would fly the airplane, but Marshall got in the cockpit, and Priest, who was just under six feet tall, sat on his lap. As he started the take-off run, the canopy slid open and hit him in the forehead. Bert reached around him and closed it. Priest managed to get the airplane off the ground, raising the left wing just in time to avoid grazing a haystack at the end of the field. It was an outstanding feat of flying skill.

Since Bert had no oxygen mask, Priest leveled off at fourteen thousand feet and managed to avoid flak areas and Luftwaffe pilots.

Priest still had his helmet and oxygen mask, and as he approached Steeple Morden, he requested emergency landing priority. "What kind of emergency?" asked the tower operator.

"There are two of us in this airplane," replied Priest.

After a five-second moment of silence, the tower operator asked, "What kind of aircraft are you?"

"P-51."

"Did you say 'P-51'?"

"Roger." Priest was enjoying himself.

Another five-second delay. Then "Cleared to land."

Instead of heading for the dispersal area after landing, Deacon taxied off the runway across the short grass to the area in front of Gremlin Villa, where the twosome soon drew a crowd of incredulous and very happy people.

It was the first successful rescue of an American pilot in Europe. It earned a Distinguished Service Cross for Priest, and a good-natured "reprimand" for Bert Marshall from Chuck Lenfest for losing the brand-new airplane that Bert had borrowed from him for this mission.

Lieutenant Colonel Stewart returned to the group in mid-August after his thirty-day Stateside leave and resumed his position as group executive officer. Shortly thereafter, Kinnard was transferred to the 4th Fighter Group as deputy commander; he took command of the group a few weeks later.

On August 28 Bert once again demonstrated his affinity for flak, and his flying skill, when he took a number of direct hits on the wings and canopy during a strafing attack on a German airfield. Pieces of the canopy punctured his helmet and lacerated his scalp. In spite of blurred vision as he tried to wipe the blood out of his eyes, he managed to get the plane to England, where he successfully crash-landed at RAF Station Manston.

Eight aircraft were shot down by flak on that mission; all but two pilots evaded capture and eventually made it back to Steeple.

The group lost twenty-eight Mustangs in August. Several more were so badly damaged that they were scrapped. Thirteen pilots were killed or captured. Only two 355th Fighter Group pilots were shot down in air-to-air combat.

Bert Marshall was notified of his promotion to major on September 2, along with Larry Sluga, Billy Hovde, and Chuck Lenfest. They were four very popular leaders, so it was the busiest Saturday night the officers' club bar had enjoyed to date.

September was the month of the shuttle mission. For this "maximum effort," the 355th borrowed twenty-two Mustangs from other groups to augment its fleet. The 355th was to escort three groups of B-17s dispatched to drop supplies to Polish Underground units surrounded by German troops in the heart of Warsaw, then take the bombers on to Russia. Pilots were told to leave their sidearms at home, carry extra spark plugs for the engines, and avoid sustained dogfights with the Luftwaffe, since fuel supplies might get a bit low trying to find the Russian airdrome at Piryatin. They were also directed not to discuss politics with the Russians, not to "fraternize" with Russian women, and to avoid any controversial situations with the Russian allies.

Originally planned for September 13, the mission was

scrubbed twice because of weather, then recalled on September 15, when the bombers encountered a wall of thunderstorms in the Berlin area. The shuttle mission was put on temporary hold when the entire resources of the Eighth Air Force were needed to support the vast airborne and armor attack known as Operation Market Garden, an attempt to achieve a crossing of the Rhine River at Arnhem, Holland.

Finally on September 18, the first leg of the shuttle was flown. Sixty-four Mustangs plus eight spares took off. Lieutenant Colonel Stewart led the group, but his generator failed shortly after landfall over Holland and he had to return. Major Bert Marshall took over the lead.

This was no milk run. The group had to ward off several gaggles of Me-109s while trying to save enough fuel to make it to Russia. Four 109s were destroyed for the loss of two Mustangs—both of our pilots killed. Heavy and intense flak over Stettin damaged several other Mustangs.

The airfield at Piryatin was a small grass strip partially obscured by smoke and haze, but the group landed without further incident. Marshall was the last to land after a flight of seven hours, thirty minutes.

Marshall led fifty-six Mustangs on the second leg of the shuttle, leaving behind several Mustangs with minor damage or equipment failures to be handled by the ground crews. It was an escort mission; the bomber target was a marshaling yard in Hungary. This one was a milk run with little flak and no Luftwaffe. The group was spread out over three bases around Foggia, Italy, and pilots spent the next two days relaxing and sightseeing.

On September 22, Bert led the group on the final leg home. It was another milk run, except that Steeple had less than half a mile visibility in a low fogbank. It was the kind of fog that you can see through from above the airfield, but the forward visibility approaches zero as you enter the fogbank for a landing. All Mustangs landed safely after a flight of nearly seven hours.

September closed with lousy weather and seventeen missions flown. The group shot down twenty-three enemy air-

craft and destroyed another twenty-six on the ground. Nine
Mustangs and eight pilots were lost. The Luftwaffe was
more active than in recent months, but most of its activity
seemed directed against the newer fighter groups in VIII
Fighter Command.

The escort mission to Giebelstadt on October 3 was rou-
tine until Chuck Lenfest decided to strafe an airfield at
Nordlingen on the way home. He destroyed an FW-190, and
Henry Brown flamed an Me-110 just before taking a direct
hit in the engine section from a 20mm shell. Henry's
coolant was lost, and he was forced to belly in on a nearby
field. The field appeared to be clear and reasonably level, so
Chuck landed his P-51 (ironically, it was actually Bert
Marshall's plane) in the same field, intending to pick up
Henry and bring him home. As he was taxiing to meet
Brown, his left wheel ran into a deep mudhole and he was
unable to free it, even with Brown trying to lift under the
wing. His engine soon overheated, and when the coolant
boiled over, Chuck and Henry headed for the woods.

When Al White realized what had happened, he landed in
an adjacent field, intending to let Lenfest and Brown take his
airplane while he took his chances to evade capture. Neither
Lenfest nor Brown saw Al's Mustang as they headed for the
woods, though the rest of the squadron tried to steer them to
Al by buzzing them repeatedly. Al waited as long as he could
before his engine overheated, then took off without incident.
Chuck and Henry became guests of a German POW camp.

In that short space of time, the 355th Group lost its leading ace—Brown, with a total of 28.7 enemy aircraft destroyed—and the 354th Squadron lost its operations officer,
Lenfest, who also was an ace. The two aircraft lost were the
only two in the squadron equipped with the new K-14 gunsight. Serendipity for the Luftwaffe.

That evening in the officers' club bar, Bert asked Al,
"What in hell were you trying to do?"

"I was going to let them take my airplane. They were
much more valuable to the squadron than I am!"

"Well, it was a damn-fool thing to do!" said Bert.

"I guess so."

"Would you do the same thing again?"

"Yes, I would," said Al.

"So would I," said Bert with a big smile.

Al told me of this conversation later and added, "That's why everybody loves this guy!"

The K-14 gunsight was a radical departure from what we had become accustomed to. The "fixed" position projected a cross surrounded by a 70-mil ring; it was used for strafing or if the gyro function failed. In the "gyro" position, the K-14 projected a circle of diamonds surrounding a central dot. Rotating a twist grip on the throttle changed the diameter of the circle. The sight could be set for long-range or short-range operation. The tech order made it sound simple, but it required a bit of practice. It was a great improvement over the fixed sight because it took the guesswork out of high-deflection shots.

On October 3 Maj. Gordon M. Graham, who had a lot of flying experience with Training Command, was assigned to the 354th Fighter Squadron as operations officer. Bert Marshall held two positions at this time: commander of the 354th and acting group executive officer. The plan was to transfer Marshall to group headquarters as group executive officer when Graham was ready to assume command of the squadron.

When I returned to Steeple on October 16, I asked Duff what he thought about Graham. "He seems like a nice guy, but nobody seems to know much about him, except that he came here from Training Command. Guess what his nickname is."

"Tell me."

"Ace!"

"All he has to do now is live up to it."

October and November 1944

I didn't get back to Steeple until October 16, more than two months after I had left. Jim Duffy, Burt Sims, Brady Williamson, and Lee Mendenhall were there from the original outfit to give me a warm welcome at the bar that evening. Bert Marshall was there and introduced me to Major Graham.

"I've heard a lot about you," said Graham with a smile.

"They can't prove any of it, Major," I said with a matching smile.

At the flight line, all the P-51Bs were gone, replaced by sleek D models. There were a few new faces at Gremlin Villa.

I hadn't flown a Mustang—or any other airplane, for that matter—for more than two months, and as soon as I finished processing in, I checked out in the new P-51D. It was a little heavier than earlier models, with an extra .50-caliber machine gun in each wing, and its top speed was reduced slightly. The new sliding canopy made for better visibility, and those extra .50s were welcome additional firepower. The B-model problem of gun stoppages—especially in high-G-force situations—had been solved by positioning the guns in an upright position and adding a few inches to the thickness of the wing to accommodate them and the ammunition feed mechanism.

Like its predecessors, it was a sweet-flying airplane. After a thirty-minute orientation flight, I was ready to get back on the schedule, but group headquarters policy required that I fly at least fifteen hours of "refresher time" in the P-51 before I could be assigned to a combat mission. The English weather hadn't improved much, so it was October 30 before I was finally scheduled for a mission, even though I had only ten hours of refresher time by then.

When Bert Marshall was transferred to Group headquarters as executive officer on October 23, Ace Graham became squadron commander. It was a tough position to be in. Some of us had been in the squadron from the day it was formed, and had quite a bit of combat experience; Bert Marshall was a well-liked and capable leader; and the nickname "Ace" didn't sit well with some of the bona fide aces in the group.

Physically, Ace was not particularly imposing: about average height and slim, wiry build; curly, reddish-brown hair topped a ruddy complexion. His face was like a boxer's face—a little puffy, with a slightly flattened nose. Wrinkles around his eyes attested to many hours of squinting into the sun, and perhaps to a sense of humor. His whole bearing and demeanor radiated a controlled aggressiveness.

Though titular commander, he wisely let Lee Mendenhall run the squadron while he observed and learned. He could have started leading the squadron right from the beginning—it would have been the safer course for him. Instead, he chose to start off flying "tail-end Charlie," the most vulnerable spot on a combat mission.

When I returned from R&R, I was A Flight leader and Jim Duffy was B Flight leader. Ace flew most of his early missions in our flights. After several missions as wingman, he moved up to element leader for a few more missions, then flight leader. Within a few weeks he had flown every position in the squadron—except squadron leader—on all kinds of missions.

At that point squadron pilots began to believe that this guy was the genuine article. He also had begun to live up to his nickname. By the end of the year he had shot down three enemy aircraft and demonstrated the aggressive leadership that made him one of the leading aces of the 355th Fighter

Group. He was a leader who never asked anyone to do anything that he wouldn't do himself.

"Where are we going today?" I asked Mendy, who was now operations officer. It was October 30, two weeks after my return to the squadron.

"Hamburg," he answered. "Ever been there?"

"Once or twice."

"By the way, Bud, we're part of the 2d Air Division now."

"What does that mean?"

"It means that most of the time, we'll be escorting B-24s, because that's what the 2d Air Division flies."

"That's fine with me. I'm not prejudiced."

The 354th launched five flights—twenty Mustangs—with Mendy in the lead. I was leading the last flight, designated White Flight, and Graham was leading my second element. I was a bit apprehensive as I eased the throttle full for takeoff. After more than two months away from combat, was I ready? It was only after the gear came up and patted me on the ass again that I relaxed. I knew what I was doing. Even the usual English overcast seemed comfortably familiar.

The weather over the Continent was lousy: Layers of clouds extended to at least thirty thousand feet. The B-24s were at twenty-four thousand feet, flying a ragged formation, skimming in and out of cloud layers. It was impossible to keep all of them in sight. There was plenty of that familiar flak to remind me that this was serious business, but the Luftwaffe, if they became airborne, couldn't find us in all those cloud layers.

It was an uneventful escort job. The only sign of the Luftwaffe was a long contrail pinpointing an Me-262 high above the bomber stream. He swung around in a wide circle and headed back to where he came from. It was an impressive sight; his speed was much greater than ours, and he appeared to be some ten thousand feet above us. If the Germans produce sufficient numbers of these, I thought, we are in deep trouble.

After five hours of hit-and-miss escort duty, we returned to Steeple. The bar did a brisk business as usual that evening. Sitting around the bar with Burt and Duff, and now with Ace Graham, I was back home. Duff had been grounded for three days with a sore throat, and was giving it the scotch-and-soda treatment. Next morning, Doc Fontenot sent him to the hospital, where they decided to remove his tonsils. "Some guys'll do anything for a few days off!" said Burt.

Six replacement pilots joined our squadron on October 31, all second lieutenants: Glenn Beeler, Marvin Castleberry, Joseph Mellen, Charles Rodebaugh, Stanley Silva, and Kirby Smith. We had received quite a few replacement pilots in the past few months; we now had forty-seven pilots assigned, an all-time high.

October was not the group's best month; only fifteen missions were flown. The fall weather was raising hell with air operations over the Continent, and the Allied armies on the ground. The group shot down six enemy aircraft and destroyed one on the ground but lost five aircraft and five pilots to enemy action. Also, Col. William Cummings, who had returned from his thirty-day R&R on October 20, was transferred to VIII Fighter Command, and Lt. Col. Everett Stewart was now group commander.

On November 1, the 355th launched twenty-four aircraft—eight per squadron—to escort B-24s attacking the synthetic oil refineries at Gelsenkirchen. The field order predicted that the weather over the Continent would be miserable, so the 8th Fighter Command, in its wisdom, advised each group to send only "experienced pilots complete with instrument cards."

Brady led our squadron (after showing his year-old instrument-qualification card to Mendy), with Graham (who couldn't find his) leading the second flight. I couldn't find my instrument card, either, so I stayed home. The weather was better than predicted.

Escort was without incident. As Brady broke off escort

and headed home, he observed two flights of Mustangs from another group cruising about three thousand feet overhead. A moment later, an Me-262 appeared out of nowhere and shot down the no. 4 man in the rear flight. Brady started a climb to intercept. The other three members of the flight under attack apparently didn't even notice the absence of tailend Charlie, so the 262 slid into the no. 4 position in the flight and started shooting at no. 3. When he saw Brady's bunch coming at him, he broke away in a steep climb, heading northwest, toward the Zuider Zee.

At that point about forty Mustangs were chasing him. The 262 pilot was obviously very cocky and maybe a bit arrogant. He performed a few aerobatics for the pursuing Mustangs, flaunting his superior speed and climb capabilities. He gradually let down to about fifteen thousand feet, diving and turning, and maintaining a speed of about five hundred miles per hour.

Then he did something stupid. He suddenly whipped into a 180-degree turn and came directly back toward the swarm of Mustangs chasing him, firing as he came. Half a dozen Mustangs tore into him head-on, with guns blazing. When Brady last saw the 262, it was in a flat spin at about ten thousand feet, and the pilot had bailed out—a victim of his own ego?

The mission was otherwise uneventful. As Burt wrote in his narrative: "But that's enough, isn't it?"

Me-262s were becoming part of the scenery whenever the Luftwaffe appeared to challenge the bombers. They were seen on four of the next five missions. They employed hit-and-run tactics against both bombers and fighters, using their significant speed advantage to avoid dogfights with Mustangs. In a turning contest, the advantage was with the Mustangs.

Ace Graham led the squadron for the first time on November 6, 1944. It was a routine escort mission—the usual flak, clouds covering the Continent, and no Luftwaffe.

Jim Duffy was back from the hospital on November 7.

He had lost a little weight, thanks to the excellent hospital bill of fare. "Actually, the food wasn't all that bad," said Jim, "but they wouldn't let me have even one small beer!"

My next mission was on November 8. The group was split into A and B groups again. I could understand the strategy when the A and B groups were given different missions, perhaps in different locations, but this was not the case.

"A Group" consisted of Maj. John "Moon" Elder's 357th Squadron plus two flights from our squadron led by Lee Mendenhall. "B Group" was Lieutenant Colonel Stewart with the 358th plus three flights from our squadron, which I led. Mendy's "A Squadron" was to provide top cover for the 357th, and my "B Squadron" was to provide top cover for the 358th. The mission—nearly identical for both groups—was to protect the 2d Task Force, seven boxes of B-24s bombing Merseburg. The only difference was that A Group would be on the left side of the bombers, and B Group would be on the left.

"Why do those folks at Fighter Command like to do this A and B group nonsense?" I asked Burt. "When we're all going to the same target and escorting the same bombers? We know how to do that! Why do those folks feel compelled to tell us how to do it?"

"Beats me!" replied Burt. "Most of those people finished a combat tour before they were assigned there. Some of them must have been with the 56th Fighter Group. They use A and B groups a lot." He shrugged. "And they're a damn good outfit."

Before we made landfall, the controller reported that the 2d Air Division mission had been scrubbed, so we were to continue inland and "freelance around the 1st Air Division." Mendy radioed that he was siphoning gas and had to return, so I took over the lead of the 354th. We continued the mission with each squadron intact—not in the A Group and B Group configuration. Except for the usual flak, it was uneventful. On the way home, my wingman, 2d Lt. Oran Stalcup, reported that he had a rough engine, so I led him to an emergency field outside of Liège, Belgium. I watched him land safely, then I headed home to complete a long, seven-hour flight. Stalcup returned the next day with his magneto trouble fixed.

On November 9 Mendy led a strafing mission against rail and transportation targets east of the fortress city of Metz, which Patton's Third Army was trying to take. Thick haze, low clouds, and occasional snowstorms made strafing difficult and caused the squadron to split up into individual flights and elements. Lieutenant Hull was clobbered by flak and crash-landed in Germany. After he slid to a stop, he radioed that he was okay, and headed for some nearby woods. Six pilots landed in France, including Lieutenant Ted Todd, whose flak-damaged Mustang was limping along at 150 miles per hour.

We would have lost quite a few airplanes on this mission had it not been for the safe havens provided by Ninth Air Force bases in friendly territory. Often the bases were relatively primitive, with pierced steel planking runways and tent cities, but they looked great to pilots in distress.

The November 10 mission was an easy milk run. Graham led the squadron, and I led his Blue Flight. We escorted B-24s to an airfield near Frankfurt believed to be the home of a number of Me-262s. Most of the Continent was covered with clouds, with tops at about twenty thousand feet, so we couldn't observe the results of the bombing. There was plenty of flak at Frankfurt and Coblenz, but for the most part we were above it.

On the way home, my engine began to run rough. At first I thought I could get back home with it, but it started cutting out every now and then, and I wasn't comfortable with the thought of crossing the North Sea with that problem. Just a few months earlier, I would have had no other option. I told Ace I was going to have to find a place to land, but I didn't need an escort. I headed west, switched to the emergency channel, and requested a steer to the nearest base.

I saw a few breaks in the overcast as I headed west, but I

stayed at twenty thousand feet to increase my radio range—
and I wanted plenty of altitude in case the engine quit completely and I had to bail out.

"Falcon Two Zero, this is Dogwood. Transmit ten seconds for a steer." I squeezed the mike button and counted
slowly to ten. A few seconds later: "Falcon Two Zero, steer
two fiver zero; repeat, two fiver zero. Over." I acknowledged the heading and asked him about the weather at his
airfield.

"Ceiling three thousand feet, visibility five miles in light
rain," he answered. I kept transmitting periodically, and he
kept refining my steer.

After about ten minutes, I could tell by his signal
strength that I was getting close, so I found a break in the
overcast and dove my coughing Mustang down below the
clouds to about twenty-five hundred feet. A light rain decreased my forward visibility to about three miles. Within
five minutes I spotted the rotating beacon of the airfield. I
switched to tower frequency and landed my sputtering P-51
on the pierced steel planking runway without incident.

P-47s were widely scattered all around the field. The
voice from the tower directed me where to park, and there
was a jeep there to meet me. I shut down the engine, entered
the pertinent information in the Form 1, and was driven to
the base operations van. This was a Ninth Air Force fighter-
bomber base, flying P-47s in close support of army ground
units. These guys lived in tents and moved often to stay
close to the front lines.

Except for the control tower (a motorized van with an
aircraft canopy sticking out of its roof), about half a dozen
blister hangars scattered around the perimeter, and a few
other motorized vans along the flight line, the rest of the
base seemed to be tent city—a soggy, dripping tent city.
This was a highly mobile outfit. I suddenly realized how
lucky I was to be in the Eighth Air Force and made a mental
note never to complain about our Nissen huts again.

"Yeah, we know," said a smiling captain in the comfortable ops van. "You need spark plugs. All you Mustang guys

come in here for the same reason. I don't think we can get to it until tomorrow sometime, but we'll take care of you."

"Where am I?" I asked.

"We're just outside of Denain, a small village with the usual church, a few shops and cafés, and nice people. We have a visiting officers' tent, if you'd like to spend the night here; or I can get you a ride to the village, if you want to take your chances there."

"How would I get back here tomorrow?"

He scribbled a number on a small scratch pad and handed it to me. "Call this number, and we'll send a jeep for you."

I looked at my watch: It was 3:30 P.M. I opted for the village.

The jeep dropped me off at a café owned and operated by Monsieur et Madame Verriez. I grew up in a bilingual family where we spoke Canadian French or English interchangeably, so in spite of the differences between the two varieties of French, I was able to converse easily with the owners.

They were thrilled to meet *un pilote chasseur Américain,* and they did have a bedroom above the café that I could use if I liked. Gaston Verriez operated the café, his wife had a hairdressing salon and barber shop behind the café, and their home was next door. They insisted that I have dinner at their café that evening, and we spent several hours talking on a wide range of subjects. I explained how I happened to be in Denain, and they told me many tales of the German occupation. It was nearly midnight before I got to bed.

Next morning, after coffee and toast with them, I tried to pay with the only money I had with me—about three English pounds—but they wouldn't hear of it. I called the number at the base, and the jeep soon arrived. I thanked them profusely, we said our good-byes, and all waved as the jeep pulled away. The weather had improved a little. It was still cloudy, but there was no rain, and the visibility was at least five miles. I looked for my airplane, but it was not where I had left it.

A major was the duty officer, but he was busy on the

field phone, trying to be heard above the roar of Thunderbolts taking off a few hundred yards away. He finally handed the receiver to a captain standing next to him. "*You* talk to him," he said. "I don't know what in hell he wants!"

"You must be the Mustang jockey," he said to me. I introduced myself and asked where my airplane was.

"In one of our hangars," he replied.

"Getting a plug change?"

"Not exactly. I have a bit of bad news for you. Last night was foggy as hell out here and one of our refueling trucks accidentally bumped into your plane and tore up a section of the wing. It'll be weeks before we can get it fixed."

It took a few seconds for the full impact of his message to sink in. "How am I going to get back to England?"

He shrugged. "I don't know," he said, and I thought he was on the verge of adding that he didn't care, but he continued, "There's a B-17 that came in yesterday with flak damage. That should be ready to go back in a couple of days. They might give you a ride back."

"Can I get through to my base on the phone?"

"I doubt it, but we can try a teletype."

I asked him to send a teletype to Station F-122 in England, giving my name and squadron, and advising them that my aircraft was damaged and I would return as soon as possible. He said he'd take care of that. He also told me how to get in touch with the B-17 pilot.

A sergeant was detailed to take me to the hangar to get my flight gear, which I could store in the ops van until I left. When I saw my P-51, I knew why it would take several weeks to repair. The entire left wing outboard of the guns was nearly sheared off and hanging limp. I dragged my gear to the jeep.

"Where's the B-17?" I asked the sergeant.

"Next hangar."

We drove to the next hangar. The B-17 looked intact and ready to fly. The pilot and copilot were standing near it; the cowling was removed from one of the engines, and a mechanic was tinkering with something on the engine. I introduced myself and was told that they were missing only one engine part. It had been ordered and probably would arrive within a few days. The B-17 would then be ready to go back to England, and yes, they did have room for one more.

I found the Post Exchange in a small building next to the main gate. They were using military scrip instead of local currency but were willing to accept one of my English pounds in exchange for a few necessary toilet articles and a small bag to carry them. Later that afternoon, I went back to the Verriez café in the village and explained my situation to them. They were delighted that I would be around for a few days and told me that the upstairs bedroom was still available. This was Armistice Day, Gaston reminded me, and there was a memorial program of some kind in the village meetinghouse; he insisted that I attend the program with them.

And so it went. For the next few days, I was a member of the family. I spent most of the days at the base, chatting with the P-47 pilots. I thought I might have known some of them from flying school, but I didn't. Since I had flown combat missions in the Jug, they offered to let me fly a few missions with them, but I politely declined.

They were fighting a different kind of war. Their missions were seldom more than thirty minutes, but they flew two or three a day. They carried bombs, or napalm, or rockets, and were in constant contact with a forward air controller or even with some of the U.S. army ground units. Surprisingly, their loss rate was not much different from ours, though they had more damage from small-arms fire than we did. The P-47 was the American weapon most feared by German ground troops.

Finally, on November 13, the B-17's engine part arrived and the pilot told me that we would leave the next day. I said good-bye to my French "family" early next morning. Gaston gave me a beret to wear as a souvenir of our friendship and several photographs of the "Café et Coiffeur" that had been my temporary quarters. I insisted that he take my remaining two English pounds for my "bread and board." He accepted reluctantly, insisting that the room was *pour la famille* and not for rent. It was an emotional parting.

The flight to England was uneventful; we stayed at about five thousand feet—an uncommon experience for the bomber crew—and landed at Steeple Morden at noon. I invited the crew to stay for lunch, but they were eager to get home.

I thanked the crew, lugged my flight gear off the airplane, and trudged to Gremlin Villa, wearing my beret. My only greeting was from Burt. "Where in hell have you been?" I answered him in rather vulgar French terms, which he fortunately did not understand.

My damaged Mustang never returned to Steeple. That mission was never credited to me either, since the Form 1, from which all such data were derived, never reached Steeple. Years later, I noticed that my Form 5, the official record of my flying time, did not show any mission flown on November 10, 1944.

My next mission, on November 18, confirmed that the 8th Fighter Command shared my misgivings about the 262. It was a strafing mission to Leipheim, suspected to be the home base of an Me-262 Staffel.

"Things haven't changed that much over here after all," I said to Mendy. "My last mission before I left was strafing 262s at Lechfeld. Now I'm going after them again, at Leipheim."

"We're seeing more and more of them," he replied, "and that ain't good!"

"Maybe we'll see a little flak at Leipheim."

"That's not a maybe," replied Mendy. "That's a sure thing!"

The bombers had the day off. Eighth Air Force fighters fanned out all over Germany, dive-bombing and strafing transportation targets, oil dumps, and airfields. Major Sluga led the group with the 358th, and Jim Duffy led our squadron. I led the flight behind Duff. Though we had plenty of pilots, we were short on airplanes, so we were able to put up only three flights for this mission. I flew WR-M on this flight, since WR-N was still on the Continent. McKibbin, Dawe, and Lowry were temporarily unemployed.

We rendezvoused with the 4th Fighter Group, which was led by Lieutenant Colonel Kinnard, twenty miles northwest of the target. We provided top cover at eight thousand feet while the 4th Group strafed, then we reversed our roles. Both groups were briefed to take out any gun emplacements spotted.

The airfield was well defended; there were at least thirty machine-gun positions and more than half a dozen 20mm emplacements. The 4th Group eliminated several flak positions as they worked the field over. Kinnard said later that he counted forty-four Me-262s scattered around the field; most were well camouflaged and hidden in the heavily wooded areas bordering the field.

The 4th Group made four passes, then climbed to our altitude to provide top cover while we dove down to strafe. By then there were at least ten fires burning in different parts of the airfield, and dense smoke made it difficult to pick out targets. The tall trees bordering the field forced us to come in at a higher angle, making us more vulnerable to the antiaircraft fire.

On my first pass, I lined up on a camouflaged aircraft partly hidden in the woods on the far side of the field and fired a long burst as I closed in on it. I saw flashes all over it, and it burst into flames just as I passed over it. As I pulled up I saw a gun emplacement on the roof of a small building to my right; two gunners were doing their best to end my career. I never enjoyed flying down somebody's gun barrel, but I devoted my second pass to putting them out of business. They saw me coming and both were firing at me, and my stomach was churning a bit, but it was no contest.

My third pass was unsuccessful. I lined up my target, only to see it blow up as another Mustang came in from my right. I had to pull up to avoid a collision.

By this time the flak had decreased considerably, but the

smoke had increased. As I started my fourth pass, a breeze blew the smoke away from the buildings at the far end of the field, and I saw a 262 parked on a hardstand in front of a blister hangar about four hundred yards away. I put the gunsight on the 262 and fired all the way in. It flared up while I was still about two hundred yards away, but I kept firing until I had to pull up to avoid flying into the hangar roof. I looked back as I pulled away from the tree line and saw the plane blazing away.

"Uncle here. Let's regroup and get out of here," Sluga called. We formed up well above the airfield and headed out. The 4th Fighter Group set course, and we followed. We left a large number of aircraft and a few buildings still burning. We had worn out our welcome, having visited devastation on Leipheim for nearly an hour. The 4th Group claimed twenty destroyed, and the 355th claimed fifteen. In our squadron, Ted Todd and I both flamed two while Jim Duffy and Tom Wood each got one. The Me-262s that had not been destroyed had plenty of holes in them. A significant dent had been made in the Me-262 inventory. The 4th Group lost two aircraft in a midair collision over the target. Flak damaged four airplanes in our squadron, but all pilots returned safely to base.

We were supposed to go strafing again the next day, but fog and rain kept us grounded. Five replacement pilots, all second lieutenants, joined us in the afternoon: Carl Decklar, Jack Fletcher, Warren Gadpaille, Donald Galer, and Robert Goth.

November 23 was Thanksgiving Day, and we were released from operations. The 354th repeated its winning 1943 performance at the skeet-shooting contest, and once again our entire squadron had a turkey dinner at the Red Cross Aero Club, with personnel from the other two squadrons acting as waiters and KPs. Our star gunners were Ace Graham, Brady Williamson, Floyd Schultz, Stan Silva, and Bill Falvey.

On November 24 I received a brand-new P-51D to replace the one I left at Denain. Apparently the group had written that one off. McKibbin and Dawe spent the day checking it over, painting our names and the swastikas on it, and helping Lowry and the armament people bore-sight the guns.

The next day, I flew it on its maiden combat flight. It was a frustrating and nerve-racking one for me, but the new Mustang behaved perfectly.

It seemed like such an easy mission: Protect the second box of B-24s trying to destroy a railway viaduct near Bielefeld, about fifty miles southwest of Hannover. There were only thirty bombers in this task force, so it didn't seem to be a difficult assignment. The first task force, consisting of sixty B-24s, was hitting the oil refinery at Misburg, a dot on the map just outside of Hannover. Another fighter group was assigned to protect them.

The 2d Scouting Force, operating from Steeple, arrived at the Misburg target area about five minutes ahead of the bomber force. Captain Bob Whitlow, who was leading eight Scouting Force Mustangs, saw the first gaggle of Me-109s streak through the bomber force before he could intercept them. "They charged right through the box!" he said in debriefing. "It was rough. I saw eight bombers go down, like somebody throwing a handful of rocks. My second flight headed off the second wave, and the flight I was leading headed off the third wave. I don't think the fourth and last wave made an attack." The Scouting Force held them off for about five minutes, charging into one wave after another as the Luftwaffe tried to regroup; they shot down five 109s, probably destroyed another, and damaged two, all without loss. They were credited with stopping the German formations from wiping out or badly damaging that box of B-24s.

Larry Sluga led the group with the 358th at the front of the last box, the 357th brought up the rear, and I led the 354th, which was assigned to roam along the flanks. I had started out with sixteen planes, but my wingman turned back with a rough engine, and two others turned back from

Duff's Blue Flight. The two spares filled Blue Flight, so with Deacon Priest leading Green Flight, Duff had eight ships in his section and I had seven in my lead section. We heard the Scouting Force fighting off the attacks at the front end of the bomber stream, but we were too far behind to help. Besides, we soon had company of our own.

Duff was well above and on the starboard side of the bombers, and I had my section low on the port side. Duff spotted a large gaggle—seventy-five plus—at twenty-eight thousand feet and heading our way from the nine-o'clock position to the bombers. Duff took his section over the top of the bombers and charged into the German formation as I climbed at full power to help out with my section. Several other Mustangs from another group (probably the group that had been assigned to protect the front boxes of B-24s) joined Duff in breaking up that attack. The dogfights sprawled all over the sky from twenty-five thousand feet on down.

"Falcon Red Three here. Another gaggle coming in from six o'clock high!" I looked behind me and saw what appeared to be at least seventy-five Me-109s and FW-190s at about twenty-seven thousand feet, heading for the starboard side of the bomber stream, and there was nothing between them and the bombers. They had suckered me and my small group out of position. This was a typical German tactic: Attack the bombers with overwhelming force where the escort fighters are thinly scattered along the route.

With my adrenaline working overtime, I jammed the throttle to emergency war power and whipped the Mustang around in a climbing right turn to intercept the first wave— about ten Me-109s that were slanting down toward the B-24s in a loose, line-abreast formation. I put my gunsight pipper well ahead of the nearest 109 and started firing. I was still out of effective range, but I hoped to break up the attack. I started a steep diving turn to chase them, when I suddenly noticed white puffs all around my airplane.

A quick look behind revealed two FW-190s coming in from above and my right rear, the first one firing away. The rest of my section was nowhere in sight. I turned sharply into the 190s. They sped past me, then climbed to rejoin a group of about a dozen FW-190s above and to the rear of the bombers. They were not in the attacking force, but seemed to be providing top cover to protect the Me-109s.

I was alone. The rest of my section had either been shot down, I thought, or were busy trying to avoid being shot down.

I headed toward the second wave of Me-109s diving toward the bombers, but once again, two 190s sliced toward me from above, firing as they came. When I turned into them, they sped by and returned to their formation two thousand feet above me. It dawned on me: They had me boxed in. They probably could have shot me down if they committed themselves to doing that, but apparently that was not their function—I would have drawn them from their assigned mission. They were there to keep escort fighters from interfering with the main attack. If they managed to shoot me down in the process, that would be a bonus.

I felt helpless and frustrated. A number of thoughts were racing through my mind—none of them pleasant. There was no way I could stop the attacking 109s all by myself. I knew that if I ignored the 190s and pressed my attack, I would be dead meat before I fired my first round. And when the last wave of 109s had started their assault, the 190s would be free to play with me—with all the advantages of numbers and altitude. I might get one of them, but they'd eventually nail me.

I heard the sounds of combat from Priest's flight on the deck, so I headed down in a steep dive. I leveled off just above the tops of the broken cloud deck, but by then the radio was quiet and there was no aircraft in sight.

I climbed back up to twenty-five thousand feet and headed home. I was the only airplane in that piece of sky. I felt dejected and humiliated; I had been unable to protect the bombers from attack, and many of them had paid the price. I wondered what had happened to the rest of my section.

I found out at the debriefing. Lieutenant Floyd Schultz,

leading my second element, reported the second gaggle behind us, and was still watching them when I made that hard climbing turn to intercept. My wingman had aborted earlier, and when Schultz turned around, I wasn't there. Assuming that I was still on my way to help Duff, Schultz kept going and joined Duff's element. Green Flight followed him.

As Duff had latched on to the tail of an FW-190, he took a quick look behind him: There was no one there, not even his wingman. He opened fire and found that the guns kept firing even after he released the trigger. He was spraying lead all over the sky, and some of it hit the enemy fighter. He chopped the throttle to keep from overrunning the 190, and the guns stopped firing. When he pushed the throttle forward, the guns started firing again. The German pilot jettisoned his canopy. "I could see him twisting his neck from one side to the other," said Duff. "He must have thought I was the most eager guy in the whole air force, shooting like that. He fell into a flat spin and jumped out." Jim's guns finally stopped firing: He was out of ammunition.

When he looked behind him again, there was an Me-109 right on his tail and firing. "I never worked so hard in my life, getting away from that guy. I thought he was going to follow me all the way to England. I couldn't do anything but try to stay out of his way; I didn't have any more ammunition."

Priest caught up with two FW-190s on the deck. When he shot down the first one and swung toward the second, the German pilot bailed out before Deacon could get a shot off.

Chuck Hauver and Joe McLear also nailed two each; and Joe Mellen and John Molnar got one apiece to bring the squadron total to nine destroyed and four damaged. The 357th destroyed nine and damaged one; and the 358th claimed four destroyed and three damaged. The 2d Scouting Force destroyed five, had one probable, and damaged three. Neither the group nor the Scouting Force had any losses, though there were a few times in that rhubarb when I thought I'd be listed in the loss column that day. I seemed to be in the wrong piece of sky the whole time.

During the debriefing and the bull session after the mission, several points were brought out: the importance of maintaining flight integrity; of wingmen staying with the leader; and above all, letting others in the squadron know what was going on. For some of the pilots, this was the first taste of combat. In several instances the teamwork among flight leader, element leader, and wingman was not what it should have been.

Another lesson we relearned from that mission: Don't be drawn away from the bombers in pursuit of an attacking force, thus leaving the bombers open to a massive follow-up attack—a lesson learned early in the game by veteran pilots.

We also discussed the Luftwaffe tactics: Concentrate a large force on a specific bomber task force, thereby overwhelming the fighter escort and limiting its ability to intercept. This was a return to early Luftwaffe tactics of concentrating huge fighter attacks against a relatively small force and inflicting unsustainable losses on that force, the classic example was the total destruction of the 100th Bomb Group on a mission early in 1943, for which the 100th was known thereafter as the "Bloody Hundredth."

A noticeable departure from previous attacks was the presence of a German "top cover" to deflect the escort fighters from the main attack.

On November 28 we were scheduled to go back to Leipheim on a carbon copy of the November 18 mission. Five minutes before briefing time, the mission was scrubbed because of lousy weather in the target area. I was not disappointed.

On November 29 the group was divided into A and B groups again. Lieutenant Colonel Stewart headed A Group, with three flights from the 354th and two from the 358th. Bert Marshall took over A Group when Stewart aborted because of a rough engine. Major Hodge Kirby led B Group, with three flights from the 357th and two from our squadron—my flight and Jim Duffy's. A Group freelanced ahead of the bomber force, while B Group provided close escort for the B-24s.

Our part of the mission was uneventful. Marshall and Graham led their flights down to attack trains. Ace destroyed the locomotive but called off the attack on the passenger cars when it became obvious that the passengers fleeing from the train were not military. Derby hats and umbrellas were not standard issue to the Wehrmacht.

Bert found another train to attack but encountered a number of flak cars in the same area. His airplane caught the brunt of the flak barrage. As he limped home, Deacon Priest provided a close escort. Bert's hydraulic system had been shot out, and he made another belly landing—his third—at Steeple. He was unhurt, but his airplane had sustained major damage—more than two hundred holes of various sizes. It was stripped for parts and consigned to the junk heap.

"What is it with you and flak?" asked Stewart. "You got a magnet in that airplane?"

Marshall finished his tour with that spectacular landing. He had elected to return to the 355th after his leave—welcome news for all of us. To top off an unforgettable day, he learned that he had been promoted to lieutenant colonel that afternoon. He had gone from captain to lieutenant colonel in fewer than three months. "At that rate," said Duff, "he'll get his first star by Christmas." He was by far the most popular officer in the group, and there was no rancor or ill will at his rapid rise.

The 355th flew seventeen missions in November; weather canceled almost as many. We destroyed seventy-three aircraft—ground and air—for the loss of nine.

December 1944

December came in with strong winds, low clouds, and blustery rain—a precursor of the foul weather to come. We were released from operations.

Al White and Norbert "Nobby" Jackson completed their combat tours and were awaiting orders to return Stateside. Al had opted to return to the 355th after his leave; Nobby had requested reassignment. "These guys are sure finishing their tours in a hurry," I said to Jim.

"That's because they're flying longer missions than we did in the 47s," he replied. "The average mission these days is five hours or more. In the Jug, it was closer to three hours—even less at the beginning." True enough. With an average of five hours per mission, only sixty missions were needed to reach the magic three hundred hours—a matter of four months or so if you didn't take many leaves and passes. When I finished my three-hundred-hour tour, I had more than seventy-five missions, more than half of those in the P-47.

On December 3 I woke up feeling like I had been run over by a truck—aching all over. I checked in with Doc Fontenot, expecting him to give me a couple of APC tablets and tell me to see him in the morning. He took my temperature, and to my surprise ordered me to the base hospital, where I spent the next three days. I was the only patient in the ten-bed ward. I read every magazine in the place, slept a lot, and bitched most of the time. Sylvia, a cute young English girl working for the Red Cross, visited me several times and brightened my spirits.

Jim and Burt visited me once to tell me about a productive mission on December 5, when Billy Hovde led his squadron into a gaggle of seventy-plus FW-190s. He shot down five and shared another, completely breaking up the Luftwaffe attack before they could reach the bombers. Duff and Stan Silva were the only two from our squadron to score. Ace Graham stopped by to say, "Get off your ass! There's a war going on!"

I was back to normal on December 7, and Doc cleared me for flight. Weather canceled all operations the next day, but I finally flew a five-hour escort mission to the Stuttgart area on December 9. I led the squadron and then the group after Major Kirby had to return when he developed engine trouble over the North Sea. Flak around the Stuttgart area was heavy as usual, but otherwise the mission was uneventful.

On nearly every mission, pilots reported seeing contrails of V-2 rockets headed for England. Most of the launch sites were in Holland or Belgium. I watched a V-2 shortly after it was launched, passing just about half a mile from us, its rocket engine spewing fire from the tail end as it soared into the stratosphere. Awesome!

On December 11 Duff led A Squadron and I led B Squadron on an escort mission to Hanau. It was another five-hour milk run.

Duff and I requested a forty-eight-hour pass and were mildly surprised when it was approved. The squadron had plenty of pilots, and the two-day-pass restrictions had eased. We hadn't done London together for several months.

We got to London before noon, and after checking in at the officers' hotel on Jermyn Street, we headed for the Rainbow Club for lunch. As we walked along Regent Street, crowded with shoppers, we suddenly heard the unmistakable sound of a V-1's pulse-jet engine. We looked up and saw it clearly, less than a thousand feet high, nearly overhead. Everyone on the crowded sidewalk stopped and stared up at it.

Then the rasping, buzzing sound of the engine stopped.

The V-1 slanted down toward the ground. It seemed to be headed right for us. We flattened ourselves against the wall of a large building, and we had a lot of company. We looked as if we were all plastered against the walls.

The V-1 passed overhead, about two hundred feet up, and crashed with an earsplitting roar about three blocks away.

Almost instantly, the traffic—pedestrian and vehicular— that had come to a standstill at the approach of the buzz bomb, was back to normal. As Duff and I stepped away from the wall, a scrawny little woman—she looked to be in her late sixties—passed us, muttering to herself, "Bloody nuisance, these buzz bombs!"

From a German standpoint, the V-1 was a good investment. For the price of one bomber (including crew training, bombs, and fuel) they could fire more than three hundred V-1s, each with a ton of TNT, a range of about 150 miles, and a better chance of reaching its target.

Wartime London was exciting and lively. There were plenty of good restaurants, nightclubs, and after-hours clubs, all bustling with activity. At times it was hard to tell there was a war going on, but after the manned bomber raids ended, the V-1s and V-2s were constant menacing reminders. The ubiquitous uniforms, the blackout curtains, and the dim lights moving slowly in the hushed streets added to the atmosphere of impending disaster—the Damoclean sword of the V weapons.

In Piccadilly Circus, the statue of Eros was packed in sandbags to prevent damage, as were most other statues and monuments throughout the city. Damage caused by earlier bombings was much in evidence, especially in the waterfront area. It didn't come close to the damage I was to see a few years later in Hamburg and Berlin, but it impressed me at the time.

The streets were dimly lit at night. Cars used soft blue parking lights, never headlights. It was easy to get around the city. Subway trains, double-decker buses, and taxicabs provided transportation throughout Greater London.

People who had been bombed out of their homes had established temporary quarters in most of the Underground stations. There were beds, suitcases, dressers, chairs, tables—everything you might expect in a home except privacy. I was accustomed to seeing them there, but I always marveled at their ability to live near-normal lives under such conditions. The subway dwellers had become oblivious to the crowds of passersby and the noise and rushing air of the trains.

London taxicabs were square and boxy-looking but very roomy. Three people could sit comfortably in the backseat, but there also were two pull-down jump seats facing rearward. Next afternoon, Duff and I were in the back of a London taxi with two young ladies we'd met the evening before, headed for a theater in Leicester Square to see *Gone With the Wind*. Suddenly the driver slammed on the brakes and ran across the street into an Underground station.

We looked at each other, wondering at the strange behavior of the driver. Then it dawned on us. We started to jump out and follow the cabbie, but before we opened the door the V-1 exploded with a deafening crash two blocks away. The driver had spotted the buzz bomb, and when he saw the little puff of smoke as the engine stopped and the bomb started its glide, he had wasted no time finding shelter.

The cabbie returned and started off again without a word of explanation or apology.

"Hey!" I yelled at him. "Why didn't you warn us?"

"No time, Guv'nor."

London cabbies liked American passengers because they usually tipped generously above the metered fare. When he dropped us off at the cinema, I handed him the exact amount shown on the meter and walked away. "What? No tip?" he yelled.

"No time, Guv'nor!" I yelled back.

On December 16 the German Army opened its surprise counteroffensive in the Ardennes sector of Belgium.

American troops were caught completely off guard, due to a
colossal intelligence failure and the complete misjudgment
at the highest levels of the Allied command of German intentions and capability. The Wehrmacht breakthrough and
progress in the first few days were startling and alarming. In
addition, it seemed that the gods of war were on the German
side, because the miserable weather on the Continent kept
the Ninth Air Force grounded. Even in England, heavy fog
and multilayered clouds stymied Eighth Air Force attempts
to provide support for the ground troops.

The "mission" on December 19 epitomized our anger
and frustration at our inability to help our army ground units
now catching hell in the Ardennes area. First, Burt Sims
came through the pilot quarters at 7:30 A.M., announcing a
briefing at eight forty-five. Just as he was finishing his
wake-up calls, he returned to yell, "Briefing's been moved
up to 0815!" We scrambled to the briefing room on a few
cups of coffee. When we got there, a message from headquarters ordered a fifteen-minute delay.

"Gawdammit!" yelled Brady. "Can't those guys tell
time?"

Just as the briefing began, another teletype ordered that
one hour be added to all the times mentioned in the field order. A heavy fog was settling in around Steeple.

We were to patrol an area around Paderborn, hoping to
entice the Luftwaffe up for a little brawl. Failing that, we
were hoping to find breaks in the overcast that would allow
us to strafe a German airfield about ten miles southwest of
Paderborn, at Geseke, where the Luftwaffe was believed to
have a large concentration of fighters supporting the
Ardennes breakthrough. Headquarters did not tell us how to
find Paderborn on a continent hidden by clouds. After the
briefing, we grabbed some breakfast. As we headed for the
airplanes, another half-hour delay was ordered.

Finally we started engines, taxied into takeoff positions,
and were told to wait for a green light from the tower. Ten
minutes later, we got word from the tower that we might as
well wait in the squadron ready rooms. We taxied back to

the dispersal areas and trudged to Gremlin Villa. The fog was still with us. We couldn't see the southeastern end of the runway. At noon the mission was scrubbed and we were released for the rest of the day.

"All this, and we didn't help those poor GIs a damn bit," said Duff. Then, seeing Chaplain Zeigler at the end of the table, he asked, "Chaplain, is God on the side of the Germans in this one?"

The chaplain shrugged. "I prefer to believe He's on ours."

Heavy fog stayed with us for the next three days. The news from the Army ground units under attack in Belgium was not encouraging. On December 23 the fog lifted just enough for the groups to take off. I led the A Group section of our squadron and Jim Duffy led the B Group section. Ace Graham's wingman, Lieutenant Goth, became disoriented in the heavy fogbank and crashed just after takeoff. He survived with minor injuries. Trying to avoid a collision, Duff's no. 4 man, Lieutenant Heaton, stalled out and crashed near Baldock. He survived the crash but suffered head injuries and minor burns. It wasn't a good start.

We escorted the bombers to the Coblenz–Trier area. About ten minutes ahead of us, the 4th Fighter Group found more than two hundred Luftwaffe fighters and shot down thirty-five of them for a loss of five of their own. Two other fighter groups in that area joined the party and nailed thirty-one more. We didn't see a single enemy fighter. "We've got to figure out how we can be in the right place at the right time!" said Graham.

Dense fog blanketed the base on December 24; visibility was one hundred yards at scheduled takeoff time. I wasn't scheduled on this one. The Mustangs taxied into takeoff positions, and the pilots were told to shut down, leave the airplanes in position, and return to their ready rooms. Two and a half hours later, the fog thinned a little; the pilots rushed out and took off before it closed in again. The mission was a milk run, and Steeple was fogged in when they returned.

Graham took eight ships into Raydon, Duff took eight into Honington, and Brady took four into Wattisham; the rest of the 355th Group landed at Leiston. And that's where they spent Christmas Eve.

The December 25 field order released the 354th Squadron airplanes at Raydon and Honington, and told them to return to Steeple when weather permitted. The rest of the 355th Group planes were to escort B-24s to Trier. Graham wasn't happy sitting on the ground at Raydon while the rest went into action, so he got permission from VIII Fighter Command to join the other two squadrons. Ace's seven ships (one had engine trouble and didn't take off) caught up with the group and the rear box of bombers near Ostend. That's when a gaggle of about fifty FW-190s came steaming in from their three-o'clock position, while another twenty-five Me-109s provided top cover for them.

"Keep your eye on those 109s," Graham told his no. 3 man. "I'm going after these 190s." He peeled off into a steep dive toward the middle of their formation. His wing-man took one look at all those 190s and didn't follow; he just kept flying straight ahead. When the ensuing wild party was over, Graham had bagged two FW-190s and broken up the gaggle; Chuck Hauver had shot down a 190 and a 109. Most of the 355th Group landed at Leiston—Steeple was still socked in tight.

On December 28, the Leiston division of the 355th escorted B-24s against marshaling yards near Hamburg. No enemy fighters appeared. Our planes finally landed at Steeple on their return to England. The pilots who had spent Christmas at Honington and Wattisham were also able to get back to their own beds.

Graham had a short talk with the wingman who hadn't followed him in his attack on the 109s. "I just couldn't do it, sir," he said. "I wanted to and I tried to, but I just couldn't!" He was almost in tears.

"I'm sending you back to the States," Graham said. "You don't belong in this outfit. I'm sending you back as 'unfit for combat.' Maybe they can find a slot for you—maybe in

Training Command. The adjutant will have your orders for you in the morning."

The pilot saluted and walked out, shoulders slumped and head hanging low.

"Maybe I should have had him court-martialed," Ace said to me later, "but I really felt sorry for the kid." Then he laughed. "I probably wouldn't be feeling sorry for him if I were sitting in a POW camp right now!"

On December 31 we escorted B-17s to Misburg. Mendy was leading the squadron, I was leading the second section, and Ace Graham was leading Green Flight behind me. On climbout, I discovered that the K-14 gunsight was stuck in the "fixed" position, and no matter where I put the switch, I couldn't get it to the "gyro" position. "No problem," I thought. But I wasted a lot of time and effort trying to find a switch or a circuit breaker that would solve the problem. It was only later that I realized that I should have been paying more attention to the "gun heater" switch. Normally, we turned that switch on right after we started engines for a combat mission, because the oil and grease congealed at the extremely low temperatures at high altitude and tended to jam the guns. For some reason—maybe I was distracted by radio contacts or conversations with McKibbin—I had neglected to do it. A stupid mistake, hardly the kind of thing you expect from one of the "old hands."

Not long after rendezvous, I heard Ace's calm voice: "Falcon Leader, I've got a bunch of Focke-Wulfs cornered back here. And there's plenty to go around."

Mendy didn't answer. I thought he might be having radio trouble, so I said, "Where are you, Ace?"

"Just make a one-eighty and you cawn't miss us," replied Ace in his British accent. I wheeled Blue Flight around and, sure enough, there were "plenty to go around."

I managed to get right behind one of them. He was in a diving left turn, right in my gunsight. I pressed the trigger. To my consternation, only the right outboard gun fired.

That one gun popped away with no effect until I finally

got a hit on his right wingtip. He straightened out and dove straight away from me, centered in my fixed gunsight. A perfect setup, but I just couldn't hit him. Chuck Hauver was just off my right wing. He could see that I was having problems. "Let me have him," he said. I slid over to the left and watched him blow the FW out of the sky. Belatedly, I turned on the gun heater switch. I felt foolish, frustrated, and furious.

Chuck broke off to the right. Just as I turned to join him, I heard my wingman, Johnny Molnar, yell, "Bud! Get this sonofabitch off my ass!"

I racked into a hard left turn and saw Johnny about five hundred yards behind me with a Focke-Wulf about three hundred yards behind him. Molnar was turning that Mustang as tight as he could, and the FW was sticking with him, but it was unable to lead him enough for a shot. I joined the rat race.

Johnny kept yelling at me to "get this sonofabitch off my ass!" and I kept trying to assure him calmly that I would do just that. It wasn't that easy.

With Molnar leading the aerobatic display, we used up quite a bit of sky and soon found ourselves down to about seven thousand feet, just above a layer of clouds. There was neither sky nor airspeed enough left for anything but tight turns, and all three of us were doing the best we could in that department. I lowered a few degrees of wing flaps—I didn't dare look down at how many degrees. "Johnny"—I tried to sound calm, but my blood pressure must have been sky-high—"did you lower your flaps a little?"

"Yeah."

"Keep the stick pressure you have now. He's not gaining on you at all, but I'm gaining on him." I tried to sound confident.

I could see the vapor trails from the wingtips of the planes in front of me, and I knew that my wingtips were producing the same pattern. All three or us were right on the edge of high-speed stalls. My Mustang kept giving me subtle clues, through the control column and the seat bottom, that it would be unwise to tighten the turn much more. If I stalled out of this turn, Molnar would be on his own. Every ten seconds or so, the wings of the 190 became blanketed very briefly with white vapor, an indication that the German pilot knew I was getting in position for a shot, that he was slipping closer to a stall. He couldn't increase his turn enough to get to a shooting position on Johnny, and I sensed that he felt he was running out of time.

The 190 pilot pulled it in a little too tightly. Suddenly his plane snapped viciously to the right and spun down into the cloud layer. The FW had a reputation of snap-rolling out of very tight turns. I watched him spin into the clouds. "Man, that was close!" said Johnny as he raised his flaps and eased into his wingman position. It wasn't hot inside my cockpit, but I had to wipe the sweat out of my eyes.

The terrain below the overcast was hilly, with some peaks rising to nearly three thousand feet, and I doubt that the German pilot had enough altitude to recover, but I'll never know for sure—I wasn't about to follow him into that overcast. I was tempted to claim it as a probable, but it was just as likely that he was "one that got away."

In the meantime, Ace Graham was adding to his score— he shot down two FW-190s, and Chuck Hauver damaged another after shooting down the one that would have been mine but for a stupid mistake. Chuck became an ace with his fifth victory on this mission, the last of his combat tour.

Nearly all of the Eighth Air Force missions during the final two weeks of December were aimed at destroying the lines of supply and communications of the German counteroffensive in the Ardennes. By the end of December the German "bulge" had been contained and even reversed, the siege of Bastogne had been relieved, and the Allied forces were getting ready for the final offensive thrust that would end the war.

The 355th Fighter Group ended the year with 590 confirmed enemy aircraft destroyed. We were in third place in that category behind the 4th and 56th Fighter Groups, which had been in combat before us. Like those units, we had paid a price.

Hitler's desperate gamble to turn the tide on his Western Front had failed. German troops were in retreat, and the Allied armies were on the move again.

January 1945

The receipt of a field order for a mission next morning curtailed our New Year's Eve party a bit. As usual, young ladies from neighboring towns had been transported to the party in GI buses—sometimes GI trucks. Because of the field order, their return transportation was scheduled to leave the officers' club at 12:30 A.M., and all pilots scheduled for the mission were to be in bed by 1:00 A.M. Some left earlier—and that's how I met Ruby.

I had noticed her at the public swimming pool at Letchworth the previous summer on one of those rare warm summer days. She looked great in a white bathing suit and she was, to my eyes, lovely. As I was trying to impress her with my prowess off the diving board, she left. Diving was not one of my finer skills. She came to the officers' club weekly dances occasionally but always sat with the same 358th pilot and another couple. When Ruby's escort left at about 11:00 P.M. on New Year's Eve, because he was on the flight schedule, I went over to her table and asked her to dance with me. She smiled and said, "Yes," and I was smitten. I wasn't much of a dancer, so after the song ended, I asked if I could join her at the table. She smiled again and said, "Of course." It was the beginning of a lovely romance.

We exchanged the usual small talk, and I learned that her name was Ruby Bradbury, she was eighteen years old (I was twenty-two) and lived with her parents in Letchworth, and that the other pilot was just a friend. "Aren't you on tomorrow's mission?" she asked. I replied that I was, but I'd be glad to keep her company until her bus left. We made a date to go to the movies in Letchworth on the following Wednesday, January 3. There was an evening "liberty run" into the nearby towns of Letchworth, Hitchin, and Baldock every Monday, Wednesday, and Friday. The trucks departed from Steeple at 6:00 P.M. and left each town at 11:00 P.M., when all the pubs closed. There was time to see a movie and not much else. It became our regular dating pattern: Wednesday night movie and Saturday night dance at the officers' club. We soon fell in love.

Dawn came with typical raw and damp English weather. From our breakfast bar in Gremlin Villa, we heard the 97th Bomb Group's B-17s taking off from Bassingbourne, a few miles to the north, and a few of our own P-51s getting a pre-flight run-up by early-bird crew chiefs. Gremlin Villa was the usual bedlam of high-spirited voices, Ping-Pong, and Benny Goodman on the record player. We ate our Spam-and-eggs breakfast and checked the schedule to make sure all the pilots were on hand. At about 8:20 A.M. we headed for the group briefing room about a hundred yards away. The last B-17 was just lifting off the runway at Bassingbourne—already in trouble.

We all heard it at the same time—the sound of engines getting closer and closer. Then we saw it. The B-17 was in obvious distress, seemingly headed right for us. The right outboard engine was on fire, and the inboard engine on the left side seemed to be just windmilling. We watched, horror-struck, as it passed a few hundred feet from us, barely missing the control tower, left wing low and skimming just above the ground. Just past our main runway the left wing hit the ground. The B-17 cartwheeled and slammed into the ground in the middle of our D Flight dispersal area and exploded. We stared numbly as the fire trucks and ambulances raced to the scene. Men were running in all directions. At least one P-51 was burning.

First Lieutenant Sheldon Prescott, the group personal equipment officer, who had come overseas with the 355th, made this entry in his diary: "Ordinary day at the base (a work day, not a holiday), except that a Fortress from Bassingbourne blew up here on the field this morning at 0800 while taking off on a mission. All its crew were killed and it destroyed 2 of our 51s and damaged 3 others. Also hurt one of our boys. I went out there about noon and there were still parts of human bodies out on the field."

Graham broke the silence. "There's nothing we can do down there," he said. "We have a job to do. Let's go." We followed him silently to the group briefing room.

The mood was somber as we went through the details of the mission. We were to escort B-17s attacking oil refineries at Derben, about fifty miles west of Berlin.

On our way back to Gremlin Villa we could see the blackened tail of an incinerated Mustang—all that was left of it. Three other D Flight airplanes had been damaged. Takeoff was delayed fifteen minutes to allow for aircraft reassignments.

Graham led the squadron, and I led Yellow Flight behind him. We made rendezvous near Lenzen at twenty-eight thousand feet, and were just settling into our escort duties when Stan Silva, flying no. 3 in my flight, called in, "Falcon, Yellow 3 here. Two bogeys coming in fast at eight o'clock high." I wheeled the flight in a sharp turn toward the approaching contrails. The Me-262s turned away and headed for the deck. Before we reached the target, two more 262s tried to get a crack at the bombers, but Graham's flight drove them away. The German jets wanted no part of a dogfight with Mustangs; they preferred to sneak up from the rear and clobber unwary victims. Even in a so-called milk run, we couldn't relax; there always was the possibility that a German pilot was looking at us through his gunsight. There was plenty of heavy flak in the target area, but the prop-driven Luftwaffe were nowhere in sight.

The 355th was split again on January 2. This time the groups had different missions. Major Hodge Kirby led the 357th, with two of its flights and one flight from our squadron—led by Lt. Herb Mann—to escort bombers to the Remagen area. The 358th, with three of its own flights, escorted B-24s from the Dümmer Lake area to Charleroi. Meanwhile, two 354th flights, led by Mendenhall, had a different kind of mission.

Early that morning, a P-38 landed at Steeple, but this was not a run-of-the-mill P-38. It was an F-4. It had no identifying letters or numbers on the fuselage, and there were no .50-caliber machine guns in its nose. It was a photo-reconnaissance plane, stripped down to minimum weight, with sophisticated cameras in the nose instead of guns, and with souped-up engines. The 354th had the unusual mission of escorting this unarmed F-4 to a target at Coblenz.

The F-4 pilot made several runs over Coblenz at about twenty thousand feet, then headed home. Apparently he wanted no company from that point; he poured the coal to those two engines and climbed away, leaving the escort far behind, unable to match his speed, much less catch up. "What the hell did he need *us* for?" asked Mendy at debriefing. "He was probably laughing all the way home."

The weather turned bitterly cold that night, and frost was heavy by morning. Our supply of coal was strictly rationed, and we spent a lot of time looking for wood to chop up for our small stoves. To make matters worse, all our extra blankets had been stripped off the beds and sent to the Continent for use by our ground forces. We certainly didn't resent that, but we sure missed the extra blankets on those bitter nights. "It could be worse," said Duff. "We could be in the infantry, freezing our asses off!" We didn't complain.

Jim Duffy led the squadron on the January 3 escort for bombers pounding German supply lines and the artillery units supporting the Wehrmacht retreat. I led Yellow Flight behind him, and Ace led the two flights of the second section. A solid overcast obscured the ground, and that may have accounted for the lack of Luftwaffe activity. As Ace Graham put it, "They probably don't enjoy the prospect of popping through the overcast to find a bunch of Mustangs on their asses." For whatever reason, it was a milk run.

Weather grounded us on January 4, but we were having other problems. In addition to the shortage of fuel for our stoves, we now had a shortage of water. The water supply was erratic: Sometimes it was on, sometimes it was off. But the worst aspect of the problem was that the hot-water boiler in the washroom was out of order. No one seemed to know why, except that it probably had something to do with the water supply problem.

"If you think this is tough, go join an infantry unit in Belgium," Mike Glantz kept reminding us. That didn't make our problems go away, but it did put them in perspective.

Graham led the group with our squadron on January 5; I led his second section as escort for Liberators attacking rail targets behind the German southern front. We saw nothing but heavy cloud cover over the Continent.

Bob Heaton came back from the hospital that evening with a head full of scars to show for his accident on December 23.

The miserable weather continued, canceling a mission on January 6 and messing up another on January 7. We escorted B-24s headed for targets in the Strasbourg area. The Continent was hidden in clouds, with tops to about ten thousand feet. As we approached Saarburg, about fifty miles north of the target area, the bombers encountered a solid overcast, with tops well above thirty thousand feet. The bomber box we were escorting bored right into the overcast. Major Larry Sluga, who was leading our group, figured that we couldn't do them much good in those clouds, so he began to orbit in the area where the bombers were expected to be on their way out. About twenty minutes later, a box of B-24s popped out of the wall of clouds, but it wasn't the group we had escorted in. Sluga decided to escort that box out and told us to stay in the area a while to see if our assigned box came out.

Five minutes later, another box emerged from the wall. This was our assigned group, so we took it home.

"War is hell, you guys!" yelled Mike Glantz. "We still have a water shortage, but there's a mission to fly. So up and at 'em, no matter how bad you smell!" It was January 8, still bitter cold, and the mission was another milk run over a continent still covered with clouds.

Burt's narrative records that there was still a fuel shortage as well as a water shortage. "The only thing there's no shortage of is—shortages."

On January 9 we awoke to a white world. Snow covered the field, the aircraft, the runways, and all of the English countryside. It was a beautiful sight to us New Englanders, but it kept us on the ground for a while. Gremlin Villa was the center of a series of snowball fights—fighter pilots venting their aggressive tendencies on each other in the absence of legitimate foes. Though the battles were hot and heavy, no serious casualties were reported.

Snow fell most of the day, and for the first time, we watched snowplows trying to keep the runways clear. There was a mission scheduled that day, but it was scrubbed even before the pilots were awakened.

It snowed most of that night, and again the scheduled mission was scrubbed early on January 10. There were a few breaks in the overcast that afternoon. Burt wanted to get some public relations photos of Mustangs flying over the snow-covered field. I led the squadron in a tight low-level formation over the field while Lt. Bill Dumas, the base photo officer, flew overhead in an AT-6, snapping pictures. Then the squadron broke up into flights and we came streaking across the field a few feet above the snow cover at about four hundred miles per hour for more photos. Some of the photographers were more concerned with avoiding decapitation than snapping photos at first, but we repeated the show several times so everyone could get a good shot. We had a ball.

The next day, we were told that none of the photos came

out satisfactorily. The photo lab said that their equipment was faulty.

Burt said, "Next time, we strafe the photo lab!"

Bill Dumas did not appear at the officers' club that night.

On January 11 the snow was deep and the clouds were low, and there was no flying. Snowball fights continued to rage with unabated enthusiasm all over the base, but the casualty list remarkably remained at zero. It rained the next day, and the snow was washed away.

The ceiling was two hundred feet and the visibility less than a mile on January 13 when the group took off to escort four boxes of B-24s from Cambrai to the Rudesheim rail bridge. I wasn't on the schedule. Lieutenant Ksanznak from the 358th was killed when he spun out of the overcast shortly after takeoff.

The weather on the Continent was no better, and the mission was recalled just after the B-24s dropped their bombs through the overcast. All of our Mustangs landed elsewhere when they returned to England; Steeple was zero-zero again. The 354th found usable runways at Everett, Manston, and Boxted, spent the night there, and returned the next morning.

On January 14, for some reason that I could never fathom, the people at the 8th Fighter Command split the 355th into four groups—A, B, C, and D—even though A and B groups were going on the same mission. Led by Major Wilson of the 357th, the A and B groups escorted bombers to Brauhschweig and back to the Dutch coast, where they dropped to the deck to shoot up sundry locomotives and trucks.

I was leading C Group, which consisted of three flights from our squadron. We escorted B-17s to Coblenz, then were directed by a ground-control station code-named Nuthouse to sweep the area east of Coblenz. Nuthouse reported enemy aircraft—rats—in the Bonn area and gave me the heading to fly. "Rats are at angels ten." I let down to twelve thousand feet and saw nothing but a few clouds.

"Nuthouse, this is Falcon Leader. No rodents here."

"Roger. We don't have them on the screen anymore. Return to Big Friends." I climbed back up toward Coblenz, caught up with the bombers, and escorted them to the North Sea. Except for heavy and uncomfortably close flak at Coblenz, it was a milk run.

Moon Elder led the third mission of the day at the head of D Group, which consisted of one flight from the 357th, two from the 354th—Graham and Duffy—and one from the 358th. They got all the action that day. In two separate encounters, Ace Graham shot down two FW-190s and finally lived up to his nickname, Lt. Newell Mills claimed two 109s and one FW-190, Lt. George Kemper and Lt. Carl Decklar each claimed two, and Lt. Tom Wood claimed one. Duff was totally frustrated because "I couldn't hit anything!," though he shot at plenty of Germans. After the mission, he found out that his gunsight had been replaced and the guns had not been bore-sighted. He had a few words to say to the armament section. Knowing Duff, I suspect it was a mild rebuke.

The target next day was Lechfeld—not exactly my favorite destination—but the home base of Me-262s. The plan called for B-17s to bomb the airfield, after which the fighters would strafe it. Major Sluga led A Group, which consisted of 358th and 357th airplanes; and Ace Graham led B Group, which consisted of four flights from our squadron and three flights from the 357th. "Why in hell do they keep up this A and B group crap?" Duff asked Mike Glantz. "We're all going to the same place!"

"It makes those headquarters types think they're winning the war with their clever tactics," explained Mike. "After all, they *are* much smarter than you are; *they're* not getting shot at!"

Lechfeld was completely obscured by low clouds. The bombers dropped their load through the overcast, but the planned strafing attack was out of the question. There were breaks in the overcast south and east of Lechfeld, so Sluga took A Group to the airfield at Landsberg, and Graham took B Group to Oberpfaffenhofen Airdrome, just outside of Munich.

"Obie," as our pilots had nicknamed it, was an active flight-training base when the 355th first visited it on April 5, 1944, and destroyed fifty-one German aircraft. Nearly a year later, its hangars and administrative buildings were battered, and only five aircraft were visible on the airfield. They were parked about twenty yards apart in front of one of the battered hangars. Graham didn't want the whole of B Group trying to shoot up five aircraft, which would have set up the potential for midair collisions, so he designated Red and Yellow Flights to strafe, and the rest to provide top cover. He was leading Red Flight and I was leading Yellow Flight.

On our first run, he set fire to a lone Me-109 and I set fire to a three-engine aircraft that looked like a Ju-52. The other three aircraft were not burning, so we made another pass. By this time the flak was getting hot and heavy, and thick black smoke was coming from the burning Ju-52, which partially obscured the other three parked aircraft. Graham got a lot of hits on one, and my wingman, Lieutenant Vickery, followed him with more hits, which finally set it on fire. White puffs from 20mm shells were all around us as we poured a lot of lead into the other two. There were plenty of holes in them, but none burned—there couldn't have been any fuel in them. The 20mm "golf balls" put a large, ragged hole in Graham's plane—outboard of the guns—and smaller holes in three other Mustangs.

We rejoined the rest of the group and set course for England. The Landsberg contingent had already left their target, where they destroyed nine aircraft and damaged several others.

At the officers' club that night, Duff gave Ace a hard time about "hogging those sitting ducks while we bored holes in the sky above you."

"There was a lot of flak down there, Duff," replied Ace, "and I didn't want you to get hurt."

"You didn't mind if Bud got hurt?"

"Bud must have a flak deflector on his airplane. Guys on each side of him on a strafing run get hammered, and he comes through without a scratch."

"Yeah. His crew chief probably puts a heavy coat of grease on his airplane. The flak just slides off."

I just sat there and smiled. I knew it was McKibbin's rabbit's foot.

January 16 was not a good day for the 355th. We lost five aircraft, but fortunately no pilots.

The villain was the weather. It was marginal at takeoff time, and went from bad to unbelievable as the group performed its assigned escort duty. I wasn't on that mission, and I went to the control tower to find out where the squadron was going to land. It certainly wouldn't be Steeple; I couldn't see the near end of the runway from the tower. Major John Elder was leading the group and requested permission from the controller to land the group on the Continent, but was told to try for Goxhill or Manston. Goxhill, more than a hundred miles away, wasn't an option for the Mustangs because of their fuel supply.

Graham managed to get our squadron, except for Lieutenant Vickery, into Manston before it closed down. Vickery landed at a fighter base in Belgium in marginal visibility and collided with a truck crossing the runway. He was unhurt, but his airplane was badly damaged. Three other pilots bailed out over England when they ran out of fuel with no place to go. Billy Hovde was trying to make a dead-stick landing at Manston after running out of fuel when a B-24 cut in front of him. He pulled up to avoid a collision, stalled out at about a hundred feet, and crashed short of the runway. Miraculously, he survived with only bruises and a deep gash in his back. His airplane was demolished, but it didn't burn—no fuel. The 65th Fighter Wing— there were four other fighter groups in our wing—lost fourteen planes and five pilots in this fiasco.

All pilots except Vickery returned to Steeple the next morning, some without their aircraft. Vickery came back via B-17 five days later after "freezing in a tent for four nights."

On January 17 the group, led by Stewart, escorted bombers to targets in the Hamburg area. Duff was leading the 354th, and I led his Blue Flight. On the way home I spotted a grass field with what appeared to be about a dozen twin-engine airplanes parked in a row. I told Duff I'd take my flight down to check it out. As soon as I started my firing pass, I realized that these "aircraft" were realistic dummies. It was not uncommon for the Germans to set up these enticing targets surrounded by flak guns. The dummies weren't real but the flak was, so, as Johnny Molnar put it later at debriefing, "We got the hell out of there in a hurry!"

Our coal supply was replenished on January 19, but still there was no hot water in the officers' washroom in our squadron area. The coal was the hard-to-light coke type, but Jim and I had a small metallic container of napalm outside the building. Having learned the hard way to use *very little* napalm, we had no problem lighting the coke.

On January 21 I led the squadron on another five-hour milk run to Heilbronn. There were lots of clouds, a little flak, and no Luftwaffe.

Captain Noble Peterson from the 358th led two flights of Mustangs on an unusual mission that day. The four planes in his flight had been modified to carry photorecce cameras, and one flight from our squadron went along as escorts. The destination was Pölitz, about a hundred miles northeast of Berlin. A 358th Mustang and a 354th Mustang returned early due to mechanical problems, so Peterson had a flight of six—including Lieutenants Dick White, Jack Fletcher, and Duran Vickery—when he reached Pölitz. The sky was clear but hazy, and they made two passes through heavy flak to take the pictures.

On their way home they were bounced by two Me-262s just north of Steinhuder Lake. The jets, which had become a common sight by then, seldom attacked Mustangs unless they caught a few of them napping. These two made several passes at our Mustangs. Our tactic was to keep turning into them, which caused the 262s to break away.

Graham left early on January 23 for Eighth Air Force headquarters. The rumor mill said he was going on a secret mission to Italy. He returned late next night, tired and disgusted that he hadn't been able to start on his secret mission. The next morning, January 25, he called Lee Mendenhall and me to his office.

"I'm sending you guys to Naples," said Ace. He handed an oversized envelope to Mendy. "This envelope has to get to General Eaker as soon as possible. His headquarters is at Capodichino Airport, just outside of Naples. You leave as soon as you can. Don't spend a lot of time packing!"

The envelope looked appropriately important, addressed to "General Ira C. Eaker, Commander, Middle East Air Force, BY HAND." The word EXPEDITE was stamped all over it in red letters.

What Ace didn't tell us—and we didn't find out until much later—was that the letter had already been delayed at least two days before it was given to Mendy.

We quickly packed a few necessities, but there was no way we could leave that day. Fog and light freezing rain that turned to snow in the afternoon kept us in the ready room, hoping for a small break in the weather. There was none. Next morning was more of the same, but we were able to get off early in the afternoon.

England, as usual, was covered with clouds, but by the time we reached the French coast, there were breaks in the overcast and the visibility was great. The ground war had passed from France into Germany by then, so there were no flak batteries to worry about.

We were approaching Paris when Mendy radioed that his fuselage tank, right behind the pilot's seat, had sprung a leak. I thought he was kidding. "Yeah, sure!" I answered. "Wishful thinking, Mendy."

"I'm not kidding!" he replied. "I'm getting soaked with gas! We're going to have to land at Orly." Later, I jokingly accused him of using his knife on the tank, but he denied it vehemently.

We landed at Orly Airport, just outside of Paris. By the time we found competent mechanics, it was dark. They drained the tank and removed our external tanks. These were made of compressed paper and were not designed to hold high-octane gasoline for any great length of time. They had begun to seep.

We spent the night at the airport, contrary to the reports circulated later at Steeple that we had gone into Paris for a bit of fun and games.

Orly was socked in the next morning—ceiling and visibility zero. No planes arrived or left. By noon, visibility had improved to half a mile, so off we went, hoping to reach Naples before nightfall. Air-to-ground visibility was limited to just a few miles because of the lingering fog, haze, and broken clouds.

The P-51 did not have sophisticated navigational equipment. It had a magnetic compass, a remote-reading compass indicator, and a clock. The four-channel UHF radio could be used to call a homing station, if there was one around. Under the circumstances, our maps were no great help.

As we approached the Mediterranean Sea, we could dimly make out the coastline but couldn't tell exactly where we were. That's when Mendy called. "Bud, I don't think I can make it to Naples on the fuel I have left. I'm going to try to land at Cannes."

"Oh, no!" I thought. "Not again!" I had enough fuel— eighty gallons more than he had—to get to Naples, but *he* had the envelope.

Mendy started calling for a steer to Cannes or Nice, but there was no reply. Thinking his radio might be weak, I repeated his calls. No answer. He switched to the emergency channel but couldn't get anything on that either.

We had let down to five thousand feet to try to get our bearings, but found no distinguishing landmarks because of the restricted visibility. When Mendy finally raised a response from a homing station, a voice with a heavy French accent directed us to "steer one three five."

"Where is this airfield?" Mendy asked.

"Bastia," replied the voice.

Forgetting his manners, Mendy said, "Where in hell is that?"

"On the island of Corsica, northeast coast," replied the voice. "It is a French air force base. Would you like a steer?"

Bastia wasn't all that far from Naples, but to Mendy it was the difference between landing at Bastia or floating in a dinghy in the Mediterranean. "Roger," he replied. "We're steering one three five."

We soon spotted Corsica, a mountainous island almost halfway between Cannes and Rome. The weather in the area was excellent, with a few scattered clouds and nearly unlimited visibility. At twenty-five thousand feet we would most likely have seen the Italian coastline, but Mendy was concentrating on his dwindling gas supply. His main objective was to land on terra firma with a few gallons left.

It was about 4:00 P.M. when we landed. By the time we managed to get our planes refueled, it was dark. Even if we had wanted to take off for Naples, we couldn't have done so, because the French closed the air base at 5:00 P.M. No lights, no tower personnel, no mechanics—nothing! The base had no accommodations for transients, so we had to spend the night in a small hotel in the town of Bastia. The old crone who ran the hotel was happy to accept our English pounds, which was the only money we had.

Bastia was a small medieval town with narrow, twisting streets and an absolute minimum of nightlife. We had dinner at the hotel and went to bed early.

We took off next morning as soon as the French opened the air base—at eight o'clock—and landed at Capodichino airport in less than an hour.

General Eaker's headquarters resembled an oversized communications trailer bristling with radio antennae. Mendy wanted me to go with him to deliver the letter, but I politely declined. I watched as he was escorted to the trailer by two MPs, and wondered if I'd ever see him again. We knew that the envelope was at least two days overdue. What we *didn't* know was that it was more like five days overdue.

Five minutes later, he came out. His face was a bit redder than usual, and his shoulders slumped forward as he walked, but he didn't appear to have been physically abused.

"Well?" I said, "What did the general have to say?"

Mendy climbed into the jeep. "The first thing he said was 'Where in hell have you been?' because he got this same letter by courier mail yesterday. I started to tell him about the trouble we had, but he wasn't listening. He said some nasty things about me and my ancestors and a few other things. . . ." Mendy shrugged. "Let's get the hell out of here!"

It was just a little after 10:00 A.M. We figured there was little point in trying to hurry back to England, so we decided to fly to Rome. We landed at a military base just outside the city before noon. We spent the afternoon gawking at the historic parts of the city, and we even had time for a guided tour of the catacombs. We stayed on the base that night— we couldn't afford to stay in Rome.

We were at the flight line early the next morning. Our P-51s had been serviced and were ready to go. We filed our flight plan and took off. Mendy thought we could make it to Paris before noon. I thought that was a great idea—no rush this time. The weather people told us that the weather in Paris wasn't great, but they thought we could get into Orly without too much trouble.

There was a high overcast as we crossed into France, and it kept lowering as we flew north. Mendy decided to stay below the clouds, so we kept getting lower and lower. The cloud layer and mountains were getting closer together. I suggested to Mendy that we should climb up through the overcast. He didn't answer.

Soon we were picking our way between the hills, trying to stay beneath the clouds. I was getting plenty nervous.

"I'm getting low on fuel," said Mendy. "I may have to belly in." I was surprised to hear this, because I thought he'd have at least enough gas to get to Paris.

About fifteen minutes later, still dodging hills and clouds, Mendy spotted an open field in a valley and decided that it was a good place to belly the plane in "while I still have power." He circled the field twice to make sure there were no stone walls or other obstructions, then lined up and brought the plane in, gear up and full flaps, for a power approach just above the stall speed, and touched down a few hundred feet from the field boundary.

The Mustang skidded along a few hundred yards and came to a stop. Mendy radioed that he was okay, and I watched him climb out of the plane and wave. I could see some people from the nearby village running toward him. They weren't waving pitchforks, so I figured they were friendly. I waggled my wings and started up through the overcast.

The top of the overcast was about twenty thousand feet, and I leveled off at twenty-five thousand feet. I saw nothing but clouds below me in all directions. I turned to the heading for Paris.

I established radio contact with Orly about ten minutes south of Paris. To my surprise, the air traffic controller said, "Is that you, Bud?"

It was one of those strange coincidences that confound logic. He was from my hometown of Nashua, New Hampshire, and had dated one of my sisters; he had seen the flight plan that we had filed in Rome and recognized my name.

"Bud," he said, "you don't want to try to get in here. I'm in the tower and I can't even see the runway. We've had no traffic in or out of here all day."

"Do you have any suggestions?" I was trying to sound calm and collected.

"It's socked in all over the Continent. Manston is reporting three hundred feet and half a mile, and that's the best weather around."

I checked my gas supply. I had used up quite a bit dodging hills and clouds with Mendy. I might be able to reach Manston, but it would be close. I probably wouldn't have enough gas for a missed approach. There weren't many options: either get to Manston or bail out, and I didn't want to bail out over the English Channel. In January, I'd have about twelve seconds to get into my inflatable dinghy before hypothermia made it impossible. Few pilots had beaten those odds.

I pulled the fuel mixture control lever back past the "auto-lean" position and reduced the engine RPMs to get the maximum fuel efficiency. About ten minutes north of Paris I started calling Manston, informing them of my fuel situation and requesting a steer to base.

Manston didn't hear me; I was too far away. Then "Falcon two one, this is Grandstand. Can we help?"

"I sure hope so!"

"We're a temporary airfield at Laon. One PSP runway. We have three hundred feet and about half a mile visibility in light drizzle. Want to give it a try?"

I said I would indeed give it a try. The confident voice directed me to descend to one thousand feet and steer zero one zero degrees. Every minute or so, he requested a transmission to refine the heading to base. I knew that the terrain in that part of France was flat and low, so running into trees or hills was the least of my concerns.

He heard the sound of my engine as I passed over the homing station. From there, he calmly talked me through a series of headings and turns designed to bring me to the airfield on the runway heading. "We'll be firing red flares at the end of the runway," he said. "Let down to two hundred feet." With gear and flaps down, I concentrated on the instruments: rate of descent, heading, airspeed, and altitude. He kept giving me heading corrections to keep me lined up.

At three hundred feet, still descending, I saw nothing but clouds. Should I go around? But then what? Bail out? Two hundred feet—and still nothing. Ease it down a little more. Suddenly I spotted a red flare to my left in the clouds, then I was below the overcast and I saw the runway a little to my left. I skidded over to the runway heading and touched down about three hundred feet down the runway. The pierced PSP runway was slick with rain, so I eased the brakes to a stop at the end of the strip. Then I breathed a huge sigh of relief.

"Thanks a whole lot, Grandstand! That was a real sweat job!" I said.

"It was for me, too! You're very welcome. Come again."

This base was home to a Ninth Air Force fighter-bomber squadron flying P-47s in support of infantry units. These guys lived in tents and moved every few weeks to a new temporary base. There were rudimentary quarters for visitors in a section of a bomb-damaged building—nothing fancy, but better than spending the night sharing somebody's soggy tent.

Next morning, I headed back to England and Steeple Morden. The weather was still miserable over the Continent and England. As soon as I could, I established contact with the homing station at Steeple Morden and asked about the weather.

"One thousand feet and two miles in light rain." Not great, but not a problem either. I landed and taxied to the dispersal area.

Ace Graham was there in his jeep to greet me. "Where in hell have you been?"

"That sounds familiar," I thought, but I said, "It's a long story."

The old order changeth, yielding place to new. Tennyson.

Brady Williamson, one of the original members of our squadron, became the first pilot to complete two combat tours. He left for the States on January 29. We were sorry to see him leave; he was always ready with a quip or a joke to brighten our days, and we knew we'd miss him.

Burt Sims was transferred to Eighth Air Force headquarters on January 31 for assignment to the public relations section. His publicity releases made hometown heroes of many of us, and his sharp wit and humor lightened many difficult situations. We knew we'd miss him, too. Mike Glantz took over his duties as squadron historian.

January began with a disaster and was not a great month for the group. We lost nine airplanes. Six were due to the weather, and three were the work of flak. We lost three pilots—one killed, and two POWs.

February 1945

The bad weather continued in England and on the Continent on February 1 and 2. The group was released both days. I led eight newly assigned pilots on a practice bombing/strafing exercise at The Wash. On February 3 Colonel Stewart led the group with our squadron, escorting bombers to Magdeburg. The Luftwaffe didn't show up, but a 358th pilot was killed while strafing a train that had a few flak cars attached.

February 4 was sunny at Steeple, but not on the Continent. I took eight more newcomers to The Wash for bombing/strafing practice.

February 5 featured three briefings in the morning and all three missions scrubbed because of weather. That evening I received a surprise phone call at the officers' club. My brother Ray, who had been training in a B-17 operational training unit in the States, called from Rattlesden, a bomber base about fifty miles northeast of Steeple. He had been assigned to the 709th Bomb Squadron of the 447th Bomb Group.

He was a flight officer and navigator of a ten-man crew captained by 1st Lt. Robert Glazener. He hadn't flown his first bombing mission yet—his crew was still in the preoperational training phase—so I suggested he try to get a forty-eight-hour pass and meet me in London. A few days later, he called again. "I have a forty-eight-hour pass this coming weekend. Can you make it?" My schedule was quite flexible by that time, so I assured him I could. The 354th had plenty of newly assigned pilots, all clamoring to get on the mission schedule, and I had no trouble getting a forty-eight-hour pass for February 10 and 11. We met at the officers' hotel on Jermyn Street late on the afternoon of the February 9. Over a few preprandial cocktails he told me of his transatlantic adventure.

They left Bangor, Maine, on December 14, in a brand-new B-17, equipped with all the latest radar-bombing equipment. This was a specialized bomber, designated Pathfinder, designed to lead bomber formations. They landed at Goose Bay. Four days later they were cleared for departure to Meeks Field, Iceland. The marginal weather at takeoff time caused a lengthy delay, with engines running, awaiting takeoff clearance. The flight engineer insisted that the fuel tanks be topped off, and the pilot had the good sense to agree.

After passing the tip of Greenland, they encountered severe icing in a solid overcast as night came. The deicer boots did not operate properly, and ice kept accumulating on the wings. The pilot was unable to maintain altitude, even with full power on all four engines. They jettisoned all their personal belongings, and every part of the airplane they could detach, to lighten it and thus decrease its rate of descent and increase its range.

The radio operator established contact with Meeks Field and obtained a steer to the airfield. By this time the airplane was below a thousand feet and the warmer air was melting some of the ice off the wings, but the fuel supply was nearly down to the "fumes only" stage. Just as it appeared they would have to ditch in the cold Atlantic—in the dark—a red flare and runway lights appeared ahead. The B-17 was still carrying plenty of extra pounds of ice, but the pilot managed to put it on the runway, using nearly full power. All four engines stopped halfway down the runway—out of fuel.

Some of the crew climbed out and kissed the cold, wet runway. It had been a harrowing, twelve-hour ordeal. They were safe, but their clothing and all other personal belongings were at the bottom of the icy Atlantic. So was all that brand-new radar equipment. The "new" B-17 was towed to the hangar, with empty fuel tanks and a stripped interior.

It wasn't until January 14 that their B-17 was declared airworthy after a short test flight. They were cleared for departure on January 19, and landed in Scotland late that day. The B-17 stayed there to be restored to its original operational condition and for subsequent reassignment. The following Monday the crew was given orders and train tickets and told to report to a replacement depot just outside London. They went through the usual processing and were able to replace some of the items they had thrown into the North Atlantic. A week later the crew was assigned to the 447th Bomb Group at Rattlesden, about eight miles southeast of Bury St. Edmonds, reporting for duty on February 2.

Ray was just eighteen months younger than I, and we had always been quite close, in spite of almost daily fights when we were kids. We had a lot of reminiscing to do in the next day and a half as we toured the sights—and nightspots—of London. I knew he was in for some rough missions, even though the Allied armies and the Russians now appeared headed for a decisive victory soon. There were still Luftwaffe fighters and plenty of flak over Germany. The war wasn't over yet. We went our separate ways Sunday afternoon, promising to stay in touch.

Mendy finally returned on February 7, and was greeted by Graham's "Where in hell have you been?" routine. He had quite a story to tell. The villagers who rushed to meet him when he bellied in treated him royally. He spoke no French at all, so when he tried to tell them he was thirsty— by pantomiming drinking a glass of water—they kept giving him glasses of wine. "I was drunk before I found anybody who spoke English," he said, but it didn't sound like a complaint.

His long homeward journey included several days in Paris, where he acquired quite a few bottles of French liqueurs and perfumes. He refused to say what he was going to do with them. "Sprinkle some of that perfume on yourself next time you're in London," suggested Long Jawn Stanton, "then walk through Piccadilly Circus in the evening and see what happens."

"You missed all the excitement," Duff said to me when I returned from London late in the afternoon of February 11. I got the full story from Mike Glantz the following morning.

Jim Duffy shot down no. 5 on February 9, making him the group's eighteenth ace. He was closing fast on the FW-190, getting solid hits all over the fuselage, when the German pilot jettisoned his canopy and popped the stick forward, catapulting himself out of the cockpit. "I thought the canopy and the pilot were both going to come through my canopy!" Duff said after the mission.

It had been nearly a month since our group had encountered German fighters, except for a brief encounter with Me-262s on January 21. The 357th bounced a small gaggle of 109s and 190s near Brandenburg; Lt. Bill Lyons nailed a 109, and Lt. Ed Ludeke got a 190. But the 2d Scouting Force, led by Lt. Col. John Brooks, put on the big show.

Brooks led his flight of four Mustangs ahead of the bombers to Magdeburg to report on weather conditions affecting their mission. As the bombers neared the target, he spotted a gaggle of about fifty Me-109s at fifteen thousand feet and climbing toward the bomber task force. He led his flight into the gaggle with guns blazing, concentrating on the lead ships. Brooks blew up two of the lead 109s, and his element leader, Lt. Bill Whalen, knocked down two more. The gaggle was completely disorganized and broke up into small units with seemingly no direction. Most of them headed for the deck, but others seemed to be just milling around aimlessly. Whalen became the first and only air ace in the 2d Scouting Force, and Brooks later received the Distinguished Service Cross for his outstanding leadership. Before this encounter, Brooks had never fired the guns on a P-51, or on any other aircraft.

On the way home, two 358th pilots reported a large park-

ing lot containing what appeared to be thousands of trucks
and other vehicles near Steinhuder Lake.

In search of such a lucrative target, the group took off
next day with a 108-gallon fuel tank on the right pylon and
an 80-pound cluster of fragmentation bombs on the left pylon. There was a heated discussion at the briefing concern-
ing the wisdom of having an 80-pound frag-bomb cluster
under one wing, and a 108-gallon fuel tank, weighing about
700 pounds, under the other. "The frag cluster has a flat
plate facing. That produces more drag and will counter
some of that uneven weight distribution," said Moon Elder,
who was leading the mission. "But you'd better crank in
that aileron trim tab," he added, pointing to a sketch on the
chalkboard showing the optimum position of the tab.

The mission included escorting B-24s to their target,
then bombing and strafing targets of opportunity while
searching for that parking lot containing all those trucks.
"That's an unusual configuration for escort duty," Graham
noted. "What happens if we get bounced?"

"You'll think of something, Ace," replied Moon.

Taking off with that combination was, as Stanton put it,
"kinda hairy." The group rendezvoused with the B-24s over
Holland, but the weather over the target area in Germany
was 10/10 cloud cover all the way up to more than thirty
thousand feet. The group had to turn back, and Nuthouse ordered it to abandon the bombing/strafing mission and return
to base "with ordnance." The wing tanks were jettisoned,
but the frag clusters were retained.

Over the North Sea, Lt. Oran Stalcup reported that his
engine was skipping. Shortly afterward he reported that the
engine had quit. He tried vainly to get it restarted, then
bailed out about thirty miles east of Great Yarmouth.
Lieutenant Charles Spencer watched helplessly as his roommate hit the frigid waters of the North Sea. Spencer circled
overhead, calling frantically for air/sea rescue. There was
no sign of a dinghy, so Spencer and his wingman, Duran
Vickery, managed to unhook their own dinghies and drop
them over the spot where Stalcup was struggling. It was too

late. Stalcup, whose Mae West was not inflated, finally disappeared under the waves of the North Sea. Hypothermia had claimed another victim.

Meanwhile, Graham was having engine problems of his own. His engine was coughing and sputtering, and it finally quit when he was within five miles of the English coast north of Great Yarmouth. He heard the unfolding tragedy of Stalcup's bailout as he mentally calculated his glide slope trajectory and elected to try to get over land and crash-land rather than take his chances in the North Sea. White cliffs, resembling those of Dover, were directly in his glide path.

He just barely cleared the cliffs and crash-landed in a farmer's garden. The impact set off one of the bombs in the frag cluster he was carrying. The armament people had said it couldn't happen, but it did, and it almost tore off the left wing. He then slammed into some trees in front of the farmer's house. Ace was dazed. He tried to open the canopy, but it was stuck. He finally got it open, and fearing that the rest of the bombs might go off, started to run away from the airplane, only to be dragged back because he had forgotten to disconnect his oxygen hose, parachute, and dinghy. He finally became untangled and ran toward the farmer's house. The farmer came out to greet him.

"You look like you've had a rather nasty accident. Would you care for a spot of tea?"

"No, thanks," replied Ace, "but I could use a spot of whiskey if you have some."

"I think the missus might be able to find some."

Ace phoned the base, and a jeep was dispatched from a nearby RAF station to pick him up. He returned to Steeple that evening, slightly battered. He had quite a few spots of whiskey to ease the pain.

On February 11, the group tried again to find the elusive parking lot, but again the weather didn't cooperate. This time the left pylon carried a 500-pound bomb instead of a frag cluster, and the right pylon carried the 108-gallon fuel tank. Duff was leading the squadron; I led Yellow Flight. Takeoff was easier. There were a few breaks around

Dümmer Lake, so Duff decided to dive-bomb a railroad bridge with his section. We dropped eight bombs, but none hit the bridge. Mendy, who led the second section, picked out a factory. Eight bombs, no hits. Strafing was not much better: We shot up two barges, an oil tanker, and some railroad traffic.

Major Lee Mendenhall completed his combat tour on February 14, and I became the squadron operations officer. On February 15 Al White, Bert Marshall, and Clay Kinnard returned from their Stateside leaves, and 1st Lt. James Jabara, who had completed a combat tour in P-47s with the Ninth Air Force, was assigned to the 354th. With an ever-present cigar in his mouth (his airplane was named *The Ceegar Kid*), "Jabby" quickly became a well-liked, gung-ho member of the squadron.

On February 16 the group launched a "minimum effort" mission providing freelance support for bombers in the Münster–Hannover area. Pilots were told that they should be prepared to land on the Continent and spend the night there. I was scheduled to lead the squadron on that mission, but Graham said, "You've spent enough time on the Continent. I'm taking your slot." Mike Glantz noted that pilots usually left their money and other personal belongings with the intelligence section before a mission, but there was very little money left with S-2 on that one. The mission was uneventful and they all landed at Chièvres, southwest of Brussels.

Graham was promoted to lieutenant colonel the next day, February 17, but wasn't around to celebrate at the monthly officers' club dance.

The Continental contingent finally returned to Steeple on February 20 with bottles of perfume, champagne, stubble beards, and empty wallets. "We stayed below ten thousand feet," said Graham, "so the champagne bottles wouldn't explode." Several of the champagne bottles were emptied that evening as we helped him celebrate his promotion.

On February 21 Lieutenant Colonel Graham led A Group, which consisted of the 354th Squadron, and Captain Hank Billie led B Group. I led A Group's Yellow Flight. Both groups made rendezvous with the B-24s over Holland and escorted them as far as Würzburg, where A Group left to find targets of opportunity, while B Group stayed with the bombers attacking targets in Nürnberg.

Graham spotted a train near Ansbach, and we let down from twenty thousand feet to attack it. At about fifteen thousand feet, with absolutely no warning, my engine quit. The silence was deafening.

I was shocked that this was happening to me. I was on my second tour of combat duty, had flown nearly a hundred missions, and now I might wind up in a POW camp just because of that damned engine!

My first reaction was to check the fuel gauges, thinking I had run out of gas on the tank in use. That wasn't the problem—plenty of gas.

I banked sharply to the west, hoping to get over France and either bail out or belly the plane in, depending on the terrain. I was doing a number of things at the same time. I radioed my predicament to the rest of the squadron; my wingman, Lieutenant Hixson, stayed with me, but the rest went on with the mission. I was checking the terrain ahead, looking for a level field long enough to belly in. And I was frantically checking and rechecking all switches, gauges, and levers.

I closed the throttle, then opened it. I experimented with different positions for the mixture control, turned on fuel booster pump switches—all to no avail. There seemed to be nothing wrong with the engine except that it simply wouldn't run! I started to concentrate on picking out a spot to belly in.

At about seven thousand feet, just as suddenly as it had quit, the engine started again. I leveled off and took a quick look at the map on my kneeboard. I figured I was about seventy-five miles east of the Rhine River. I started climbing to regain lost altitude and leveled off at ten thousand feet. I eased the throttle open a bit to get more speed. The engine shook and sputtered, and my progress toward the Rhine was agonizingly slow. Ten minutes later, the engine suddenly quit again, and once more I began looking for an open field. At eight thousand feet, the engine came back to life. This scenario kept repeating—engine quits, search for open field; engine starts, climb back to ten thousand feet—as I inched slowly across my map toward the Rhine.

Finally, through breaks in the clouds, I saw the Rhine below me. I knew that Patton's troops were getting close to the river at that time, and I breathed a bit easier. I switched to the emergency channel on the VHF radio and requested a steer to Verdun, less than a hundred miles away.

"Falcon one one, steer two-six-zero degrees." It was a welcome American voice, loud and clear. Now if that engine would just keep going a while longer . . .

I kept transmitting for a steer, trying to maintain altitude as the engine stuttered on and off. It sounded like a Model T Ford on a cold morning.

Soon I saw the airfield about ten miles straight ahead. I maintained altitude until I was right over it, then set up a circular pattern for landing. I wanted to be sure I could still make it even if the engine quit for good.

The main gear rattling on the PSP runway was one of the sweetest sounds I'd ever heard. Thunderbolts and Mustangs were scattered around the airfield. I taxied to what looked like the Mustang maintenance area and parked by a temporary hangar.

Less than three hours later, the spark plugs had been replaced, and Lieutenant Hixson and I were on our way back to England.

Lieutenant Colonel Stewart was transferred to the 4th Fighter Group and Lieutenant Colonel Kinnard assumed command of the 355th on February 21. Kinnard had not particularly enjoyed his brief stint with the 4th. Some of the 4th Fighter Group pilots had served with RAF American Eagle squadrons and had picked up some of the RAF slang. Kinnard thought it was silly that "good American boys were sayin' things like 'I pranged my airscrew on the tarmac,' like they were in the Battle of Britain." He was glad to be back with the 355th, ". . . where folks speak good old American English." And we were delighted to have him back.

On February 22 we lost Lt. George Kemper to flak when we strafed a marshaling yard near Dümmer Lake. He had narrowly avoided electrocution a few weeks earlier when he bailed out and slipped between high-tension lines on his parachute descent. This time he bellied in and was soon captured.

The next day, February 23, Lt. Bob White survived a spectacular low-altitude bailout near Ingolstadt after getting clobbered by flak while strafing the airdrome. He became a POW.

On February 24 I was leading the squadron on a fighter sweep to the Hannover area when my engine threw another tantrum. It didn't quit this time—at least not then—but I had no intention of going through a repeat performance of the February 21 scenario, so I returned to base. Graham took over. It was another milk run.

Duff led the squadron next day, and I led Yellow Flight, in a three-flight squadron on a strafing mission to Brandenburg, just outside of Berlin. Clouds hid the target area, so we strafed west of the city, concentrating on rail lines, switch houses (a high-priority target), locomotives, freight cars, and anything else we could find. The flak was meager for a change—though two of our planes came home with a few holes—and we worked over the area thoroughly. Our wing tanks had been fitted with detonators to make them into incendiary weapons, and they caused several fires in the area.

Our last February mission—on February 28—was typical. We escorted B-24 forces attacking rail targets in the Ruhr Valley. Graham then led our three flights to the

Schweinfurt area, where he spotted an airdrome with hangars that looked like they might contain aircraft. Typically, he said, "I'll make a high-speed pass across the airfield, and you guys watch to see if there's any flak. If you see any, wipe 'em out."

He streaked across the field at better than four hundred miles per hour. "There's no flak down here!" he radioed.

I said, "Look behind you, Ace." There were white puffs of 20mm fire and black puffs of 40mm stuff following just a hundred yards or so behind his airplane and gaining on him. We saw at least fifteen flak positions all around the perimeter of the field, and a few flak towers by the hangars.

"Kee-rist!" he said. "Let's get the hell out of here!"

He decided to concentrate on railroad targets instead. Some colonel at higher headquarters had estimated that one locomotive destroyed was worth two enemy aircraft destroyed on the ground, but he probably hadn't been on a strafing mission. We did good work that day, however. Mike's narrative: ". . . one switch tower destroyed, 15 goods cars damaged, 12 passenger cars damaged, one oil car destroyed, others damaged, and roughly fifteen Supermen (running from the passenger cars) were sent to meet Wotan, with hospitalization probably required for at least ten others." Mike was a student of Scandinavian mythology.

By the end of February, the Western Allied armies had penetrated the German Siegfried Line and were trying to get across the Rhine, the Wehrmacht's last natural defensive position. The Battle of the Bulge offensive by the Germans had drawn much of the German reserves from the Eastern Front, and the Soviets had begun their biggest offensive thrust into Germany. In addition to our usual escort duties, many of our missions included strafing designed to destroy the German communications and supply lines, well behind their defensive positions.

March 1945

By March 1, the ground war was obviously heading toward a conclusion. The Soviets were closing in from the east, and the Allied armies were pressing relentlessly forward from the west. With VIII Fighter Command fighters roaming at will all over Germany, the German transportation system was grinding to a halt. We had plenty of pilots, and every one of them wanted to get "combat time" and maybe shoot down an airplane or two; all of them clamored to be on the schedule every day. Graham was just as insistent. He wanted to get this war over with, so he could go to the Pacific and fight the Japanese.

Kinnard led the group with our squadron on March 1 to escort bombers to Regensburg. It was a milk run. Six pilots landed on the Continent, claiming fuel shortage. Our pilots took no chances with low fuel supplies, as long as the welcome havens of Ninth Air Force fighter bases were available. The six returned to Steeple late in the afternoon.

Also on March 1, someone at 65th Fighter Wing headquarters with nothing better to do decreed that all five fighter groups in the wing would establish a physical fitness program for all personnel. The program would consist of a minimum of three hours of *supervised* athletics per week. At the bar that evening, Graham appointed Jim Duffy, sometimes referred to as Round Boy, Supervisor of Athletics for pilots—SAP for short. Duff modestly insisted that he didn't deserve the honor, but Graham was adamant. "I want the best man for the job, Jim," he said, "and that's you."

"It'll take me at least a week to get it organized," said Duff.

"That's fine," replied Ace. "Just as long as it's a good program."

On March 2 the field order specified that there would be *no strafing* on this mission. Graham led the squadron that day and was furious when he returned. "I spotted at least a dozen fat train targets, and I couldn't do a damn thing! What kind of a war is this?" He saw no sign of the Luftwaffe, but two other fighter groups encountered gaggles of 109s and 190s and shot down sixty of them. "It's the same old story," said Ace. "Wrong place, wrong time."

Mike knocked on our door at 5:00 A.M. on March 3. "Briefing at 0615!"

Duff rolled over and muttered, "It's for you. I've gotta work on the fitness program."

I led B Group, and Les Minchew led A Group. We had become accustomed to the A and B group designations and had quit griping, since there was nothing we could do about it anyway. We escorted B-24s to Magdeburg. Les Minchew's A Group swept the area ahead of the bombers and was bounced by three Me-262s. When they broke into them, Lt. Bill Lyons managed to get a few hits on one before the Germans sped away.

Just as we were getting ready to break escort—another group came in to relieve us—I spotted ten jets heading for the bombers in a high-speed climb from below and behind the bomber stream. This was a surprise. Their usual tactic was to attack from six o'clock high, using their superior speed to fly past the escort and into the rear of the bomber stream, then climb away. They were at ten o'clock low to us.

I racked into a full-power dive, trying desperately to get between them and the bombers. I knew I was out of range, but I started shooting, hoping to distract them by spraying lead in their direction. I could feel my Mustang picking up speed fast, but it wasn't fast enough. They were too far away and moving too fast. They quickly shot down two B-24s and headed for the deck before I could get my flight in position to intercept. We chased them but couldn't match their speed. "Damn!" I thought. "Outmaneuvered again!" I was beginning to get a complex.

Mendy left for the States on March 4. Ace asked me to move in with him in his more spacious quarters in an adjacent building. I was reluctant to leave Duff but had little choice. Ace's quarters had two beds and couple of dressers, and even a closet. Compared to the small cell with double-decker bunks that Duff and I had occupied for a year and a half, it was luxurious. It even had a field phone!

Duff's athletic program finally got in high gear on March 6, when the group was released until the next day. It was quite stressful, inasmuch as most of the pilots had been celebrating something or other at the bar the night before, and were consequently participating with painfully enlarged heads. The regimen consisted of volleyball in the morning, gin rummy and censoring mail in the afternoon, and a movie in the evening. Lieutenant Colonel Graham praised Captain Duffy lavishly for having "the best athletic program in this group, and possibly any other group!" Duff accepted the praise with his usual modesty.

When Mike Glantz banged on our door early on March 10, Ace groaned and said, "You go." His usual policy was that one of us would stay on the ground when the other flew a mission. The operations officer was second in command, and one of us would always be available to "mind the store."

"The bomber types must be running out of targets," observed Stan Silva when he saw the target of the day: the Bielefeld viaduct. "We've been to that one at least half a dozen times."

"Eight, to be exact," said Mike. "The Krauts are either

masters at speedy viaduct repair, or those bombardiers need more training."

I led A Group, and it was a complete milk run—not even flak, and that was a rarity. The newly assigned pilots were getting terribly frustrated. They were eager, even desperate, to get an aerial victory or two—and even become aces—in the dwindling opportunities and the short time left before the war ended. They all wanted to fly every mission.

By then, German resistance was crumbling and, except for occasional appearances of Me-262s, the Luftwaffe was no longer a serious threat to our bombers. The few prop-driven fighters that were encountered appeared to be flown by inexperienced pilots.

Graham led the squadron on March 11. It was a long, boring escort mission to Kiel. On the way home, after breaking escort, Ace's engine started skipping and sputtering. "I knew I was over the North Sea," he said later, "but there was a solid cloud cover below and I had no idea how far I was from land." He switched to the Air/Sea Rescue channel and stayed in contact with them until he reached England. "That was a real sweat job," he told Mike at debriefing. "I kept thinking of Stalcup every time the engine skipped a beat or two."

The target on March 12 was the seaport town now known as Świnoujście, Poland—it was then part of Germany and known as Swinemünde—about a hundred miles northwest of Berlin. It was only twelve miles from the nearest Soviet troops, nearly off the right side of the large map in the briefing room. Because of the proximity to Soviet troops, this was a Pathfinder-led mission for the bombers. I scheduled myself to lead the squadron.

After the briefing, Graham took my name off the schedule board and put his name on. "Why did you do that?" I asked.

"This looks like the kind of mission that might draw some Krauts up," he said, "and I'm going!"

"You can't do that, Colonel," said Walt Randall. "Your plane wasn't fueled and we don't have time to fuel it before takeoff."

"No problem," replied Ace. "I'll take Bud's airplane." Turning to me, he said, "You stay here and mind the store."

"That's a lot of water you'll be flying over," I said. "After yesterday's flight, I thought you wouldn't like that."

"I'm getting used to it. Besides, we'll come back by way of Berlin, and I'll stay away from the North Sea."

I knew better than to argue with him. Besides, I didn't like flying over the North Sea either.

The no-strafing rule was still in effect. When Graham saw seven Ju-188s on the ground at Flensburg, he was "mighty tempted" to ignore the rule but resisted the temptation. It turned out to be another long, boring milk run.

"It's a good thing you didn't go after those Ju-188s," Mike told him at debriefing. "That airfield has twenty-one 40mm cannons, twenty-eight 20mm cannons, and a bunch of machine guns protecting it. You'd have had a warm reception."

Captain Jonas "Doc" Proffitt joined the squadron on March 13. He replaced Reed Fontenot, who headed home to the bayous of Louisiana.

The mission on March 15 dramatized the change in the air war in the closing days. Seven hundred fifty bombers attacked German General Headquarters on the southern side of Berlin. Weather was good, with only light haze obscuring the city. To everyone's surprise, there was no flak over Berlin, and the only Luftwaffe aircraft to appear were three rocket-propelled Me-163s that made a pass at Jabby's flight but zoomed away when the flight turned into them. This was our squadron's first encounter with these aircraft.

The Me-163 "Komet" was the most unusual German aircraft we encountered during World War II. It had a vertical stabilizer with a standard rudder arrangement, but no horizontal stabilizer, depending instead on "elevons" in the wings for elevator and aileron control. It was only nineteen feet long, with a wingspan of thirty feet. Its maximum speed was six hundred miles per hour, and it had an initial climb rate of sixteen thousand feet per minute—much greater than any of our fighters. It was armed with two 30mm cannons. Only 279 Komets were delivered to the Luftwaffe by the end of the war.

The Germans planned to have small units of Komets at dispersed sites to intercept Allied bomber formations. The only Me-163 group formed, JG 400, shot down nine Allied airplanes, but lost fourteen Komets, mostly in unrelated accidents. The Komet had a lot of technical problems, including the hazardous nature of its fuel, which sometimes exploded without warning, often killing the pilot. Its combat range was only about fifty miles, and it could remain airborne only about ten minutes.

Major General William Kepner was scheduled to visit the base on March 16, and a "big show" was scheduled for his benefit, including a "pass in review" by all units on the base. We expected to be placed on stand-down status for the big show, and we were surprised when a briefing was scheduled at 8:00 A.M. for an escort mission to Nieuburg.

When we got back to Gremlin Villa after the briefing, the mission was scrubbed. The general's big show was on again. He had come to present awards and decorations, but the 354th Squadron had no scheduled recipients. We were all in place in our designated positions at least thirty minutes prior to the start of the parade. For a change, the weather was great—sunny and cool, with a light breeze. According to Mike's narrative:

"The feature of the ceremony was the 'pass in review.' The entire station turned out in force, and it was a grand sight to see the parade. Spirit in the marching ranks was high but most comments compared this parade to the one we hope to participate in down 5th Avenue in New York City soon."

Mike watched it from the sidelines and took photographs. My recollection is somewhat different. Most of the participants had marched in formation very little since training days, so we were working hard to keep a reasonably straight row and column as we passed the reviewing stand. We managed to remember the commands like "Eyes left!" and "Column right!" and all that stuff, but we were far indeed from the precision of West Point cadets on graduation day. When we passed the reviewing stand, at "Eyes right!" I thought I detected a suppressed smile trying to escape from behind General Kepner's salute.

"I'm glad he doesn't come here often" was Duff's comment after the grand march.

The next morning, March 17, I led the squadron on an escort mission to Münster, a target that once might have elicited a strong response from the Luftwaffe. Not anymore. Just the usual flak, but no Luftwaffe. The hilly terrain around Münster was reminiscent of the hills of New Hampshire, where I had once practiced loops, rolls, and spins with Al Hirsch—without the flak. I felt sorry for the farmers and villagers who were in the path of the approaching juggernaut.

That evening was our St. Patrick's Day celebration and the Saturday night officers' club dance. It was a wild one. Mike had a rough time rousing pilots for the next morning's mission. Walsh, Hixson, and McLeod were out of it. Falvey said he was fine, then fell asleep again and missed briefing. Al White, one of the sober volunteers for the mission, led the squadron. Another trip to Berlin and again, no Luftwaffe, no flak.

Captain Charles Spencer, who had flown combat missions in the Pacific and shot down three Japanese fighters as a gunner on a B-17, led the 354th section in Maj. Hodge Kirby's B Group on March 19. An Me-262 made a tentative pass at Spencer's flight, and broke away when Charlie turned into him. Spencer and his flight followed the 262, unable to catch up but keeping him in sight. The 262 pilot became aware of the pursuit and tried to shake them by climbing and speeding away, but Spencer stayed within sight of him, hoping to catch him when he had to land. Several minutes later, the 262—apparently short of fuel— slowed down and headed for an airfield. Charlie was slowly closing on him and fired a burst from extreme range. Five seconds later, the Me-262 crashed and burned short of the field. This was Spencer's first victory in the ETO.

Graham left for the Flak Home on March 19, and things settled down in the 354th—for a while, at least.

On our large situation map in the group briefing room, thick red arrows indicated the thrusts of the U.S. Army groups. To the north, Field Marshal Sir Bernard Law Montgomery's 21st Army Group was shown as a rocking chair. Since the failure of Operation Market Garden in September 1944, Monty and his staff had been planning their next operation—crossing the Rhine. By March 20, rumors abounded that Monty's long-awaited offensive was imminent. In addition to the British and Canadian armies under his command, he had the U.S. Ninth Army, commanded by Lt. Gen. William Simpson; the U.S. 17th Airborne Division; and massive U.S. artillery. This was to be a dual operation: Operation PLUNDER, crossing the Rhine in boats; and Operation VARSITY, the airborne attack. It would involve 250,000 men initially, then 250,000 following up, with an ultimate buildup to nearly 1 million men. The full resources of the Eighth Air Force, the Ninth Air Force, and even RAF Bomber Command would be available to support the offensive. It would be like D day all over again.

On March 21 the no-strafing rule was lifted. On the first mission in support of Monty's offensive, the 355th escorted bombers against German airfields. Lieutenant Colonel Larry Sluga led the group, and Duff led our squadron. The plan was to strafe the airfield after the bombers had dropped their bombs. A flight of Ninth Air Force Mustangs strafed the airfield at Egmond as the bombs were dropping, and one was seen to crash and explode during his run. Sluga told the 354th to stay with the bombers, and took the other two

squadrons down to strafe. The German gunners were waiting. Sluga took a direct hit in his right wing. He pulled up
and headed home, but his aircraft caught fire, and he had to
bail out for the third time in his career. This time his luck
ran out, and he became a POW.

Stanton led the second mission of the day, also in support
of Monty's imminent offensive. It was a fighter sweep under Nuthouse radar control. They didn't see any aircraft except some RAF bombers coming off a bomb run. They
landed after dark.

There were two missions again on March 22. Captain
Hank Billie led the 357th, escorting bombers in support of
Monty's offensive. No strafing—no Luftwaffe.

Bert Marshall led the second mission, with five flights
from our squadron. I had forty pilots begging—even threatening—me to put them in one of the nineteen slots. After an
escort stint, they strafed Memmingen, Würzburg, and
Kitzingen airfields. They reaped a good harvest: five Me-
109s, three Me-262s, and four He-111s destroyed, and several other aircraft damaged. The Me-262s destroyed by Stan
Silva's flight were not on the airfield at Kitzingen but
parked along the edges of an adjacent autobahn. In the wan-
ing months of the war, autobahns were used extensively as
runways for Luftwaffe aircraft, because of the continuing
attacks on German airfields.

Lieutenant Tuholski's plane was hit by flak. He reported
that his engine was cutting out and he was trying to get back
to the U.S. lines. He didn't quite make it, but he did manage
to evade capture and returned to Steeple three weeks later.

Bert Marshall was again clobbered by flak over
Würzburg, but managed to reach Steeple Morden, where he
made his fourth successful belly landing in his brief career.
"If you keep this up, Bert," Kinnard greeted his old friend
right after Bert's airplane slid to a stop, "we're gonna run
out of airplanes."

————

The big news on March 24 was "Monty's on the move!" He had ordered a large-scale smoke screen to hide his preparations during the two weeks prior to his move, apparently unconcerned that this would give the Germans a pretty good idea where he would attack. Heavy bombers had been pummeling the Germans on the eastern bank of the Rhine for two weeks. At 1:00 A.M. on March 24, he ordered a massive artillery bombardment of the German positions on the east side. At 2:00 A.M. the powered boats started across. A few hours later they had established a foothold on the eastern bank of the Rhine, and more than twenty thousand British and American troops landed behind enemy lines by parachute or in gliders.

Meanwhile, General Bradley's 12th Army Group, comprised of General Hodges's First Army and General Patton's Third Army, had already crossed the Rhine in two places on March 22, without massive support and without self-serving fanfare. They were quietly massing for the final assault into the heart of Germany.

On March 24 Kinnard led our squadron—with Bert Marshall in his no. 3 slot "just to keep him out of trouble"— and I led the second section. We patrolled the area of Monty's offensive for about three hours. Nuthouse vectored us to several phantom bandits, but the Luftwaffe didn't show up on our watch.

Four more replacement pilots were assigned to the squadron on March 25, all second lieutenants: James O'Neill, Gilbert Plowman, Ronald Rood, and Adolf Scheid.

Graham returned on March 26 and immediately put himself on the schedule for the next two missions. The mission he flew on March 27 was "the worst I've ever been on!" The bombers were off course, not where they were supposed to be in the bomber stream, and "flew lousy formation." It seemed they were having the same problem we were: plenty of replacement pilots all wanting to get in a mission or two before the war ended.

On March 30 Ace pulled rank on me again. I was scheduled to lead the squadron until he saw the target,
Wilhelmshaven. After escort, we were to patrol into the
Danish peninsula, and that's what drew his attention. Again,
he told me to stay home and mind the store, and replaced
my name on the schedule with his.

After breaking off the escort, he headed up the peninsula
on the deck. It turned out to be a frustrating mission for
him, because he saw ten Ju-52s lined up on a taxiway on an
airfield near the edge of the German–Danish border, and he
couldn't attack because of the no-strafing order. He vented
his frustration by diving from seven thousand feet, spraying
lead all over the area where the Ju-52s were parked, and
pulling up at five thousand feet. "I wasn't strafing," he said,
"but maybe I put a few holes in some of them."

He returned to Steeple just as General Carl Spaatz, who
now commanded all U.S. Army Air Forces in Europe, was
in the middle of a "presentation of awards" ceremony. In
the reviewing stand were Lieutenant General Doolittle,
commander of the Eighth Air Force; Major General
Kepner, commander of VIII Fighter Command; and
Brigadier General Auton, commander of the 65th Fighter
Wing.

Ace requested permission to perform a "low-level pass in
review." There was a hurried consultation with the dignitaries; then the tower officer said, "Permission granted."
The 354th Squadron then put on an excellent grass-cutting
pass in review. The brass loved it.

The visiting dignitaries spent the night at Steeple. Major
John DeWitt, a World War I combat pilot and an old friend
of Spaatz and Doolittle, joined them in the VIP quarters that
night. Next morning, Spaatz wanted to know who in hell
had "short-sheeted" his bed. DeWitt just smiled and said he
had no idea who could have done such a thing.

The last mission in March was uneventful except for the
2d Scouting Force, which ran into several Me-262s near

Braunschweig. Marvin Castleberry shot down one and Dick Nyman put a lot of holes in another, but they claimed only one damaged.

The visiting dignitaries left early that afternoon. The mystery of the short-sheeted bed had not been solved to everyone's satisfaction.

April 1945

April 1 was Easter Sunday. American ground forces were pushing far into central Germany, and the Soviets were closing in on Berlin. The air war was winding down, and our newly assigned replacements were almost frantic in their eagerness for a taste of war. A critical fuel shortage, the result of nearly two years of bombing German oil refineries and storage facilities, stranded the bulk of the Luftwaffe fighters on the ground, where they were destroyed in concerted strafing attacks.

The 355th did its share, destroying a total of sixty-nine aircraft on what had to be an unlucky Friday the thirteenth for the Luftwaffe; then flaming seventy more on the sixteenth. These were not always turkey shoots. The German planes couldn't fly, but the flak gunners still could shoot. To minimize our losses, we assigned part of our force to circle the airdrome to spot gun emplacements and put them out of action while the others strafed. Even so, we lost seven airplanes on those two missions. Colonel Kinnard put it best: "Much as I like to shoot up all those airplanes, I hate losing good pilots at this stage of the game."

At the beginning of April we had about a dozen replacement pilots who wanted to fly missions but needed several training missions to learn a few of the fundamentals. Graham nominated me to "teach them what they need to know" to become productive members of the squadron. "Fly with them. Talk to them. Get 'em ready," was his directive. "We'll manage to do without you for a few days."

On April 2, Graham led A Group with our squadron on a twenty-minute escort chore, then a freelance sweep of an area that he had surveyed on his previous mission. To his disgust, the mission was completely unproductive.

Captain Al White led the squadron on an escort mission to Kiel on April 3. It was one of those 10/10 cloud coverage missions—with a lot of instrument time for flight leaders and wingmen—and not much else. There were no "veterans" on this one, but the flight and element leaders had been battle-tested.

The April 4 mission turned out to be the toughest in months. Kinnard was leading the group with our squadron, but he had to abort the mission with mechanical problems, so Duff took over. The group's assignment was to freelance in the Lübeck area.

Al White's Yellow Flight bounced four long-nosed FW-190s about two thousand feet above the Ludwigslust airdrome. In the ensuing dogfight, Al nailed one FW-190, then tried to pick off another that had latched onto his wingman, Lt. Tom Truel. Before Al could get into position to help, Truel stalled out of a tight turn and crashed. Another 190 shot down Al's element leader, Lt. Bob Goth.

Meanwhile, Red and Green Flights hit the deck. Hixson, Molnar, and Decklar each destroyed a seaplane at a naval base northeast of Lübeck. Lieutenant Dick Gray, Duff's wingman, flying his first mission in Mustangs after finishing a combat tour in bombers, was hit by flak as Blue Flight strafed eight freight cars. He radioed his intention to fly in a westerly direction as long as he could, but was not heard from again. Although initially reported KIA, he turned up at Steeple three weeks later.

Missions on April 5 and April 6 were long, boring milk runs. Our missions were getting longer, because the unoccupied parts of Germany were shrinking. On the other hand, our "safe zone" behind the fast-moving front lines was expanding daily.

On April 7 the gods of war reminded us that this war

wasn't over. Kinnard led A Group with 358th and 357th airplanes; Graham led B Group, which consisted of four 354th
flights—Duff leading Yellow Flight, Joe Mellen with Blue
Flight, and Newell Mills with Green Flight. Both groups escorted three boxes of B-24s against a munitions factory
complex about fifteen miles southeast of Hamburg. A Group
covered the front end of the three boxes; B Group was at the
rear. The weather at the target was CAVU—ceiling and visibility unlimited.

Just before the IP, six Me-262s sneaked in from behind
in a roller-coaster attack. They dove past the fighter escort
about a thousand feet below them, attacked the front end of
the bomber formation from below in a high-speed climb,
and split-essed for the deck. Graham told Blue Section to
stay with the bombers while his Red Flight and Duff's
Yellow Flight gave chase, but they couldn't catch up with
the jets. A Group, at the front of the three boxes, shot down
one 262 and damaged two others.

Seconds later, several flights of Me-109s and FW-190s
came barreling through the 354th Blue Section and attacked
the right rear flank of the bomber force. Joe Mellen and
Glen Beeler each nailed an FW-190, and Paul Vineyard got
an Me-109, but three bombers were shot down and several
were damaged.

On withdrawal, Lt. Newell Mills and Lt. Gil Plowman,
who was flying his first mission, were last seen entering a
cloud bank southeast of Bremen and were not heard from
again. They were later reported KIA.

Ace was angry with himself for "letting those jets sucker
me out of position. I should have known I couldn't catch the
bastards!"

On April 8, Bert Marshall led A Group with the 357th
and two flights from the 354th Squadron—Graham's Red
Flight and Mellen's Yellow Flight—escorting B-24s bombing Roth Airdrome, a few miles south of Nürnberg. Escort
was broken at Würzburg, and A Group headed south toward
the Augsburg area to look for targets.

Things did not go well for the 357th. Captain Bill Cullerton, who had destroyed five German aircraft in the air and fifteen on the ground, was clobbered by flak over the airfield at Ansbach. He bailed out of his burning Mustang and was immediately captured by an SS troop. The troop commander took Bill's .45-caliber pistol, shot him in the stomach with it, and left him to die. Fortunately, some civilians took Cullerton to a hospital in a nearby town, where doctors saved his life.

Graham took his two flights to the 355th's old hunting grounds, the airfield at Oberpfaffenhofen, a Luftwaffe training base. Three Me-109s had the misfortune to be in the traffic pattern, gear down and trying to land, when the 354th arrived.

Graham quickly shot down two of them and was diving down toward the third when Carl Decklar blew the 109 out of the sky from below and behind. At the debriefing later, Ace kept referring to Carl as "Pfc. Decklar." In the same vein, some pilots were referring to Graham as "old Hog It All."

"We're seeing quite a few aircraft on the ground, but where are the airborne Krauts?" Jabby asked Mike.

"Out of gas. From a standpoint of numbers, the Luftwaffe still has a lot of aircraft. What it *doesn't* have is a lot of gas and a lot of experienced pilots."

"Well, why don't we air-drop some gas to them so they can come up and play?"

"I'll relay that suggestion to the top brass," said Mike.

Graham was Uncle on the April 9 escort mission to Memmingen Airdrome. The bombs devastated the northern half of the field, including the fuel storage area and headquarters building. Uncle then directed the other two squadrons to stay with the bombers while he took the 354th down to strafe. Six He-111s were destroyed. two by Graham and one each by Al White, Phil Barnhart, Jim Jabara, and Don Langley.

I spent most of that first week in April with the new pilots. I flew with them in mock dogfights almost daily—sometimes two missions a day; spent hours discussing tactics, and flight characteristics of the 109s and the 190s, took them through cloud layers; and answered a hundred questions. It was wearying work, and by the end of the week, they—and I—had had enough. As far as I was concerned, they'd have to learn the rest through experience. They were eased into the schedule, and I wrangled a forty-eight-hour pass from Ace.

Ruby and I saw a play in Leicester Square in London on Saturday afternoon and had an early dinner in a nearby restaurant. We then took the Underground to North Cheam, a suburb in the southern part of Greater London, to visit her older sister, Vi. Vi's husband, Jim, was in the Royal Navy. Like most English servicemen, he disliked Americans because they were "overpaid, oversexed, and over here." He came home most weekends when his ship was in port, but Vi wasn't expecting him that night.

Ruby told me that her sister liked an occasional drink of gin, so I bought a bottle to take along. Vi had a drink with me—Ruby didn't drink—and we chatted for an hour or so, then went to bed. Ruby slept with her sister, and I had the guest bedroom.

At about midnight, Jim came home and climbed into the house through the downstairs living room window—which he did often because he was always losing his key. The first thing he saw was the bottle of gin and two empty glasses. He stepped into the hallway and saw my coat and hat hanging there. He charged up the stairs to the bedroom. Ruby heard him coming and covered her head to surprise him, so when he flipped the light switch on, he saw two shapes in the bed and thought the worst. Just then, Ruby popped out from under the blanket. Jim's face was a hodgepodge of surprise, wonder, anger, and a touch of relief. Vi explained the American coat and cap.

Ruby said, "I'll go sleep on the settee."

Perhaps fearing a little hanky-panky with the American in the house, Jim quickly said, "No, no! You stay here with Vi, and I'll go sleep on the settee."

I slept through the whole episode. I was quite surprised in the morning when a man came into the guest bedroom with a cup of tea. We got better acquainted and I tried to modify his notion about American servicemen. I'm not sure I succeeded.

We caught the early-afternoon train out of King's Cross Station. Ruby got off at Letchworth, and I continued on to Royston. I was back on base Sunday evening and told Ace of my little adventure. "You're lucky he wasn't armed," he said.

Graham led B Group on April 10, and I led his Blue Section. The Liberators were bombing the Rechlin Airdrome and Experimental Center, about halfway between Berlin and Leipzig. After the bombing, Graham said, "Blue Section, stay with the Big Friends" as he took his section down to strafe.

From Bill Marshall's *Angels, Bulldogs, and Dragons:* "There were all kinds of aircraft on the ground, including captured B-24s and P-38s, Me-109s, Me-410s, He-111s, Ju-52s, Ju-188s, Ju-88s, and Do-217s." The 354th destroyed eleven assorted aircraft, including a captured B-24 by Graham, and damaged fifteen others that probably didn't contain fuel—they didn't burn even though they absorbed heavy strikes by API ammunition. None of our pilots reported seeing any flak.

"Thanks a lot, Colonel," I said to Ace after we landed. "My section had a great time escorting those bombers while you courageously shot up all those aircraft on the ground."

He was grinning from ear to ear. "You did a wonderful job, Bud."

More than 250 German aircraft were destroyed on the ground that day. The once-intimidating defensive shield around German airfields was disintegrating. "Kills" on the ground had become gunnery practice.

When the 355th became operational in September 1943, the Eighth Air Force policy—carried over from World War I—was to include aircraft destroyed on the ground in the definition of "ace." Later that policy changed when large-scale strafing missions became commonplace; only aerial victories would be counted. Our new and eager replacement pilots were hoping for a reversal of the current policy.

Lieutenant Colonel Kinnard led the group on April 13, and again a large number of aircraft were reported destroyed. The 355th claimed sixty-nine aircraft destroyed and thirty-one damaged. One 56th Fighter Group pilot claimed *ten* aircraft destroyed.

I suspected that some of the newer pilots in the group were becoming "claim-crazy." On every strafing mission, a few replacement pilots claimed four or five aircraft destroyed. They were probably unaware that a claims committee at VIII Fighter Command reviewed all claims, and the committee awarded credit for kills based on an analysis of the gun-camera film. Many of their claims were drastically reduced; more often than not, five kills turned into one.

On April 16 Ace Graham led the squadron and I led Blue Section on an escort mission to Traunstein. There was no sign of the Luftwaffe, but we did spot a number of twin-engine aircraft at the airfield at Eger. With ten minutes of escort duty left, Ace told Yellow Flight to finish the escort job, and he led the rest of us back to Eger.

"Blue Section, take care of the flak," he said as he headed for the deck. I took the two flights of Blue Section to about fifteen hundred feet in a high-speed orbit of the field. We spotted five gun emplacements—one 20mm cannon in a concrete revetment and four sandbagged machine guns—and silenced them. Just shooting up two or three had the effect of silencing the others; they didn't want to give away their positions and engage in an uneven duel with the six .50s of the Mustang. Uneven though the duel was, I was never comfortable looking down enemy gun barrels.

After two passes, Graham called, "Okay, Blue Section, your turn." He led his section into the circular pattern and we took over the strafing. I put a twin-engine aircraft, probably a Messerschmitt 410, in my gunsight and kept a steady stream of fire into it until I saw a small explosion in the wing root. Then flames enveloped the entire fuselage.

On my second pass I was busy dodging other Mustangs, and all the targets I saw were already burning, so I squirted a few hangars with no visible effect. More than a dozen aircraft were burning or smoking badly.

"Blue Section, join up," said Graham, "We're heading home."

In the meantime, Johnny Molnar had completed the escort chore and was heading home with Yellow Flight. They dropped down to about five thousand feet and soon spotted ten twin-engine aircraft parked in a wooded area along the edge of an autobahn. The Luftwaffe's use of autobahns stretched their supply lines and, coupled with their fuel shortage, left a lot of aircraft stranded along the highways. Yellow Flight lost no time demolishing this small fleet of aircraft—they destroyed six and damaged at least two others.

That was our last strafing mission of the war.

On April 18 word came from VIII Fighter Command: No more strafing! The edict was all-inclusive: no airplanes, airfields, trains, barges, or trucks—no more strafing, period! Pilots in the briefing room reacted to this news with moans and groans, but I'm convinced that most of us were relieved. Everyone knew that it was just days before the Germans would have to quit, and everyone wanted to get home in one piece.

Our mission was to escort B-24s to Passau, about a hundred miles northeast of Munich on the Austrian border. Lieutenant Colonel William Gilchrist, recently assigned as group executive officer, led the group; I led the 354th. The bombers were late, and it was a long (six and a half hours), boring milk run. The Luftwaffe didn't react, but flak batteries kept us awake along the route. On our way home we saw a few airfields that would have been fair game two days before, but they were now off-limits.

Seven more replacement pilots reported that day. "They'll be lucky to get one or two missions in," said Duff.

With the air war obviously winding down and the newly assigned pilots almost fighting to get on the schedule, many of the veterans wound up sitting a few out. But not Graham; he was just as gung-ho as when he first reported to the squadron six months earlier.

On April 20 Kinnard led the group on an area support mission for B-24s hitting targets near Prague, Czechoslovakia—a mission seven and a half hours long. On the way home he spotted dust rising from the Letnany Airdrome—German aircraft preparing to take off. The Germans shut down their engines as the 355th approached, and because of the no-strafing directive, they could not be attacked on the ground. Kinnard led the group twenty miles past the airfield, then turned back in time to catch about a dozen Me-109s forming up two thousand feet above the airdrome. Eight of them were shot down; the others managed to escape. Hearing the sounds of combat on the radio, Ace hurried back to join the fun, but he was too late. The combat—if it could be called that—was over. Kinnard later said he wished they had all stayed on the ground and survived.

There was another long, uneventful escort mission on April 21—uneventful except for the B-24 that was shot down by heavy flak over Regensburg. Duff was leading the squadron, and I was leading the second section. On the way home we spotted an airfield in Holland with plenty of potential targets, but the no-strafing rule was in effect, so we passed them by. After the mission, Mike greeted me with, "Congratulations, Major Fortier!" I was stunned. I was about a month short of my twenty-third birthday, and the promotion was completely unexpected.

That evening, I was celebrating at the officers' club Saturday dance party with Ruby and a group of friends when Captain Phil Haimovit, the club officer, came over and tapped me on the shoulder. "Phone call for you," he said.

Puzzled, I followed him to the office. "This is Sergeant Berry," the voice said. "I'm with the 709th Bomb Squadron at Rattlesden. I'm afraid I have some bad news for you. Your brother's plane was shot down two days ago. Some chutes were seen, but I'm not sure how many."

I was in a state of shock, and couldn't think of anything to say, so I just hung up the receiver. I went back to the table, told them about the call, and excused myself. I walked back to my quarters, trying to sort out my feelings. I decided to fly to Rattlesden next morning to find out all I could and then let my parents know.

I was up early Sunday morning. The 355th was on stand-down status—no mission scheduled. I got Ace's approval and flew to Rattlesden. The 447th Bomb Group was also on stand-down status. I found my way to group operations, where the operations officer gave me all the information he had so far.

Ray's crew had flown their first fifteen missions in the B-17 *Dead Man's Hand*. The last four digits of the tail number—1188, aces and eights—accounted for its name. It had already survived more than a hundred missions, and this was the third crew assigned to fly it. Sergeant Hobart, the radio operator, kept a diary account of the crew's missions. The following is excerpted from his entry for the crew's fifteenth mission to Hamburg, on March 30:

Enemy fighters, both jets and conventional, were out again in force, attacking our formations going in and coming off the target. Heavy flak protected the target city. The combined opposition resulted in damage to nearly half the planes in our group.

Our plane suffered major damage when an antiaircraft shell burst in the angle formed by the nose and right wing. The explosion shattered the Plexiglas nose that sent flying splinters into the eyes of Fortier, our navigator. The twenty-pound explosive shell from a

German 88mm cannon also knocked out the right inboard engine, setting it afire. The cockpit crew successfully extinguished the fire but could not feather the propeller as the control mechanism was destroyed. Fortier remained partially blind throughout our return and the "windmilling" propeller posed a worry that should it break free, it would strike the fuselage with buzz-saw effect.

Upon reaching our base, the flight surgeon removed the Plexiglas from the eyes of Fortier and applied medication. The damage did not keep him from accompanying us on the next day's mission. Not so fortunate was old *Dead Man's Hand*. This seven-hour combat mission was the 112th for our old Fortress, and after assessing the extensive damage, aircraft No. 42-31188 was relegated to the scrap heap to be cannibalized for parts.

On April 18, to everyone's surprise, more than two weeks after its apparent demise, *Dead Man's Hand* was back on the flight line, ready to go. Glazener and his crew, having bonded with the old combat veteran, were delighted.

Their mission on April 19 was a return to Dresden. It was no. 27 for the crew and 113 for *Dead Man's Hand*. Just two days before, the 447th Bomb Group had returned from Dresden with fifteen of its twenty-six planes damaged, one of them carrying a severely wounded waist gunner.

Dresden had been the target of a furious two-day attack by RAF and USAAF bombers on February 13 and 14, resulting in the near total devastation of the city. Thousands of residents died in the ensuing firestorm. This attack provoked considerable criticism and denunciation throughout Europe and even in the United States, because Dresden was a cultural center and not considered a vital military target.

By April it was one of the most heavily defended cities in Germany, with hundreds of heavy antiaircraft guns blackening the skies overhead. The Luftwaffe usually could be counted on to appear in large numbers, as if attempting to avenge the February attack. Dresden itself was still not considered a vital military target, but the Soviets had requested an attack on a marshaling yard in the small town of Pirna, just a few miles southeast of Dresden, to cut the supply lines of German troops still opposing the Red Army advance. At the bomb-group level, the consensus was that the mission should not have been ordered at this late stage of the war.

I returned to Steeple with a heavy heart, knowing only that Ray's aircraft had been shot down and that Mustang pilots assigned to escort the bombers had sighted four or five parachutes. I could only wait for further information and hope that one of the chutes sighted was his. It was the first time I had heard about his Plexiglas injuries.

I tried to send a cablegram to my parents, informing them of what I had learned at Rattlesden, but I was told I could not send such a message until the War Department had sent its "missing in action" telegram. I wrote a letter instead. My parents received my letter three days before they got the War Department telegram.

On April 25 Graham led the squadron and the group, and I took over when he had to return because of radio trouble. It was an uneventful escort mission to the Munich area— and it was the last combat mission for the 355th Fighter Group in World War II. The war was not officially over, but the air war had ended.

On April 26, Chuck Lenfest and Henry Brown showed up at Steeple, a few days after American GIs liberated their POW camp. The pilots all gathered in the briefing room to hear of their adventures. Soon other former POWs found their way back to Steeple, on their way home. Korky, limping a little from his bail-out injury, stopped by for a day and was warmly greeted by the only two remaining members of his original A Flight: Duffy and Fortier. "I might have known that you two characters would manage to get through this!" he said. It was a time of happy reunions and reminiscences.

The 355th Fighter Group gave a good account of itself in the air war against Germany; we destroyed 340 German aicraft in the air and 506 on the ground, for a total of 846. The 354th Fighter Squadron accounted for 133 in the air and 197 on the ground, a total of 330—39 percent of the group's total.

In the loss column, the group had 91 pilots either killed in action or missing, and 58 who became prisoners of war. The 354th had 30 killed or missing and 18 who became POWs.

The 355th Fighter Group was awarded the Distinguished Unit Citation.

May and June 1945

On May 1 we learned that Hitler had committed suicide in his Berlin bunker the night before. The end of the war was now just a matter of protocol and formalities. Finally, on May 8, came the announcement on the Tannoy: "Your attention, please! Germany surrendered unconditionally yesterday at Reims, France. THE WAR IS OVER!" They should have added, "Here in Europe, that is."

All over the base, men poured from their billets and offices, cheering, shaking hands, and back-thumping. Some fired their .45-caliber pistols or their carbines in the air until the MPs put a stop to it: "Those bullets have to come down, too!" The officers' club bar and the NCO club opened at noon and stayed open all day and well into the early morning hours.

We were advised to stay on base. The message from Eighth Air Force headquarters explained, "Let the British people have their celebration. They have been at war a long time. Let them have this day to themselves."

I had mixed feelings. Naturally, I was delighted at the war's end, but my concern was what had happened to Ray. I flew to Rattlesden again, but they knew no more than what they had already told me. It wasn't until May 22 that I received a teletype message that he was in the 101st Army Hospital in Paris and that he was all right except for having lost a lot of weight. That message lifted a lot of weight from my heart and mind as well.

Ace obtained clearance for me to fly my P-51 to Orly Airport, just outside Paris. It was a joyous reunion when I hugged my brother again on May 23, though he weighed closer to 100 pounds than his usual 150. It was a beautiful, sunny day. We took the Métro into Paris and sat in a side-walk café on the Champs Élysées, drinking beer and enjoying Paris in the springtime.

We were both in uniform. Two ladies of the evening were sitting at the next table, sizing us up as potential customers, unaware that we spoke and understood French. We listened as they estimated our financial situation and speculated about our various physical dimensions. Then Ray offered them a cigarette and asked them for a match—in French. They left a few minutes later.

That's when I heard the story of his last mission.

The mission was uneventful until they encountered heavy flak as they approached Dresden. The Glazener crew was flying left wing on the lead bomber. Bombs were released on target, and the group began its withdrawal at twenty-one thousand feet. That's when all hell broke loose. "Bogey coming in fast at eight o'clock high!" one of the crewmen yelled. It was an Me-262, streaking past the Mustang escort, trying to destroy the lead bomber. Its firing burst was short of the leading B-17 but hammered no. 2, *Dead Man's Hand*.

Ray heard the earsplitting explosions as 20mm cannon shells struck the left wing and engines. He looked up out of his Plexiglas window, saw the no. 2 engine engulfed in flames, and said to himself, "I'm dead!"

The B-17 fell out of the formation, vibrating and losing altitude. "Bail out!" yelled "Pappy" Glazener on the intercom. "Everybody bail out! Acknowledge!"

A few years after the war, the survivors had a reunion, and each one wrote of his experience. A few excerpts from Ray's account follow:

> . . . when Pappy said, "Bail out! Bail out!" with the plane on fire and Percy urging "Let's go, let's go!" I didn't take time to collect my escape kit, my walking

shoes. . . . I did grab and put on my parachute before releasing the escape hatch door.

Noting how frightfully close those spinning propellers were to the opening and fearing being struck, I grasped the lower catwalk and pushed off as hard as I could. My fear of being struck by the plane led me to wait a long, long time before opening the chute, almost too long.

. . . I recall it being a bright sunny day as I touched down in an open field with not another person in sight. The wind at ground level prevented collapsing the chute, which dragged me across the clearing and into the woods. I unbuckled the harness and dived for cover recalling the instructions given for this situation: "Find a place to hide, stay there, and don't move for at least twenty-four hours." Taking stock, my entire possessions consisted of a package of Chesterfield cigarettes and some matches. My feet were slightly injured in the landing, and steadily worsened with the passing of time. While hidden, I heard people moving about, but they made no effort to approach my hiding place. I can only assume that they were as afraid of me as I of them.

After traveling for some distance through the woods, I discovered what appeared to be a safe place to remain. The spot was on the slope of a hill among pine trees and at the foot of the hill was a creek. I remained there for twenty-one days without food. Each night I went to the creek, drank my fill of water and returned to my spot. After eight or nine days without food, I found the desire gone and sensed no need for food, but a greater need for water. Psychologically, that spot was like a cocoon in which I felt safe and secure. Possibly due to lack of food, and my injured feet, I drifted into a state that could be described as lethargy. In no particular sequence, I recall nights that snow fell and nights of brilliant moonlight. I recall that on one night a deer approached very close and on another, a fox did the same.

Thoughts of "You can't stay here, you're going to die, you must at least make an effort to get out" began the end of my hibernation. At or near the same time, I heard the noise of a very heavy artillery bombardment. Like rolling thunder, the noise was continuous and had the ground shaking beneath me. Unknown to me at the time, this was a prelude to the Russian arrival.

Sometime after leaving the area, I approached a farmhouse and, able to speak the language, told the German family that I was an American in need of food. My appearance and the approaching Russians had them petrified with fear. They did take me inside the house and give me some potatoes and carrots. Immediately after wolfing down the food, I began suffering severe stomach cramps. The arriving Russians found me doubled over in pain with my head cradled between my hands. Taking one look at me, a Russian officer grabbed my arm and confiscated my navigator's watch, then they all left. My German hosts were afraid that my presence would jeopardize their safety, so I went outside, became violently ill, and left.

Probably less than an hour later, I knocked on the door of another house. Inside were an elderly couple, Mr. and Mrs. Weiss, and two or three lady guests of the same age group. I told the couple that I was an American, and they immediately took me to the barn loft and hid me in the hay. None of us knew that the war had ended, so they kept me a few more days, nursing me back to a measure of health. This was one of the ironies of war. All of their sons that were in the German Army had been killed and yet they showed compassion to one of the enemy.

It was from disarmed German soldiers passing by that we learned of the war's end.

Ray got a motorcycle ride to Chemnitz from a Frenchman who had "confiscated" the cycle after being liberated from a nearby concentration camp. Ray was then taken to the military airport and flown to Paris.

    I walked into the dining room of the 101st General Hospital and bumped into Pappy. He said, "Fort, you S.O.B.! I thought you were dead!" His face was a mess from landing in a tree. . . .

All crew members had bailed out successfully, but the copilot was beaten by German civilians as soon as he landed, then shot and killed. The flight engineer also was badly beaten by civilians. He survived but never fully recovered from the severe physical injuries to his head. Ray was the only one who evaded; all the others were briefly prisoners of war.

He had managed to get through to our parents by phone. "I talked to Mom and the conversation got pretty weepy." He reassured them that I was okay. We spent the evening reminiscing and swapping war stories; then I found an empty cot in the same ward that Ray was in and slept soundly.

    I returned to Steeple next morning. Graham was pacing back and forth in his office at Gremlin Villa. "What's the matter?" I asked.

"I found out this morning that the 355th is going to Germany next month for occupation duty. I was hoping we'd go to the Pacific. I just called a buddy of mine at VIII Fighter Command to get transferred to an outfit that's going there."

"What's wrong with occupation duty?"

"Too damn dull! Besides, my brother's still a POW of the Japs and I want to get at those bastards! Why don't you come along with me?"

"No, thanks. I'll go if the 355th gets sent there, but not with a strange outfit. Besides, I don't like flying over all that water. Gets monotonous."

For the next three weeks, he made many trips to the 65th Fighter Wing and VIII Fighter Command, trying to pull all the strings he could to get himself transferred. On June 1, Ace finally received orders transferring him to a P-51 group that had arrived in England three months earlier and was slated to be sent to the Pacific Theater within a month or so. He was to report for duty on June 18.

His farewell party on Saturday night—June 16—was one of the wildest on record at the officers' club, and extended well into Sunday in his quarters. In his seven months as squadron commander he had finished one combat tour and a fifty-hour extension, shot down seven German aircraft, destroyed nine and a half others on the ground—and increased the officers' club bar profits by a substantial margin. He had been an outstanding combat leader. I hated to see him leave.

On June 18 Ace bundled all his belongings into a jeep and left for his new outfit, which was only a one-hour drive from Steeple. "I'll be back to visit you guys!" he yelled as he departed.

"Don't threaten us!" yelled Duff.

Bert Marshall was there to see him off. "Who's taking over the squadron?" I asked Bert.

"You are!" he said. "I told you that Saturday night at the party, don't you remember?" I had to confess that I didn't remember much about the party.

Two and a half years after joining the squadron as a second lieutenant, and after 113 combat missions, I was, at age twenty-three, the "Old Man." I spent three months in that capacity in Germany, then decided that I'd better head home and get back to the books. I had no desire at that time to stay in the service, but I retained my reserve commission.

That's another story.

Epilogue

I commanded the 354th Fighter Squadron from June 17 to September 24, 1945, at which time I turned the reins over to Jim Duffy and headed home. I was discharged from active duty on February 4, 1946, and enrolled at the University of New Hampshire in pursuit of my Bachelor of Science degree. My major was premed, and upon graduation in June 1947, I applied for admission to three medical schools. At that time—with the influx of students with the GI Bill—there were at least twenty applicants for every opening in any medical school, and many of those applicants had better grades than I did. Fortunately for the medical profession—and me—I wasn't accepted at any of them.

Duff resigned his USAAF commission late in 1946 and was soon flying for Meteor Air Transport, a nonscheduled airline operating out of Teterboro Airport, New Jersey. I joined him at Meteor in the fall of 1947, when I realized that flying was the only salable skill I had. Within a year, Duff was flying for American Airlines, and I was with Northwest Orient Airlines. Duff stayed with American and retired as a senior captain in 1982. I was recalled to active duty to fly the Berlin Airlift.

Duff and I kept in close touch over the years. When I retired from the Air Force in 1965, we visited and golfed at least twice a year. Duff died suddenly in 1994, victim of a heart attack. I still miss him.

Burt Sims returned to California in late 1945, to his job at the *Los Angeles Examiner*, and to his first love—writing.

In addition to newspaper work, he wrote for several magazines, did freelance writing, wrote TV scripts, and edited several weekly and biweekly newspapers. He was an avid skier and wrote many articles for various ski magazines. We saw each other often in the ten years after the war, but less frequently as the years wore on. In recent years, health problems have slowed him down a little. He can no longer ski, but he still writes. We keep in touch by phone and the Internet.

At least five of the 354th "alumni" became generals: Chuck Lenfest, Dick Cross, and Bob White were all brigadier generals. Henry Kucheman retired with two stars, Ace Graham with three.

As a major, Bob White was first to fly the rocket-powered North American X-15 research aircraft. This was the first space flight by a winged airplane, achieving an altitude of 314,750 feet, 60 miles from the surface of the earth. He was the first pilot to receive astronaut wings. He makes his home in Germany.

Al White became chief test pilot for North American Aviation and became one of the nation's great test pilots. He flew the first flights of the prototype F-100C/F aircraft; conducted the Mach 2 store drop demonstration; was assistant project pilot for the X-15 research aircraft; and was the chief project pilot of the XB-70 *Valkyrie*. He flew the first flights of both XB-70s, the first two-thousand-miles-per-hour flight, and all subsequent Mach 3 exploratory flights. He has received half a dozen highly coveted aviation achievement awards. He makes his home in Tucson, Arizona, and still serves occasionally as an aviation consultant.

Another distinguished 354th Fighter Squadron alumnus was James Jabara, although he was an alumnus of the 363d Fighter Group in the Ninth Air Force before he joined us in February 1945. Jabby went on to become the first U.S. Air Force jet ace during the Korean War, and earned an impressive collection of medals in the process: a Distinguished Service Cross, a Silver Star with one oak leaf cluster, six oak leaf clusters to the Distinguished Flying Cross that he had earned in the Ninth Air Force, and twenty-four oak leaf clusters to his Air Medal. He had volunteered for a combat tour in Vietnam, and was in the process of moving his family to South Carolina prior to his departure, when he was killed, along with his daughter, in a tragic automobile accident in 1966.

Gordon Graham shed his "Ace" soubriquet when he left the 355th and began his upward climb. An account of his adventures and multifaceted careers would fill a book; in fact, it does. He has written a highly readable memoir of his fascinating multiple careers in *Down for Double,* published by Brandylane Publishers, White Stone, Virginia, in 1996. When he retired as a lieutenant general in 1973, Gordon M. Graham had flown more than 9,000 hours in more than 75 different types of aircraft. He had flown 78 missions in the 354th Fighter Squadron, and 146 combat missions in Southeast Asia. Shortly after retirement, he accepted a position with McDonnell Douglas Corporation as vice president for regional sales, stationed in Japan. Ten years later, he retired from that career to concentrate on hunting, fishing, and golf. We (my wife Jane and I) visit Ace and Vivian at least once each year—I'm probably the only one left who still calls him Ace; to most everyone else he's Gordon or Gordy. We play a little golf, have a few cocktails, and reminisce about the good old 354th days.

Clay Kinnard left the service soon after the war ended. His impaired hearing probably had much to do with that decision. He went back to Tennessee and took over the family precast concrete business. Under his management, the business grew into a multimillion-dollar enterprise. His wife, Ruth, an attorney, became Tennessee's first female federal judge appointed to the U.S. Tax Court. The future for the Kinnards looked bright indeed. They had two children and raised fine horses on the family farm. Then in 1969, he died suddenly of a cerebral hemorrhage at age fifty-two.

Bert Marshall Jr. returned to private business early in 1946. Two years later, he was back on active duty. He held a variety of staff and command positions in the U.S. Air Force, and flew several night-intruder missions over Korea from Japan in B-26s. His final assignment was as deputy commander, Missiles Division, Air Defense Command. He left the service in 1958 for a position with AVCO. Shortly thereafter he became vice president of Fairchild Hiller operations in Florida. He returned to Texas in 1966 as director of the A-7D program. He died of complications after suffering a stroke in March 1979.

While I was stationed in Germany, I flew to England several times to visit Ruby. Our plan was for me to go back to the States and finish my college degree—I had a year and a half to finish—then I would return to England and we would be married.

Time and distance were against us. Caught up in the academic and social life at the University of New Hampshire, my letters became less and less frequent—less and less ardent. As some wag put it, "Absence makes the heart grow fonder—of somebody else."

When I returned to England in June 1947, it was the beginning of my summer-long bicycle tour of Europe with my college fraternity roommate, Wally Curtis. Ruby was on her honeymoon, so I didn't get to see her. We've kept in touch spasmodically through the years—mostly through Christmas cards. She now lives in California with her husband; we are in more frequent contact via the Internet. We are old friends.

Glossary

Abort: Return to base without completing a mission, caused by mechanical or other problems.

Airdrome (A/D): Airfield.

Ammo: Ammunition.

Angels: Altitude in thousands of feet. Angels 12 = 12,000 feet.

Anoxia: Condition caused by insufficient supply of oxygen to the blood. Can result in loss of consciousness or even death.

APC tablet: Aspirin, phenacetin, caffeine. Used to relieve pain and reduce fever.

API: Armor-piercing incendiary. A type of .50-caliber machine-gun ammunition whose projectile ignited a small pellet in the base at impact, causing a flash and enabling the pilot to see where his bullets were hitting.

B-17: USAAF Boeing (Flying Fortress) four-engine heavy bomber.

B-24: USAAF Consolidated (Liberator) four-engine heavy bomber.

B-26: USAAF Martin (Marauder) twin-engine medium bomber.

Babies: Code word for disposable fuel tanks attached to fighter aircraft to increase their range.

Bandit: Aircraft identified as an enemy.

Barrel roll: A maneuver in which an airplane rolls around its axis while it spirals around its original flight path.

Batman: Personal orderly/valet for officers in British armed services.

Blackout: The extinguishing or screening of all lights, especially as a precaution against air raids.

Blister hangar: Temporary corrugated steel hangar in a semicircular shape, open at one or both ends; shaped like an oversized half pipe.

Bogey: Unidentified aircraft.

BOQ: Bachelor officers' quarters.

Bounce: To attack, usually from above with a speed and altitude advantage.

Break: Sudden, violent turn into an attacking force.

Briefing: Detailed instructions given to pilots prior to mission takeoff.

C-47: USAF Douglas-built twin-engine transport plane. Military version of the DC-3.

Ceiling: Height above the earth's surface of the lowest layer of clouds.

Compressibility: A condition caused by excessive dive speed in fighter aircraft, resulting in mild-to-severe buffeting and in some cases to control surface locking. Sometimes caused structural damage or failure.

Contrail (Condensation Trail): A visible white cloud-like streak trailing behind aircraft or missiles at high altitudes.

Controller: See Type 16 control.

C rations: Canned food such as stew, hash, beans (and even brown bread to go with them), etc. When possible, cans were heated in boiling water, then opened and eaten from GI mess kits.

Dead-stick landing: A landing without engine power.

Debriefing: Information gathering by the intelligence officers from pilots returning from a mission. Pilot observations, enemy defenses, combat activity, target information, and the like were summarized in the intelligence summary report to higher headquarters.

Deck: The surface of the ground. Zero altitude.

Dogfight: An aerial battle between aircraft.

Dumbo: Air-sea rescue airplane.

E/A: Enemy aircraft.

Echelon: A formation of several aircraft, all on the same side of the leader, evenly stepped back and down. Used when each aircraft has to peel off, either to attack a ground target or to enter a traffic pattern for a landing.

E&E: Escape and evasion.

Element: Basic combat unit of two fighter aircraft—leader and wingman.

Empennage: The tail section of an airplane.

Essing: Making a series of turns resembling the letter S. Used while taxiing because the airplane's nose obstructed forward vision. Also used in escort duty to maintain position relative to the slow-moving bombers.

Feather (as in feather an engine): Rotation of propeller blades until they are edge-on to the slipstream to reduce drag.

Fighter sweep: A fighter mission to an area without a specific target.

FLAK: Antiaircraft gunfire. From the German Flieger Abwehr Kanonen.

Flight: Four-ship formation consisting of two elements; also the organizational setup within a squadron—normally consisting of four flights.

Flying Fortress or **Fortress:** B-17.

Full bore: At full speed and power.

FW-190: A first-line Luftwaffe single-engine fighter, built by Focke-Wulf.

G: The force of gravity. Three Gs would be three times the force of gravity.

Gaggle: A large assemblage of German fighters flying together, seemingly without organization or cohesion.

Gruppe: Group (German). Basic Luftwaffe administrative and combat unit, comparable in size to the USAAF squadron.

He: Heinkel, German aircraft manufacturer of Heinkel He-111, twin-engine bomber.

IP: Initial point, the point where the bomb run began.

Jink or **Jinking:** Making quick, uncoordinated maneuvers to throw off the aim of a pursuing aircraft.

Ju: Junkers, German aircraft manufacturer of Ju-87 (Stuka dive bomber) and twin-engine bombers Ju-88 and Ju-188.

KIA: Killed in action.

Kill: Slang for a confirmed victory or a destroyed enemy aircraft—not an enemy pilot's death.

Landfall: Crossing from an ocean or sea to a land formation.

Lufbery: A tight circle used as a defensive measure. Originally conceived by World War I flying ace Raoul Lufbery.

Luftwaffe: German air force.

Magnetos (sometimes referred to as mags): Devices used to produce an ignition spark in aircraft engines.

Marauder: See B-26.

Me: Messerschmitt, German aircraft manufacturer, produced the famous Me-109 series and the first jet-propelled operational fighter of World War II—the Me-262. Also produced the heavy fighter series Me-110, Me-210, and Me-410.

Mess hall: Eating facility. Also called chow hall.

Milk run: An easy mission—little or no enemy resistance.

Mission summary report: See Debriefing.

MP: Military Police.

Musette bag: Small canvas bag for carrying provisions and/ or personal effects. Worn suspended from a shoulder strap.

Napalm: Highly incendiary mixture of polystyrene, benzene, and gasoline mixed in a container like a drop tank.

NCO: Noncommissioned officer.

Nissen hut: A prefabricated sheet-steel building resembling a long half cylinder lying flat on the ground. Similar to a Quonset hut.

Orderly room: The administrative section of a squadron.

P-38: Lockheed-built twin-engine, twin-boom fighter aircraft.

P-40: USAAF Curtiss (Warhawk) fighter made famous by the Flying Tigers.

Pip or pipper: Dot in the center of the gunsight indicating the aiming point.

POW: Prisoner of war.

Prop wash: Turbulent air behind an aircraft caused by a combination of propeller and wingtip vortex.

PSP: Pierced steel planking, used as runways over sod or field airstrips.

Pulk: Combat box (German). An American heavy bomber formation.

PX (Post Exchange): A retail store on a military base.

RAF: Britain's Royal Air Force.

Red line: The red line on an airspeed indicator that marked the maximum safe airspeed limit.

Rendezvous (R/V): A planned joining of forces—fighters and bombers—at a specified time and place.

RPM: Revolutions per minute.

R&R: Rest and recuperation, a vacation from combat operations.

S-2: Squadron-level intelligence section.

Scrub: To cancel, as a mission.

Slow roll: A roll around the longitudinal axis of the aircraft, keeping the axis in line with a fixed point in space.

Snap roll: A violent rolling movement of an aircraft, often the result of a high-speed stall. Usually results in a spinning maneuver from which the aircraft can be recovered.

Spitfire: British-built Supermarine fighter made famous in the Battle of Britain.

Split S: A maneuver in which the aircraft reverses direction by half rolling to an inverted position, then diving vertically toward the ground and leveling off in the opposite direction.

Staffel (German): A squadron in the Luftwaffe, but much smaller than the USAAF squadron.

Stand down: To go off duty or (as an organization) not be available for duty.

Tannoy: The public address system, characterized by its harsh and brassy sound, used at most military bases in the United Kingdom.

Taxi: To move the airplane from point to point on the ground, under its own power.

Torque: Force that causes a twisting or turning tendency in an internal combustion engine. Example: On takeoff, the airplane had a strong tendency to turn left when full power was applied. A right rudder force was required to keep the plane rolling in a straight line.

Tracer: Projectiles with a magnesium core, which gave a visible bright trajectory when fired. Tracers were supposed to allow the path of the projectile to be followed visually, but because they had greater resistance in flight, were usually well below the path of the other projectiles and therefore poor indicators. Often they were placed in ammo trays to indicate to the pilot that he was down to his last fifty rounds.

Type 16 Control: Missions flown under radar observation from England. Controller call signs included Snackbar, Colgate, and Nuthouse.

USAAF: U.S. Army Air Forces.

Vee formation: A formation in which equal numbers of aircraft fly on both sides of the leader, forming a V shape. It was seldom used tactically—just for show.

Vertigo: Dizziness, or the sensation that the aircraft is turning or whirling around. Occurs mostly while flying on instruments or in close formation in clouds.

WAAC: Women's Army Auxiliary Corps (U.S.).

WAAF: Women's Auxiliary Air Force (Britain).

WASP: Women's Air Force Service Pilots (U.S.).

Wingman: Second aircraft and pilot in a two-ship element.

Wrack (in): Sudden steep turn.